ERASMUS

A portrait of Erasmus in 1517 by Quentin Matsys now in the Galeria
Corsini, Rome (Mansell Collection)

ERASMUS

GEORGE FALUDY

STEIN AND DAY/*Publishers*/New York

First published in 1970
Copyright © 1970 by George Faludy
Library of Congress Catalog Card No. 70-108315
All rights reserved
Printed in the United States of America
Stein and Day/*Publishers*/7 East 48 Street, New York, N.Y. 10017
SBN 8128-1288-3

To
Jane de Sabran-Sully
and Eric

Contents

Preface   ix

I The Early Years   1

II The Collège de Montaigu   49

III The English Influence   73

IV 'Citizen of the World'   112

V The Leader of Humanism   144

VI 'I Concede to None'   195

Epilogue   256

Table of Events   264

Bibliography   274

Index   281

Lists of Illustrations

Frontispiece   Erasmus in 1517

Following Page 112

1   Petrarch (?) by Bellini
2   Aeneas Sylvius (Pope Pius II)
3*a* Pico della Mirandola
3*b* Marsilio Ficino, Angelo Poliziano, Cristoforo
       Landino and Gentile de Becchi
4   Poggio Bracciolini (?)
5*a* Erasmus's 'Terminus' device
5*b* Title page of the *Adagia*
6   Sir Thomas More
7*a* A drawing of John Colet (?)
7*b* Bishop John Fisher
8*a* From *In Praise of Folly*
8*b* Melanchthon *c.* 1543
9   Erasmus at about 55
10*a* 'Martin Luther in Pathmo'
10*b* Luther in about 1527
11*a* Title page of the *Opera Omnia*
11*b* Erasmus's Statue in Rotterdam
12   Erasmus in about 1532

Maps (drawn by Edgar Holloway)
The Low Countries, in about 1475   *page* 28
Western Europe about 1475   127
Western Europe about 1547   255

Preface

The biographers of such men as Leonardo, Columbus and Rabelais are wont to complain of the paucity of available information and of the unending necessity of conjecture. The biographer of Erasmus might well bemoan the superabundance of material, and the fate of being reduced to the status of a copyist in an area where scarcely a stone has been left unturned.

Erasmus's *Collected Works* and his thousands of letters comprise some sixteen million words – one hundred and fifty sizable volumes. Still more first-hand information is provided by the writings of his contemporaries, the diplomatic correspondence of the time and his first two biographers, Beatus Rhenanus and Paulus Jovius. Since their day works dealing with Erasmus have piled up until now there is a veritable mountain of them. There have been at least eighty scholarly monographs which explore one or another aspect of his life or thought. The six volumes by the late A. Renaudet alone contain nearly everything that is known about him between his youth and the year 1527.

More than two hundred biographies and biographical essays have been written on Erasmus since 1700. Pierre Bayle's article in his *Dictionnaire historique et critique* (1702) summarized his life admirably; and Bayle's opinions are, on the whole, still valid. Equally commendable is Denis Diderot's entry in the fourteenth volume of *La Grande Encyclopédie* (1765). Only slightly less reliable are such massive eighteenth-century works as the *Vie d'Erasme* of the abbé Burigni and the *Erasmus* of the Swiss theologian S. Hess.

Among more recent books are such interesting studies as those of the American scholar Preserved Smith and the Austrian novelist

Stefan Zweig. Zweig's book, though full of errors, exaggerations and banalities, must nevertheless be defended as being the only popular work to date which provides the less informed reader with anything resembling a comprehensive picture of Erasmus's role in history. The study by Margaret Mann Phillips, *Erasmus and the Northern Renaissance* (1949), is a far more authoritative work. Towering above all other popular studies, however, is the *Erasmus* of the Dutch historian Johan Huizinga, whose insight into Erasmus's mind is matched by his knowledge of the fifteenth century. His biography, like his *The Waning of the Middle Ages*, is a classic of its type.

In the face of so much previous work, the present-day writer on Erasmus must resign himself to the fact that there are no new facts waiting to be brought to light, at least none of any great significance. The best he can do is to try to reassess Erasmus's life and place in history in the light of changing attitudes and his own position. Thus it has been attempted in the present work to break with certain traditions and take the emphasis off Erasmus's letters, so lively with gossip and minutiae, and place it on his works – less entertaining, perhaps, but presumably more vital. The danger of this is that, straying from the safer ground of concentrating on Erasmus's personality in order to deal with his historical role, one is easily lured into the treacherous bog of elusive generalities – where Zweig, among others, came to grief.

As opposed to Huizinga, who as a devout Protestant tended to side with Luther on the religious question, or to those scholars who have looked at Erasmus from a rigorously Catholic point of view, the author has been in the somewhat unusual position of agreeing whole-heartedly with his subject, and has sometimes taken up the cudgel in his defence with more passion, perhaps, than is seemly. Likewise, in spite of a persistent scholarly tendency to bypass Erasmus's efforts for peace and tolerance, an attempt has been made in this book to stress them. Contemporary writers such as J. Lecler and J. K. McConica have been followed in this, as well as some from an earlier period, e.g. Bayle and Diderot.

1969   GEORGE FALUDY

ERASMUS

I

The Early Years

The story of Desiderius Erasmus of Rotterdam should begin with the facts of his family and birth and then move to more important matters. As it happens, however, Erasmus had no intention of letting posterity know the true history of his origins. Depending on which documents are chosen from amongst his own papers, we might deduce that he had been born in Rotterdam in October, 1466, 1467 or 1468. After many years of dispute it has finally been established with something akin to certainty that the date was in fact 27 October, but the year 1469.[1] We know that his parents lived at Gouda, in the County of Holland, and that he was born there in the house of his father. His father was a priest called Gerard, according to Erasmus, but is mentioned in a letter from Pope Leo X to Erasmus as Roger. In any case the son of Gerard, or Roger, was baptized Erasmus, a name quite common at that time, as it was of one of the fourteen Auxiliary Saints[2] whose statues could be seen above or in a semicircle before nearly every church door, as protection against fire, pestilence and other calamities.

Erasmus's childhood, of which nine years were spent in the rectory at Gouda, was evidently very unhappy, as indeed was the whole of his youth. He was seldom to mention it without bitterness, especially towards his elder brother, his teachers, his

[1] See R. R. Post, *Geboortejaar en opleiding van Erasmus*, Medelingen der Koninklijke Nederlandse Akademie, No. 8, 1953.
[2] The cult of the fourteen Auxiliary Saints was abolished by the Council of Trent (1546–52).

guardians and the heavy-drinking burghers of Gouda who were, in his words, greasy of mouth and palate. A chief reason for this rancour was his illegitimacy and the unhappy family life it caused. The early death of his parents probably played its part as too.

We know that the family, which besides Erasmus and his father consisted of the mother, Margaret, and his brother, Peter, all lived together in the rectory, which was probably little different from those which have survived to the present day: dwellings roofed with blue slate, standing at odd angles to both church and street, with wooden beams daubed with pitch and windows covered not with expensive glass but with oil-paper or membrane.

The relationship between father and mother could scarcely have been an entirely happy one. The parishioners must have been scandalized that his paramour lived under the same roof with their priest and, as happens in such cases, may have made the children the objects of their contempt. It is perhaps not too fanciful to imagine that the parents themselves were tormented by the situation; at least this seems to be indicated by the fact that Margaret (probably in 1478) left Gouda with both children and took them to Deventer, where Erasmus and his brother attended school. Margaret earned her living there as a washerwoman and never returned to the rectory at Gouda.

Erasmus was to struggle against these memories and the humiliation they brought him until the day of his death. It may have been chiefly for this reason that he usually maintained that he had been born at Rotterdam, and refused to follow the usual custom of using his father's Christian name as his surname, or the newer custom of taking his name from his birthplace. Later on he may also have wished to deny the burghers of Gouda the privilege of claiming him as a native son. He chose instead Rotterdam, the home of his grandparents. At first he used *Rotterdammensis*, but later settled for the more mellifluous *Roterodamus*. Once he had freed himself from poverty and dependence upon others he presented himself, probably on his thirty-fifth birthday, with the additional appellation Desiderius. Thus in the end scarcely anything was left to point an accusing finger at the circumstances of his birth.

That evidence which was left, however, Erasmus tried to obscure by inventing a romantic tale for posterity. In Basle, on 2 April 1525, haunted by the fear of death, he sent an autobiographical sketch to his friend Conradus Goclenius to ensure 'that his friends know the truth', i.e. to ensure that his own version of his life would survive. In this letter he related that his father Gerard had as a young man fallen in love with a girl named Margaret, the daughter of a physician of Zevenbergen. They maintained a secret liaison, intending to marry, but Gerard's family would not give permission. Gerard, he continued, was the second youngest of eleven brothers, and his parents insisted that he became a priest (to keep the family fortune from being divided even further). Gerard secretly left the country and went to Rome. There he earned his living by copying books, acquiring in the meantime a good knowledge of Latin and Greek. Then he heard from his parents that Margaret had died. He decided to become a priest. After being ordained he returned home to find not only that Margaret was alive but that she had borne him a son. Gerard took the child, Erasmus, into his house, but would have nothing more to do with Margaret.

This fanciful account, on which Charles Reade's popular novel *The Cloister and the Hearth* was based, is untrue in many details, and Erasmus knew this better than anyone. His brother, Peter, was three years his senior, and he had previously mentioned him in many letters. The existence of this brother had to be forgotten, however, if he was to prove that his father had not yet been ordained at the time of his love affair with Margaret, and that consequently he himself had not been conceived 'in the most damnable intercourse of mortal sin'. It may well be that Erasmus's father was ordained as late as 1466 and that Peter had been born a few months before. This could explain why Erasmus claimed to be older than he was, designating 1466 as the year of his birth and thus taking the place of a brother who, presumably, was no longer living at the time of this letter.

How much Erasmus was tortured by his illegitimate birth can be seen by comparing this autobiographical sketch with another letter which he wrote in 1516 to one Grunnius, ostensibly a

papal secretary, when he was seeking dispensation from certain
of his monastic vows. In this letter Erasmus confessed his illegitimate birth and wrote at length about his brother and about his
unhappy childhood. The letter was not sent to Rome, however,
for Erasmus had invented the papal secretary, evidently in order
to have someone to confess to – if only his own desk drawer.

It is generally believed that Erasmus's obsession with this
problem must be attributed to his neurasthenic nature, especially
since it persisted after he had gained universal fame. He was
courted by kings and popes and yet remained afraid that the circumstances of his birth would hamper the spread of his posthumous fame – although it had by no means hampered his career.
Historians have more than once pointed out that during the fifteenth century and the early decades of the sixteenth illegitimate
children were, as a rule, brought up in the house of their father
and were treated as equal members of the family. An astonishing
number of the most famous of Erasmus's contemporaries were
of illegitimate birth. To name only a few: Caesare Borgia and
his sister Lucrezia (children of Pope Alexander VI); Federigo de
Montefeltro, duke of Urbino; Pope Clement VII; and Erasmus's
own favourite pupil, Alexander Stuart, son of James IV of
Scotland.

Since the powerful were impervious to attacks against their
origins, it is sometimes erroneously assumed that no attacks were
made. On the contrary, Leonardo da Vinci, for example, sustained them often but with little concern. The first Dutch
humanist, Agricola, ridiculed his detractors on this score as
'anachronistic nincompoops'. But Erasmus, otherwise well-
balanced, if overly sensitive, lived in fear of the viciousness of
those who flaunted his origins before the public eye. The following quotation is from a letter to Erasmus, then at the peak of his
fame, from Julius Caesar Scaliger, a literary historian of great
repute. Disagreeing with Erasmus's criticism of those humanists
whose writing had degenerated into inane rhetoric, Scaliger sent
him an open letter. In the first lines we find, 'it is said that you
were born of incestuous intercourse, of sordid parents, one of
them a little priest and the other a whore; and it is said that your

father was castigated again and again by the pope'. Little wonder
that Erasmus was disconcerted.

Nor were his enemies the only ones to harp on this painful
theme. It is related that during his long stay in Basle, when he
was already quite old and half-crippled, Erasmus improvised a
little verse in Latin each morning to list the things his servant
was to buy. One morning Johannes Froben, the famous printer
who was Erasmus's publisher and devoted friend and a kind-
hearted and amiable man, came upon the servant in the street.
The poor fellow had forgotten his verse and was in tears. 'Never
mind,' the printer consoled him, 'I'll teach you another verse,
one easy to remember. Listen: *Orto de scorto pede torto poma
reporto.*' After learning that his servant was sent 'to fetch apples
for the crooked-legged bastard' Erasmus was hostile towards the
printer for years to come, and Froben complained bitterly about
the thin skin of his peevish friend.

At the time of Erasmus's youth the counties of Artois, Flanders,
Brabant and Holland were all part of the Burgundian realm.
Compared with the large French-speaking cities of Antwerp,
Bruges and Brussels, the Dutch cities of the north, Rotterdam,
Gouda and Utrecht, were insignificant and provincial. Artists
from the area had to migrate southwards to find employment,
and students left as well, the only university of the country being
at Louvain. Those who could afford it, however, went as far as
Paris.

It was for a long time assumed by historians that those areas
of the Low Countries around the mouth of the Rhine had
become wealthy only during the period of independence and
sea-power. Thanks to the work of such scholars as Henri Pirenne,
among others, it is now known that this wealth was in large part
amassed much earlier. Two rather humble occupations, coastal
trading and herring-fishing, a modest style of living and the
comparatively limited effects of the Hundred Years War all
combined to permit the burghers of the area to attain a level of
material well-being unknown to their French neighbours. Nor

did they lag behind in learning or religion, although the Burgundian knights, unable to adjust their medieval and static concept of society to altered realities, continued to consider them, rich patricians and poor peasants alike, as inferior creatures belonging to the same 'wretched Third Estate' condemned by God to eternal servitude. They were wont to sneer at the wealthy townsmen of the Low Countries as bumpkins and to exclude them from state service, and this at a time when a number of cities in the neighbouring Holy Roman Empire, and all the cities of Switzerland, were already enjoying self-government. It seems, however, that the reflective and rather parsimonious nature of these burghers – who were given to that pompous sobriety typical of beer-drinkers – stood them in better stead in a period of change than chivalrous dreams and the splendours of court life did the Burgundian knights.

The French-Burgundian wars began shortly before Erasmus was born and lasted, with the resultant rebellion, famine and piracy along the Frisian coasts, all the years he spent in Holland. The war was, ultimately, a conflict between the old and the new. Charles the Bold, duke of Burgundy, was a partisan of the chivalrous ideal; he wanted to unite the two parts of Burgundy by conquering the provinces of France which separated them, as well as Lotharingia, Switzerland, Milan, Venice and the Tyrol, thus carving out for himself an oblong empire with the Alps at its centre, one composed of Dutch, French, German and Italian-speaking peoples. The duke's other great plan was the reconquest of Constantinople – by means of that same type of cavalry so crushingly defeated by the Turkish regulars at Nicopolis (1396) and Varna (1444).

When Charles married Margaret of York at Bruges in 1468 the wedding guests were required to swear an oath to take part in a crusade against the Turks; but it was their host himself who, four years before, had accepted the leadership of another such crusade, organized by Pope Pius II, and then had failed to appear at Ancona where the army, the fleet and the pope stood waiting for his arrival. Equally revealing of this singular personality is the fact that when Charles captured Louis XI of France he humiliated the monarch in every possible way, and then, in a fit of chivalry, set him free. It was on this occasion that Italian diplomats, some of whom had long since suspected the duke of being mad, began wagering at odds of a hundred to one on his imminent downfall. The incident was indeed to have fatal consequences for him.

It was Charles's habit to have portions of the *History of Lancelot* read to him each night before he slept. In the extraordinarily old-fashioned mentality of the duke there was only the haziest borderline between the world of dreams and that of reality. In his mind naïve playfulness alternated with uncontrolled passion, and tearful piety was likely at any moment to give way to savage pride. His court, it must be admitted, was the most splendid in Europe, and he patronized poets, musicians and historians (although the best of these, Philippe de Commines, deserted to Louis XI). At his feasts gigantic pies were served in which dwarfs, monkeys and even small bands of musicians were enclosed; on his walls hung the latest paintings of Dirk Bouts, Rogier van der Weyden and the brothers van Eyck. Contemporaries reported that the whole contrived to be stupefyingly tasteless.

Charles's adversary, Louis XI of France, known as the 'Spider King', was preeminently a shrewd politician and a coldly practical man. Possessed of almost uncanny insight into the psychologies of those he dealt with, unerring instincts and untiring patience, he was also a man of detached ruthlessness and cruelty. His court, in contrast to that of Charles, was famous for its filth and slovenliness and its foul-mouthed, brawling and impoverished courtiers. Louis had neither time for nor interest in the arts. His political thinking, however, was so advanced as to be appreciated by no one in France except the historian Commines, though it was watched and eagerly commented upon by the princes of Italy.

While Charles the Bold was an ardently religious man, in his way, Louis XI appears to have been devoid of any truly pious sentiment, mixing as he did Christian doctrine with the crudest sort of superstition. He boasted of having 'purchased the grace of God for more gold than ever king did', and he collected relics by the hundredweight in the hope that they might prove efficacious in prolonging his life. Next to his bed he kept the chrism used at the coronation of French kings. It had never before been removed from Rheims, but Louis intended to use it as 'oil of the sick' should he ever need it. He maintained 'a great number of male and female bigots', as Commines put it, for the purpose of perpetual prayer to God that 'the king might never die'. He also had the hermit Francis of Paula (later canonized) abducted from his Calabrian cave, hoping that his presence would draw forth blessings from heaven. Francis of Paula was an ascetic of the most ferocious sort. He never touched money, always slept in a sitting position, refused all foods except roots and certain fruits, and screeched at the sight of women. The king, true to form, ordered his pages to place dishes of meat in his cell and then stand guard at the keyhole to see whether the holy man touched them or 'committed any other gross indecency when alone'.

Louis had no intention of conquering Constantinople, nor had he any designs on the territories of the Holy Roman Empire, the Swiss Confederation, the dukedom of Milan or the republic of Venice. His aim was to transform his loosely-knit feudal realm into a strong, modern state. To do so he knew that he would first have to counter the aspirations of Charles the Bold, and to restore Burgundy to France. He accomplished his task by means of 'Italian politics', i.e. those methods successfully employed by Italian despots for over a century and described some fifty years later by Machiavelli.

Louis first of all hunted down and hanged by the hundred the highwaymen within his realm, thus bringing order to the roads and helping to establish the supremacy of French commerce in Europe. And with his badly paid but strong army he put French military power in the ascendancy. Thanks to his policies France, later than Portugal and Hungary but somewhat earlier than England and Spain, joined the historical trend towards strong, autocratic national states.

After several indecisive wars and innumerable skirmishes – in which Louis seldom had the upper hand since the Burgundian knights knew what they were fighting for, while his own nobles were far from apprehending the strange and unattractive modernism of their king – he patiently prepared for the kill. In the battle of Nancy in 1477 Charles the Bold was slain and Louis, almost as if to appease the spirit of his enemy, chivalrously gave him a funeral as pompous and tasteless as any Charles might have planned for himself.

The people of the Low Countries had sympathized with the French against the Burgundians, but the outcome of the war brought them few benefits. Louis did not succeed in occupying the Low Countries, because Mary, scion of Charles the Bold, had been hurriedly married to Prince Maximilian of Habsburg, future emperor. Thus the northern half of the Burgundian realm, the 'Lowlands by the Sea', fell to the Habsburgs. After several years more of civil strife peace returned to the area under Philip the Handsome, son of Maximilian and Mary, and prosperity came with it. But as far as liberty, or even any measure of municipal self-government was concerned, the burghers were worse off than they had been under the Burgundian knights.

During the years Erasmus lived in the rectory at Gouda the two armies had fought their battles in the south, mainly in France. It was therefore in a comparatively peaceful atmosphere that he received the rudiments of his education from his father, who knew Greek, was familiar with the humanism of Italy and possessed a library. At the age of four he began to attend the school of one Peter Winckel, but, by his own admission, made little progress as he 'was not born for those unlovely studies', by which he chiefly meant that the instruction was in Dutch and dog-Latin.

Little else is known about the first nine years of Erasmus's life, and we must draw our conclusions from the few facts at our disposal. We may assume that family life in the rectory was joyless and made dreary by poverty. We know from his letters that Erasmus had always disliked his brother, and that he was to

remember the schoolmaster, Peter Winckel, who later became
one of his three guardians, with hatred. In all probability his
parents enjoyed little or no social life, and Erasmus must have
been extremely lonely. Gouda, like Deventer and 's Hertogenbosch, where he was to spend the next nine years, was a small,
dull and oppressive place. Because of the collapse of civil order
during the war, it is unlikely that he was even able to walk at
liberty with his friends in the nearby forests or to explore the
surrounding countryside. At night the gates of his schools, like
those of the towns, were shut tight; and, in any event, such forms
of idleness as games and country walks were not encouraged in
the schools he attended. We know, moreover, that he was a
sickly child, the embodiment of that type who, in the fifteenth
century, generally died before reaching adulthood.

The loneliness and unhappiness of Erasmus's childhood contributed to his neurasthenic character and, we may safely assume,
to that longing for love and friendship which is much in evidence
in his letters after the age of eighteen. But the circumstances of
his childhood produced a much more general crisis in him, and
one which threatened to destroy him. He eventually overcame
it, but he was never to recover completely from the struggle.

One part of his being was inclined towards submission. This
meant an acceptance of his compatriots with their rude ways,
their conceited ignorance and their hypocritical and grasping
piety; an acceptance of the schools in which coercion rather than
persuasion was the method of instruction; and, in general, that
whole way of life in which men vacillated, in permanent dis-
equilibrium as it were, between the extremes of servility and
arrogance, penitence and pride, cruel asceticism and unrestrained
sensuality. There was in Erasmus a temptation born of despair
to accept with meekness the world of his youth as his permanent
domicile, and to become resigned to his own place in it as a
penniless young man of frail health and no special talents. The
logical choice for such a youth was to enter a monastery, to
spend his allotted years there (life expectancy was in any case
only thirty years on an average at that time) and to look forward
to eternal bliss in the hereafter. To Erasmus, in his weakness,

the appeal was overwhelming, and later he was never to forgive himself for having succumbed to it.

Innate rebelliousness was also a part of Erasmus's character, however, and this too can be traced to his childhood. From his earliest years he detested the rigidity of a society which allocated to everyone a preordained and permanent niche. He despised the pettiness and backwardness of his countrymen, the bleak schools he was obliged to attend and, indeed, the whole manner of living to which he had been born, even down to its heavy cuisine.

It was in part rebellion against all this which was eventually to drive him away from the monastery and from Holland, to liberate him from penury and dependence upon others, and which when he finally freed himself from the clutches of his superiors, from princes and even from his friends and followers, was to be his self-justification. It was rebelliousness as much as anything else which, tempered by a wry sense of humour, provided him on occasion with a strength and tenacity out of all proportion to his weak constitution. He was to write *The Praise of Folly*, for example, while tormented by bladder stones. When he was over sixty and half-crippled from the effects of syphilis of the bones he still wrote 14 to 16 hours a day, often standing at a lectern.

If we may speculate further on the results of his childhood in Holland, we might mention the prevalence of horror stories, in circulation during the wars, concerning the incredible cruelty of the Burgundian knights, and link these with Erasmus's predilection for France and the institutions of authoritarian monarchy. Only much later in his life, after he had lived in Venice, visited the free city of Strasburg and found refuge in Basle, did he alter his views and come out in favour of republican government. His hatred of everything connected with the age of chivalry, the cult of heroism, feudal oppression and knights-errant 'reconciling chivalrous pride with occasional highway robbery', stemmed at least in part from the same sources. This hatred was in fact one of the few things which he shared with the majority of his compatriots, without however joining them in their enthusiasm for court poetry, tournaments and 'similar advertise-ments for massacre'.

Finally there is one last aspect of Erasmus's character which is directly traceable to his earliest years: fear. He lived in continual fear of war, catastrophe, plague, destitution, dependence, a host of enemies and even, at times, his friends. Being a man of moder-ation, with a classicist's instinct for proportion, he maintained an admirable equilibrium between these fears and his need for dig-nity and harmony; and his courage in intellectual matters, as will be seen, went very far. He was the first man of the modern era openly to preach pacifism and tolerance and this during a period of general strife, sectarian squabbling and savage oppres-sion. His courage was all the more remarkable in that he admitted his own sometimes hysterical fear – a singular trait in an age when braggadocio and vainglory were the usual paths to public recognition. Compared with his more colourful contemporaries, such men as Charles the Bold, Lorenzo de' Medici, Pope Alexander VI, Henry VIII, Francis I or Martin Luther, Erasmus, the advocate of moderation in the face of violence and the incorrigibly reasonable adversary of fanaticism and bigotry, appears very pale indeed. In this sense, certainly, he does not blend well with the background of his time. His personality was unheroic and his life was not such that it can be dramatized. Against this, however, lies the fact that, so far as concerns the spiritual and intellectual heritage of the age it is the pallor of Erasmus which has proved the more enduring. The Reformation is with us still, to be sure, but the colours of its makers are faded.

When Erasmus was nine (in 1478 or 1479) his mother took him and his brother to Deventer and stayed with them there for the next five or six years. The school there was a widely-known institution run by the Brethren of the Common Life, a lay society distinguished for its piety and humility. The Brethren led a life of almost Cistercian simplicity, living in near-poverty and every evening pooling such earnings as they had in a com-mon purse. The children of the well-to-do paid fees in proportion to their parents' wealth, but those of poor families paid nothing, being given room and board.

The Brethren of the Common Life were adherents of a religious movement known as the *devotio moderna*, which had spread during the fifteenth century across the Low Countries, northern Germany, France and, to a lesser extent, England. It had been founded during the time of the Great Schism (1378–1429) as a means of escaping the excessively worldly preoccupations of the Church, to permit its followers to turn instead towards genuine piety and the teachings of the Gospels. Scrupulously avoiding heresy, it nevertheless came close at times to holding the Bible rather than the Church as the chief authority in matters of faith.

The founder of the movement, Gerard Groote, had been under the influence of the great mystic Jan Ruysbroeck, who had taught that prayer, meditation and Bible-reading were in themselves sufficient for communion with God. Groote advocated, beyond this, the reform of the monastic orders; he attacked the depravity of monks and advised his followers, with largely successful results, to turn their backs on the elaborate systems of scholastic theology. The movement was, nevertheless, welcomed by the Church at the Council of Constance (1414), and eventually received the blessings of Pope Eugene IV.

It was after Groote's death (1384) that the first so-called frater houses were established. In these the Brethren, bound by no solemn vows, spent their lives 'in the imitation of the primitive Christians', as it was set down in their charter, and 'supported by their own labour, namely the copying of books'. When the advent of book printing deprived them of their major source of income they turned to teaching.

A hundred years after its appearance on the scene the *devotio moderna* had become the most influential religious movement in northern Europe, making itself strongly felt in Germany and the Low Countries and even in that bastion of unyielding scholasticism, the Sorbonne. It united the three reformative trends of the day within its framework: a return to the teachings of the Bible and to simple piety; a retreat from the fossilized structures of

Thomism, Scotism and Nominalism and from the whole medieval tradition of theological disputation; and, finally, an ever-
increasing tendency to criticize the corruption of the monastic
orders.

Although we are well informed about the thought and activity of the Brethren, it is impossible, though often attempted,
to give a single and universally valid definition of their doctrine.
In reality they had no fixed doctrine, as such. Some of them,
Egbert ter Beck for example, the rector at Deventer a few years
before Erasmus's arrival, were outright ascetics. Beck banned
plays, games and even laughter. When his duties required him
to speak to a woman he would avert his face and keep his eyes
tightly closed. He considered modulated singing an unnecessary
display, ruling that humble Christians should sing 'as frogs
croak' if they wished to please God.

Gerard Zerbolt of Zutphen, on the other hand, had been a
mystic. With the permission of his superiors he never left his
cell, except on Sunday mornings when he played tag with the
children before the monastery or, it is said, sat for hours con-
templating a blade of grass, a flower or puddles of water, 'those
dim and pale mirrors of His eternal beauty'. It was said that a
beatific smile never left his face. In his cell he alternately wrote
and prayed, never sleeping more than two hours at a time.
When he died, at the age of twenty-one, he left behind two books,
The Reformation of the Faculties of the Soul, and *Spiritual Ascensions*. In the first he maintained that man is capable of improving
the quality of his soul and, similarly, that the mind can be improved by exercise in the same way that a carpenter's hands
become more skilful with practice. In the second book, following the footsteps of such mystics as Dionysius the Aeropagite,
Meister Eckhart and Ruysbroeck, Zerbolt gives his vision of
the 'overly vast desert', the 'formless abyss' of the 'silent and
eternal Divinity', knowledge of Whom can only be attained by
losing all our knowledge and discovering in ourselves 'bottomless un-knowing, when, beyond all names given to God we
immerge in His namelessness and merge in His unknown darkness and vast absoluteness without form, mode or name'.

Both books were to have great influence in France and Spain until the close of the sixteenth century, most notably on Ignatius Loyola.

The Brethren maintained a variety of attitudes towards learning. Some were in favour of literature, and others feared its pernicious effects. But mistrust of dogmatism and scholastic theology was almost universal within their ranks, and during the second half of the fifteenth century they became increasingly outspoken against both. Godfried Toorn, rector of Deventer until his death in 1450, counselled his flock against reading Aquinas because 'he was too subtle for simple-minded folk'. Johan Wessel, one of the first humanists within the order, had spent many years in Rome, and when he addressed the Brethren and students on Sunday mornings he expounded the new ideas in no uncertain terms: 'Read the ancients, sacred and profane; the doctors, with their robes and distinctions, will soon be drummed out of town.'

According to the previously-mentioned autobiographical letter of Erasmus, the school at Deventer was 'still barbarous' when he arrived there. There were two hundred and seventy-five boys in one classroom under one master, and the level of teaching was always geared to the slowest members of the class, all of which was usual practice at the time. Discipline was strict and students were struck for the slightest infraction of the rules, though never, we are told, in anger. A medieval proverb had it that 'Children must become accustomed to suffering upon this earth, and the sooner the better'; to which Egbert ter Beck had added: 'And they enjoy suffering anyway'.

Erasmus was never to cease lamenting his years at the school of the Brethren; not because of the beatings or the strict orders which forbade the playing of games, but because of the antiquated teaching, the senseless cramming and the textbooks written in jarring verse which had to be memorized from beginning to end. Any student doubts concerning the texts, or criticism of them, were inevitably brushed aside with references to the incontestable authority of the author. 'Heavens, what an age that was,' Erasmus wrote decades later, 'when with so much ceremony the couplets of Ioannes de Garlandia were read to the boys accompanied by a complicated commentary, and a large part of the time in school was consumed in dictation, repetition and the memorization of silly verses.'

While Erasmus was still at Deventer the first Dutch humanists arrived there to teach. Thus like many of his contemporaries he witnessed at first hand the clash between scholasticism and humanism, or, to be more precise, the slow and truculently unwilling retreat of the former. It was one of the most important issues of the age, and it had to be fought over anew in each school and university, except of course where the local prince had for the time being decided the matter according to his own lights.

The humanism of the Renaissance had been born of a preoccupation with the poets, writers and philosophers of antiquity. These studies, the *studia humanitatis* as they were called, were held to consist loosely of all those pursuits which would in some way improve man's situation in the universe. In the eyes of the humanists antique society had been in every way superior to that of the Middle Ages; and classical writers were held to be the only competent thinkers and stylists, as opposed to the 'scholastic muddleheads and stammerers'. The result was that for perhaps the first time in history a large and influential part of a society was attempting, not so much to imitate, as to revive a culture dead for over a millennium.

At first only Latin authors were read, or those who had been translated into Latin; but later knowledge of Hebrew, and especially Greek, began to be widespread. Humanism, although much more an outlook and a way of life than a philosophical system, instilled in its followers an ardent desire to solve every sort of human problem. Yet it never lost sight of its original aims: philology, which would elucidate the writings of the ancients, and pedagogy, which would disseminate their ideas.

Petrarch was generally held to be the father of the movement. It is true in any case that he had been the first writer 'of sufficiently fine mind to recognize the grace of the lost antique style and to attempt to revive it'. He was said to have 'led mankind from the barbarities and the darkness' of the Middle Ages 'to the light of a new day'. Petrarch had complained of his studies at the University of Paris that he had only heard the name of Cicero mentioned there, but was unable to find any of his works. He kept a Greek Homer in his library, looking at it longingly and, as he says, lovingly, but was unable to read it.

A few decades after Petrarch's death humanists, most notably the Florentine Poggio Bracciolini, began searching intently for 'lost' Latin classics. They soon unearthed large numbers of them, and from the most unlikely places. Then, in 1440, some of the Byzantine scholars who had attended the Council of Florence stayed on in Italy. Greek scholarship was soon firmly entrenched in many parts of the country. During the decades before the invention of book printing manuscript-copying was at its height, and the 'Italian' custom of collecting libraries spread rapidly over the whole of Europe. The ideas which inevitably accompanied these trends were soon being discussed in universities, at the tables of princes and, in Italy at least, in every house with any pretentions to culture.

Humanists were not only eager but insistent in upholding the philological requirements of the new learning. Medieval Latin, very much alive and wonderfully adapted to the needs of the Church and medieval thinking, had nevertheless abandoned much of the vocabulary and complex syntax, and all the marmoreal elegance, of the classical language. The humanists, not surprisingly, dismissed it as barbarous and useless. As far as their own purposes went they were undoubtedly right: whatever objections may be put up against the Latin of Cicero as a vehicle of lucid thought, it was undeniably the best such vehicle available to the humanists.

To see the problem clearly one has only to imagine Thomas à Kempis's *Imitation of Christ*, medieval pietistic writing at its best, put into classical Latin; or Pico della Mirandola's *On Human Dignity* transcribed into medieval Latin. Kempis would lose his Dutch-uncle persuasiveness, while his harshness and naïveté

would be magnified to the point of making him sound very
much the provincial propagandist. Pico's work, on the other
hand, would suffer the obscuration of its logical structure, the
supreme elegance of its style and, for that matter, its dignity.
Moreover, Pico was dealing with many concepts for which the
language of Kempis simply had no terms.

Humanism was in its essence concerned with all the phenomena of the world, but especially with literature, jurisprudence,
pedagogy, philology and rhetoric. Scholasticism, on the other
hand, no matter in what directions it sometimes ventured, was
inextricably rooted in the thinking of medieval theology. To the
scholastics the world appeared to be permanently in that state
ordained for it by God. The state was obviously a bad one, and
the only possible hope for it was faith, which would at least
remedy the situation in the hereafter. Humanists, though believing Catholics as a rule, were convinced that man could be made
better through learning. They branded the attitude of the scholastics as barbarous, illiterate, ignorant and the deplorable remnant of a bygone era; to which the scholastics replied with
charges of pedantry, demagogy and insanity.

The real difference between the humanists and their adversaries lay not so much in the emotional involvement of either
with classical antiquity, but in the manner in which that age
was viewed. The fact is that the scholastics had no real grasp of
history as such, and the humanists had. No history was taught in
medieval universities, and the civilizations of the past were
obscured in vague legends. Alexander the Great, like Caesar,
was seen by the scholastics as a medieval knight in armour,
tilting against turtles and starlings, serenading beneath the balcony of Roxane in the dress of a troubador. Alcibiades, having
wandered long beneath the vaults of medieval learning, had
gradually changed his sex and was believed to have been an
Athenian courtesan by the name of Archippiada. The *Metaphysics* of Aristotle was taught in all the universities in a hopelessly inaccurate version translated from the Greek through
Syriac, Arabic, Hebrew and, finally, into dog-Latin. To this
version was added a forged last book to enforce the view that

Aristotle had believed in a personal God and in immortality, which of course he did not. The result was that he came to be regarded as something close to a Christian philosopher and an only slightly lesser personage than a Church father.

With the advent of humanism, Caesar, Alexander, Aristotle and even Virgil, though well known during the Middle Ages, began only now to be seen in historical context. Far from thinking of Caesar as a medieval knight, the humanists argued whether he had been the bearer of civilization to all Europe or the grave-digger of Roman liberty. They made more than one translation of Aristotle, and from the Greek this time. They tried, moreover, to understand him in the framework of previous Greek philosophy and the Athens of the fourth century B.C.

All this activity depended on the humanist preoccupation (or obsession if one prefers) with philology. In previous ages this science had been largely ignored. Texts had very rarely been scrutinized for authenticity, this as a rule having been decreed by popes, princes and councils. Thus it had occurred to few to bring textual criticism to bear on the Bible, for example, the various copies of which were often at odds with one another on many points, and riddled with the errors of copyists. The *Canon of Medicine* of Abu Ali ibn Sina, known as Avicenna, had been used as the basic textbook in the schools of medicine of all the universities of Europe since around the year 1200. Many untimely deaths would have been laid at the doorstep of its translator, Gerardus de Cremona, had anyone dared to find out how badly he had bungled his work. The faulty translation of the twenty-ninth of Averroes's theses left all Europe with the misapprehension that anyone who sailed south or southwest from Spain would perish, since the extreme heat would cause his brain to boil. It may be held as fortunate that Columbus (if Salvador de Madariaga and others are right in their contention) was familiar with the Arabic original.

It was the spirit of criticism, sadly missing in previous centuries, which the humanists revived. Salutati, a disciple of Petrarch, insisted that whenever face to face with a philosophical or theological text one should refrain from empty disputation but attempt to get at the author's exact meaning. From the beginning of the fifteenth century the humanists exercised with increasing severity the most exacting textual criticism on every manuscript that came into their hands. Attempting first to date it, they proceeded to seek out corruptions, to compare different readings and to employ both common sense and historical knowledge in correcting, appraising and annotating it. Their methods and resources were, compared with ours, severely limited; their confidence and optimism were not.

The pedagogical aspirations of the humanists sprang from much the same sources. Aside from being the answer to a growing public interest in education, this tendency, which had been perceptible as a Socratic trend in the movement from its inception, soon grew into ambitions to take over the universities and public offices. Petrarch, having visited the University of Padua, had complained of its Averroistic impiety and its corruption of youth. Marsilio Ficino, friend of Lorenzo and head of the Platonic Academy in Florence, maintained: 'The city does not consist of stones, but of men; it is necessary to tend men like trees while they are young and to guide them to bear fruit.' This was a general view amongst humanists, all of whom in one way or another considered it their duty to instruct. That they were ultimately successful in this is perhaps best seen in the fact that, when after the Reformation they had become suspect in the eyes of Catholics and Protestants alike, they found refuge in the schools – which by then could no longer be run without them.

Humanist objections to medieval pedagogy were manifold. Most important was the charge that the scholastics had no actual method of teaching but simply coerced their students into mindless submission. This was substantially true. The humanists, for their part, attempted to teach by arousing enthusiasm, explaining and illuminating their subjects during informal lectures which were really dialogues at times, and by taking the students out of the classroom to teach such things as botany and astronomy. Open-air gymnastics was encouraged as well. Perhaps the most vivid description of the differences between scholastic and humanist pedagogy is the rather malicious one found in chapters

XIV to XXIV of the *Gargantua* of François Rabelais, an admirer of Erasmus.

More particular objections against the scholastics were the inadequacy and inelegance of their Latin and its lack of any standard orthography. In consequence of the latter, words were both written and pronounced according to variations in ecclesiastical usage, or else succumbed to the pressures of the various vernaculars until they became unrecognizable from one district to the next. Thus *caeleste* (heavenly) became *cieleste* in France, *coeleste* (pronounced *tsöleste*) in Germany, and, though the spelling remained the same, was pronounced with the usual soft *c* by the Italians. The name of the great theologian Pierre Abélard was variously spelled, in Latin, as Abalard, Abelart, Abaelard or Esbaillart. Another theologian, from Bamberg, signed his name as Bambergensis on some occasions and as Papenpergiensis on others. To the scholastics a name was only the insignificant symbol of a higher essence, and such practical considerations as consistent spelling could be disregarded.

The virtual nonexistence of a standardized spelling and grammar made the adoption of the classical language imperative, in the view of the humanists, if philology was to progress. Added to this were the facts that there were no dictionaries; neither Greek nor Hebrew was taught in the universities; and of extant encyclopedias the best was that of Vincent de Beauvais, printed around 1480 in eight enormous volumes but arranged neither in alphabetic order nor, indeed, in any other.

Humanist anger centred, however, on the two dozen or so textbooks invariably used in primary and secondary schools during the preceding three centuries. The most famous were the Latin grammar of Ebrardus, the *Parables* of Alanus and the book of Ioannes de Garlandia, previously mentioned as Erasmus's pet hatred. These too, by the way, were mercilessly lampooned by Rabelais. A few lines of the text should suffice to show what aroused Erasmus's ire in the case of Garlandia, who was an Englishman who had taught grammar in the University of Toulouse from 1229, the year of its foundation.

In his book, a collection of Latin synonyms and equivoques

printed in some twenty editions during the latter half of the fifteenth century, Garlandia devoted a little verse and a prose commentary to each entry. Thus under *salt* we find: *est salus prelatus*, which means that salt denotes the prelates of the Church, for, as the commentary explains, it is written in the Gospels that 'Ye are the salt of the Earth'. Under *dog* we find *humble* and *vile* (since Saul said to David: 'After whom is the king of Israel come out? After a dead dog?') Further on we discover *dog* connected with *deny* and *stick*, since the heretical dog denies God and sticks to his heresy. The book continues with some three hundred other words, each belaboured in the same way. To make matters worse, on the rare occasions Garlandia did touch upon anything significant he usually erred. Thus in the above example he mistakenly supposed the word *heretic* to be derived from the Latin *haeret* (sticks).

This was the extent of philology during the Middle Ages, and it would not be unfair to say that *magister* Garlandia represented this facet of medieval learning at its best. It would be ridiculous to blame him for not knowing that which he could not have known; but once men had begun to put the situation right there was little justification for defending such work as scholarship from any point of view.

There is, however, another side to this problem, one which goes beyond the effects of formal pedagogy within the schools, and one of which every humanist was aware. Everyone who had gone to school had copied out hundreds of times such phrases as *The prelates of the Church are the salt of the earth*. They had been the very essence of his education, and afterwards were the warp and woof of his intellectual life. He heard them in church, from his children and in everyday conversation. Thus when he saw a cleric it can scarcely be doubted that 'salt of the earth' was hovering somewhere in the back of his mind. The salt-cellar before him at dinner necessarily reminded him of the prelates of the Church. Whatever caught his attention presented itself to him in the form of an allegory, a parable, an equivoque, a proverb or a synonym – but seldom as the thing itself. His thoughts progressed in a preordained way in a world where every possibility was delineated within the patterns of a pre-established order.

Thus the pedagogical and philological rebellion of the humanists became the rallying-point in their more general revolt against the past. In it they substituted a programme of concrete research for the great logico-theological systems of the Middle Ages, already petrified by now, and declared war on the hierarchical and oppressively closed system of Aristotelianism in the name of Platonic liberty – which is to say, in a recognition of the possibility of many systems, and of the infinite varieties and contradictions of Being.

It was during Erasmus's last years at Deventer (probably 1482–1484) that two humanists Alexander Hegius and Ioannes Synthen, who were also adherents of the *devotio moderna*, came to the school, the former as its rector and the latter as a teacher. They began immediately 'to introduce better literature', as Erasmus says. Hegius was an enthusiastic teacher and a lover of books. It was probably at his lectures that Erasmus first became familiar with the basic ideas, or rather the basic requirements, of humanism: an enthusiasm for classical authors and history, a mastery of classical Latin and a gift for elegant and unambiguous expression. But Hegius, for all his love of teaching, was, like Synthen, a poor writer and a narrow personality. The first humanist Erasmus was to meet who fully deserved the title was Rudolf Agricola, a scholar who possessed a truly radiant mind.

Agricola was not a priest, nor did he have any connection with the *devotio*, except perhaps in his friendship with Hegius. It was at the request of the latter that the famous man agreed to come every Sunday to Deventer, for no fee, to lecture the two thousand boys on humanism. He was the first Friesian humanist of repute, and in every way a colourful character. His compatriots regarded him with both pride and horror. His love of poetry, literature and, above all, music, was unbounded. In his childhood he had been in the habit of following strolling pipers, and was often found by his father two or three days' journey from home. He studied everything that was offered at the universities of Erfurt, Cologne, Louvain, Paris, Pavia and Ferrara, lived a long time in Italy, and remained all his life a light-hearted and generous bohemian.

Being a man of the world and a veteran of many disputes, Agricola knew how to speak to both masters and boys at once without lowering his standards. These lectures no doubt contributed greatly to Erasmus's intellectual development, but other and more personal impressions may have been left behind as well. First, Agricola was a fellow countryman of his and from that same region which Erasmus never tired of calling the home of obscurantism, dullness and pettiness. Erasmus had before him the example of a Dutchman who had risen to knowledge and fame.

Moreover, for the innocent victim of an illicit union there was something which may have been an even more stimulating revelation: Agricola was also the son of a priest, and the circumstances of his origin were well known throughout Northern Europe thanks chiefly to a jest of his father's. On 17 February 1444, Agricola's father, Henri Hausman, had been appointed abbot ('Father') of a convent near Groningen. As he received this news a messenger arrived to inform him that his paramour had given birth to a son. 'God's blessing on it,' he is reported to have said. 'Today I have twice become a father!' This anecdote was known to every schoolchild in Holland. Almost certainly it was not lost on Erasmus that here was a man who, forced to carry the same burden as himself, had simply risen above it by becoming a famous humanist.

Evidently, however, Erasmus was anything but a good pupil, and, as with many who later display extraordinary mental ability, his early development was slow. In his own cryptic reference to this, he 'acquired some knowledge' during his years at Deventer, which is to say until he was fourteen or fifteen. It was probably his lack of success at school that prompted his mother to remove him finally and secure a place for him as a choirboy in the cathedral of Utrecht. A position in the cathedral choir was well paid and life-long. At Utrecht he came under the tutelage of Jacob Obrecht, sometimes considered the greatest master of counterpoint of the fifteenth century. But after a year or so Erasmus was found unsuited to the work and his mother took him back to the school.

The years at Deventer ended either in 1483 or 1484 in sudden tragedy. Plague had broken out again, and Erasmus's mother fell ill and died. With his brother Peter he walked home to Gouda only to find that their father was also seriously ill. Within a period of a few months he lost both parents, neither of whom had reached the age of forty.

Erasmus's father had appointed three guardians to look after his sons. These were Peter Winckel, the schoolmaster at Gouda, Winckel's brother and a third man whose name is unknown to us. According to Erasmus, his father left what would have been a substantial legacy, 'had it been faithfully administered'. Although ready for university by now, he was sent to yet another secondary school, that run by the Brethren at 's Hertogenbosch. The school there was still untouched by humanist influence, and it must have made Erasmus furious to find himself trapped in an atmosphere which, thanks to Hegius and Agricola, he had long since outgrown.

The autobiographical letter, written as usual in the third person, tells us:

> The boy was now sent to 's Hertogenbosch . . . where he spent, that is lost, nearly three years in the House of the Brethren, as it is called, in which Rombold taught at that time. This type of teacher is spread widely throughout the world, the destruction of good intellects, using the schools to promote monasticism. Rombold, who was much pleased with the boy's ability, began to encourage him to become one of his flock. The boy excused himself on the grounds of youth.

In the other letter, to the imaginary papal secretary, Erasmus tells how Winckel saw to it that the boys were safely out of the way in the school of the Brethren:

> Who, having nested everywhere, make a regular business of bringing up boys. Their chief concern, should they chance to see any youth of unusually high spirits and quick disposition, is to

break his spirit and to humble him with blows, threats, scoldings
and other means, which they call 'breaking in'. . . . They suffer from
a lack of good authors and live in their own obscurity . . . and since
they measure themselves by themselves and not by others . . . I
do not see why it is permitted them to instruct youth.

In spite of these difficulties, Erasmus says, he acquired a fairly
fluent style at 's Hertogenbosch and had access to some good
books. During his last year there he suffered from quartan fever,
and when plague broke out again the Brethren sent the students
home. This was probably towards the end of 1486, when Erasmus
was seventeen.

This time it was one of his guardians who died of plague; and
the other two, Peter Winckel and his brother, combined forces
to convince Erasmus and Peter to enter a monastery. They
argued that the country was torn by rebellion, piracy, robbery
and famine. Erasmus was frail and unable to work long hours.
What better solution, they reasoned, than the peaceful, carefree
life of a monk?

Erasmus tells us that he was under pressure from every side,
and that quartan fever had weakened his willpower. By chance
he met a former schoolmate from Deventer, now a monk in the
monastery at Steyn, not far from Gouda. The monk, Cornelius,
eloquently praised the spiritual life in the monastery and described the great library, the abundant leisure for reading and
the tranquillity of the monks' lives. Would Erasmus not take the
habit as well? After so much persuasion, Erasmus continues,
this was the push which took him over the brink. He agreed to
his guardians' demands and became a novice in the Augustinian
monastery at Steyn.

The decision was to prove unfortunate from many points of
view. Erasmus had no ascetic leanings, his field of interest was
predominantly secular and he was physically unsuited to the
rigours of monastic life. As this became more and more obvious,
however, he blamed his initial decision on his own lack of good
judgement, the situation he had been in and, not least, the pressures which others had brought to bear. Later he was to shift
all the blame on to Winckel and the Brethren of the Common

Life, whom he attacked in books and letters, whenever the opportunity presented itself, until his death.

There can be no doubt that he was less than just in this. It was in the school of the Brethren at Deventer that he had become acquainted with humanism through Hegius and Agricola. Moreover, he was inclined to forget that not only he, but the Brethren too, were changing during this period: by the end of the century they had adapted themselves with almost incredible ease to the demands of the time, and there was to remain little difference between their methods and the pedagogy of the humanists.

After nearly ten years of daily contact with the teachings and mode of life of the Brethren, Erasmus evidently did not notice, or at least never admitted, how thoroughly he had assimilated much of their viewpoint, especially in religious matters. On the contrary, he was consistently and vigorously to deny the direct and lasting influence they had in fact had on him. It is true that in his religious views he was to go much farther than the Brethren, but his simple piety resembled nothing so much as that primitive Christianity which they preached. Even more significant is the fact that his basic attitude towards religion, like that of Luther at the first stages of the Reformation (Luther was also thoroughly familiar with the teachings of the Brethren), was derived from the *devotio moderna* in its three essential points: acceptance of the Bible as primary authority, rejection of the systems of medieval theology, and unflagging criticism of the monastic orders. However curious the fact may be, it was in all this that the ideas of the *devotio* were to survive, though scarcely recognizable as coming from the same source when dealt with by such disparate men as Thomas à Kempis, Martin Luther and Erasmus.

It was probably late in 1487 when he was eighteen that Erasmus entered the monastery in which he was to spend six years. The priory at Steyn was an old foundation of the Augustinian order, a large building of a type found in many parts of Europe. It was later destroyed by fire, but a good description has been preserved in the *Analecta Daventria*. The cloister enclosed

EDGAR HOLLOWAY

NORTH

SEA

ENGLAND

FRIESLAND

Emden

Groningen

Bremen

UTRECHT MÜNSTER

Amsterdam

HOLLAND

GELDERLAND

The Hague

Utrecht

Münster

Rotterdam

ZEELAND

MÜNSTER

River Rhine

Dover

Calais

Bruges

Ghent

Antwerp

BRABANT

Malines

FLANDERS

Brussels

Louvain

Cologne

Artois

Liège

Aix-la-
Chapelle

PICARDY

HAINAUT

Namur

Dinant

Dieppe

Amiens

LUXEMBURG

Luxemburg

Mayence

Frankfort

Rouen

Beauvais

Trèves

Worms

Heidelberg

Reims

Verdun

Metz

LORRAINE

Paris

CHAMPAGNE

Chartres

Nancy

Strasburg

Stuttgart

Sens

Troyes

Orléans

Epinal

Colmar

River Rhine

DUCHY

FREE

NEVERS

COUNTY

Mülhausen

Nevers

Dijon

OF

Basel

SWISS

Besançon

Dôle

BURGUNDY

Berne

CONFEDERATION

Mâcon

SAVOY

Geneva

Lyons

100 MILES

0

0

160 KM

The Low Countries, c. 1475.

a square courtyard with a large chestnut tree in each corner; the small low-lintelled cells stood off long corridors, and the single, tiny window of each opened on to the courtyard. On one side of the monastery was a large vegetable garden which provided the monks with the bulk of their diet. It was safe from the ravages of rebellious peasants and wandering mercenaries, both of whom respected the inviolability of the enclosure. Next the kitchen was the library, which was fairly large: it contained besides the works of St Thomas, St Augustine, St Bernard, Albertus Magnus and the usual edifying works, a surprising number of classical poets and philosophers, including Virgil, Plautus and Aristotle.

There was little similarity between the monastery at Steyn and those foundations in which, at that time, ruffian and idle monks revelled on the money extorted from pious old women, and in which the priors and the majority of their flocks were terrorized by the ruffian elements. The rules had been somewhat relaxed, however, during the previous half-century under the influence of the *devotio*. Thus Erasmus was able to spend a good deal of time in the library, studying classical literature and writing the first of his poems.

Although there was a measure of freedom within its walls, Steyn was still a monastery and not an institution of classical learning. Some of the monks were inclined towards mysticism; others simply devoted themselves to those ascetic practices which are a foundation stone of the contemplative life. Both varieties of spiritual life were alien to Erasmus, and he openly admitted his inability to understand mysticism. While others attended to the mortification of the flesh, he professed temperance rather than asceticism, considering the latter both contemptible and worthless as a means to salvation. 'Perhaps God wishes to tempt us,' he wrote, 'but surely He does not want to torture us.'

He was painfully aware of his physical unsuitability to the life, and 'suffered atrociously' during periods of fasting. Looking back on it later he added contemptuously: 'One may find others who, having filled their bellies, can go without food longer than a vulture.' The complaint sounds less childishly petulant when we note that in later years his stomach troubled him so much that his doctors prescribed only the lightest of well-cooked food, and even that to be taken frequently and in small amounts. But perhaps in this case the causal interconnection should be reversed: when Erasmus maintains that he could not endure fasting and was consequently unable to live in the monastery, it seems likely that in reality he could not endure life in the monastery and, therefore, could not bring himself to fast.

The majority of the monks, being of peasant stock, were ruddily healthy, phlegmatic types who kept the rule as best they could and expressed their outlook in such proverbs as 'No learning, no doubts', 'Knowledge puffeth up' and 'Much learning maketh mad'. It is likely that Erasmus's intellectual pretensions, his constant studying and his hopes of earning eternal fame with his poetry met with a certain amount of derision in this atmosphere. Learning was his consolation, however, and he gathered a small circle of young monks around himself. Together they pursued the study of classical literature and poetry and practised writing letters on non-religious subjects (stylistic models, they hoped, to be used in the textbooks of the future). They criticized one another without pity and praised one another to the sky. At Steyn the monks were free to visit their neighbours' cells, and from Erasmus we learn that whole nights were spent discussing humanism or in reading aloud the plays of Terence.

One of his companions at Steyn was his former schoolmate at Deventer, Cornelius Gerards, the young man who had helped persuade him to enter the monastery in the first place. Two others were William Hermans of Gouda and Servatius Rogers of Rotterdam, the latter a tall and handsome young man who was later to become prior of the monastery. Both Cornelius and William had entered the monastery to escape the extreme poverty of their homes, and, though good Christians like Erasmus, they also lacked any real vocation to the religious life. Both wrote neo-Latin poetry of some merit, 'Solacing themselves with their studies,' in the words of Erasmus, 'as prisoners might.'

It was the humanists' universal custom to write innumerable letters, for the stylistic exercise involved if for nothing else. Erasmus had few people outside Steyn to write to; thus with the playfulness of youth added to the essential motive of improving his prose style, he often wrote to his friends within the same building. These letters testify to the rapture he felt at having at last found real friends, *des amis particuliers* as it were, after a lonely adolescence. In them he discussed the poetry of Cornelius and William, copied out his own latest verses and engaged in arguments concerning the Italian humanists Poggio and Valla, defending the latter for his style and erudition and censuring the former for obscenity. He added outspoken passages on the monks' philistine surroundings and on the generally lamentable state of Dutch culture.

His third friend, Servatius, seems to have lagged behind the others in intellectual and poetical skill. However, the most intimate and impassioned of his letters were addressed to Servatius, letters in which his enthusiasm for humanism and classicism gave way to romantic sensitivity and protestations of devotion. These letters, characterized by their lack of restraint and by phrases reminiscent of Dante's 'sweet new style' and later to be echoed in the prose of the late eighteenth century, are of a type found nowhere else in the ten thousand folio pages of Erasmus's collected works.

'My mind is such,' he wrote to Servatius, 'that I think nothing in life can rank higher than friendship, that nothing should be more ardently desired or more jealously desired.' He reminded Servatius of the famous friends of antiquity, Orestes and Pylades, Theseus and Pirithous, Damon and Pythias, all examples for them to follow. 'I place my hopes in you alone. I have become yours so completely that you have left me naught of myself.' And later: 'When you are away nothing is sweet to me; in your presence I care for nothing else. When I see you happy I forget my own sorrows.'

I would write to you more frequently, my dearest Servatius [begins another letter], if I knew for certain that you would not be more fatigued by reading my letters than I am by writing them;

and your comfort is so dear to me that I would rather be tortured
by that which gives you rest than fatigue you by that which gives
me pleasure. But since lovers find nothing so distressing as not
being allowed to meet one another . . . I long . . . to see you face
to face as often as we please. That joy is denied us. I cannot think of
it without tears . . . Farewell, my soul, and if there is anything
human in you, return the love of him who loves you.

Servatius evidently replied in rather lofty style and, as often
happens in such exercises, displayed his eloquence better than
he did his feelings; for Erasmus soon encouraged him to disregard classical Latin, a most untypical piece of advice and one
certainly never to be repeated. 'Don't write,' he answered, 'with
borrowed sentences or, what is worse, by compiling sentences
from Bernard and Claudian; you need not be ashamed of barbarism when writing to me.' In another letter he mysteriously
gives himself up to resignation: 'I have left nothing untried
which might affect the young mind, but you persist in your
resolve, more than adamant.' We are not told what resolve it
was that Servatius persisted in.

Friendships of this kind were anything but rare in the religious life of the time, and, within certain well-defined limits,
were approved of even by the Brethren of the Common Life.
It may be that Servatius, fearing Erasmus's jealousy and the
violence of his affections, asked his friend to be more moderate.
Perhaps, being more at home in the monastery and with the
discipline it required, he remembered the warning of the theologian Gerson of the Sorbonne, much quoted throughout the
fifteenth century: *amor spiritualis facile labitur in nudum carnalem
amorem* (spiritual love easily changes into naked carnal love), and
was retreating before the danger. In any case, Erasmus changed
his attitude and never again mentioned his love to Servatius,
limiting himself instead to lectures on literature, philosophy and
humanism, and, if anything, with more spirit and wit than before.

After a year in the novitiate Erasmus took his solemn vows and,
as he says, 'immediately began to repent of it'. In spite of his

habit of lamenting the years lost at Steyn, it is unlikely that he was as consistently unhappy there as he would have us believe. At any event the six years undeniably furthered his intellectual development and were well spent in preparation for the future.

From this point on, thanks to Erasmus's collected works and his voluminous correspondence, we are able to follow the development of his mind, even down to the sequence of his reading, until the last days of his life. According to his own testimony he acquired much of his stylistic ability while at the school. Those of his writings which date from Steyn do indeed show a thorough knowledge of classical Latin, their style being based largely on Cicero, Sallust and Quintilian; and yet this style was not pedantic, nor even quite puristic. Even at this stage of boundless enthusiasm for the classics Erasmus did not limit himself to the vocabulary of a society dead a thousand years. He was already modernizing his Latin, adapting it to the needs of his time and not, as Machiavelli said of certain humanists, 'attempting to resurrect the dead things of the past'.

For the time being, however, his style remained not so much over-embellished as too complicated and fastidious, a reflection perhaps of his youthful rapture at having acquired the skill to play with the language with confidence. Later on his style was to become much simpler and clearer, not least of all because he wanted to be unequivocally understood by the widest possible audience.

His knowledge of classical writers increased steadily, especially of the poets from Virgil to Claudian; and to these he added his first Greek author, Plato, probably in Marsilio Ficino's splendid new Latin translation, published in Florence in 1484.

It seems to have been at Steyn that he also acquired his real familiarity with the scholastics, though he was later to deny that he knew them well. One of the humanists' favourite jibes at the scholastics was to maintain that they had been unable to struggle through their books. There are only a very few references in Erasmus's writings to scholastic reading, and perhaps because of this some of his biographers have maintained that he had no inkling of those theological systems against which he

fought so single-mindedly. It would be hard to reconcile this
view, however, with the fact that Erasmus later acquired a doctorate in theology – let alone the obvious fact that he was
scarcely able to resist reading anything which passed through
his hands. Some scrutiny of his books as opposed to his letters
and especially his annotations to the New Testament, his
polemics against the Inquisition and much else of his later work
serves amply to demonstrate a thoroughgoing familiarity with
the most important writings of Aquinas, Scotus, Albertus
Magnus, Abelard, Bernard, Lombardus, and even many lesser
figures. On one occasion he went as far as to confess to a youthful infatuation with the works of Gerson, the last great scholastic
of the Sorbonne and the persecutor of Jan Hus, a man whose
very name one might have expected him to loath.

By far the most important aspect of Erasmus's years at Steyn
was his gradual but wholehearted conversion to the humanist
cause. Throughout much of his life he had no doubt heard much
about the 'glorious and legendary humanists, who should be
listened to with awe and followed, even though they cannot be
fathomed by ordinary mortals'. It was said quite pointedly and
in exact reflection of the humanists' view of themselves that
they, with their discovery of classical antiquity and their programme of learning, were the harbingers of a new age; that the
earth was not, after all, necessarily a valley of tears, the habitat
of misery and irreversible decay it had seemed to preceding ages.
Human affairs, it was asserted, could be altered and directed
towards the better, for the soul of man is a divine spark, even
a part of God Himself separated from Him by nothing more than
the barrier of free will; God has set no limits on human endeavour in order that man might reasonably strive for perfection
– which aim, universally pursued, would inevitably result in a
rebirth of the Golden Age.

This was at least the gist of the sentiment which spread north-
wards from Italy and fanned out across the Continent, and it
must have been very much in Erasmus's mind as he decided to
escape from the monastic life and become a humanist, a man of
letters and a poet. The pull of a true vocation, belatedly dis-

covered, probably added to his intention. It would be impossible to say, however, which came first: the desire to escape from the monastery by means of a literary career, or the intention of becoming a humanist and its attendant necessity of leaving the monastery.

Knowledge of the classics, elegant style, perfect command of Latin, appreciation of antique wisdom, predilection for poetry, literature, rhetoric, history, law and Platonism: these were the weapons which humanism pitted against scholasticism. And against these the scholastics held up their theological systems, Latin Averroism, dialectics, medicine, predilection for the natural sciences and Aristotelianism. This controversy between scholastic syllogisms and Florentine letters, Aristotelian categories and neo-Platonist dreams, Padovan agnosticism and humanist piety, was, roughly speaking, the order of battle throughout the whole age. It was as well the line of propaganda which the humanists employed in their attack, often for purely polemical reasons and almost always with demagogical methods. The scholastics replied with an equal amount of demagoguery, to which they frequently added charges of heresy and denunciations to the Inquisition.

For the man of the fifteenth century humanism appeared a rather complex science, an intellectual and anarchistic guild in which each member was perfectly free to entertain the most radical and individualistic views, to continue the work of his predecessors or else to demolish it at will. Thus to Petrarch (1304–74) it meant the exploration of man's inner life as well as a deep concern with civic virtue. Seeing an antithesis between humanist piety and the agnosticism of the Padovan professors, Petrarch adopted an extremely hostile attitude towards the scientific bent of the latter.

Colluccio Salutati (1331–1406), chancellor of the republic of Florence, maintained that 'Thomistic Aristotelianism', by which he meant dialectical gymnastics for the adept but not for the masses, had been foisted upon the Church with the result that

Christianity had been robbed of its original nature. His own philosophy was culled from the teachings of Christ, Socrates and St Francis, whom he considered the only messengers of truth.

Leonardo Bruni d'Arezzo (1369–1444) was interested chiefly in politics, holding that 'among the moral doctrines through which human life is shaped, those which refer to states and their governments occupy the highest position'. Against Stoic asceticism and monastic withdrawal, he insisted on 'the obligation of men to live among men'. He advocated a Socratic devotion to one's fellow citizens, claiming this to be nothing more nor less than that love of one's neighbour which Christ demanded.

Poggio and Valla, as we shall see, were chiefly interested in the moral sciences and philology; they quarrelled, however, vilifying one another in scurrilous pamphlets as long as they lived. And finally there was Leon Battista Alberti (1404–72), the greatest architect of his time, who gave the Santa Maria Novella in Florence its present form and built much else throughout Italy. Alberti, long called the 'discoverer of nature', was the inventor of the *camera obscura* and the science of geodesy. A mentor of Leonardo da Vinci, he was a champion of the natural sciences and was especially devoted to mathematics, which he called the 'secret code of the universe'.

It was only after he left Steyn that Erasmus was to read the works of the next generation of Italian humanists, the Florentine neo-Platonists, especially Angelo Poliziano (1454–94) and Giovanni Pico della Mirandola (1463–94), who were still alive while he was in the monastery. His acquaintance with the French, English and German humanists was as well of a later date. It must be remembered that he had no opportunity to read systematically; many of the humanists had not yet been printed, and he had to satisfy himself with such books as he could find in Dutch libraries or could borrow from friends. But even with this taken into consideration it is amazing that he read none of Petrarch's works until 1527, 35 years after he left Steyn.

Four humanist authors were especially favoured by Erasmus while he was in the monastery. One of these, Francesco Filelfo

(1398–1481), served him as a sort of cicerone among the writings of the others. Filelfo was a prolific writer who had been personally acquainted with the greatest personalities of the fifteenth century and had carried on a staggering amount of correspondence with many of them. He had witnessed and recorded the most important events of his time. As one of his colleagues wrote after his death, 'Filelfo always heard more than he was told and always wrote down more than he understood, leaving after an undeservedly long life an enormous heap of chit-chat utterly without value'. A revealing, if somewhat unfair assessment. For his contemporaries Filelfo's work had been a sort of sporadically appearing gossip column, the unofficial minutes of the Platonic Academy and a who's who of humanism. In short, he provided an unserious but nonetheless invaluable handbook of the movement; and Erasmus could hardly have found anyone better to start with.

Gianfrancesco Poggio Bracciolini (1380–1459), whom Erasmus had mentioned as an 'obscene brawler' in a letter written at Steyn, was an indefatigable discoverer of lost manuscripts and the author of *Facetiae*, a collection of ribald anecdotes. It may be assumed that the letter in which Poggio was referred to in this manner was written during Erasmus's early period at Steyn, when he played, or perhaps was, the perfect figure of a contented monk, displaying even an unwonted measure of Pharisaism. His opinion of Poggio may have changed when, still in the monastery, he read his famous *Contra hypocritas* (*Against Hypocrites*), a furious attack against monasticism and asceticism.

At first scandalized by Poggio, Erasmus was later delighted by the man who denounced monks as 'pseudo-humans' for preaching poverty and 'making our life sour' while 'we keep them alive and build cities'. In a Platonistic dialogue begun at Steyn we find an equally strong denunciation of monasticism, seclusion and martyrdom, its train of thought borrowed from Poggio. In his later years Erasmus was to lavish especial praise on Poggio and to maintain that he was one of the humanists he had most preferred throughout his life.

The humanist who was highest in his esteem, however, and to

whom he was most indebted was Lorenzo di Valla (1407–57), secretary to Pope Nicholas V. To Valla humanism meant a positive evaluation of life. It was he who wrote the first studied criticism of the wealth and secular power of the Church, and whose self-appointed task it had been to reestablish classical Latin as 'the worthy vehicle of the living Spirit become word'. At Steyn Erasmus first read Valla's treatise *De libero arbitrio* (*On Free Will*), a spirited assault against Aristotelian theology and an enthusiastic proclamation, with somewhat Pauline overtones, of Christian faith. It would perhaps not be an exaggeration to say that Erasmus's own strongly Pauline Catholicism was, in many ways, close to Valla's, as was his belief in free will as a prerequisite of human dignity.

Valla's other famous work, the *Elegantiae*, served Erasmus, as it did his whole generation, as a textbook of Latin style. It concerned itself with elegance, accuracy and shading; elegance being, perhaps, over-emphasized. It was from this book that Erasmus really learned how to read; that is, not to accept the written word as having a magical authority of its own, but to demand that it make sense, that texts have concrete significance and that every assertion, idea or theory, no matter how sacrosanct, be carefully examined.

From a letter written by Erasmus to Cornelius we know that he had read Valla's *De voluptate* (*On Pleasure*), as well. In *De voluptate*, a dialogue, Valla had asserted that pleasure is a serene movement of the soul, the reward of labour and an aspect of beauty, i.e. of God. He maintained that both ascetics and Stoics disfigure the truth by seeing in the universe nothing but warfare between sensuality and reason, body and soul, black and white. This, he insisted, is the extreme dualism of Manichean heresy, a slander against the supreme chastity of nature and its eternal harmony.

It would be false to claim that Erasmus shared these views in their entirety; and yet the substance of them was approved by him, as by nearly every major humanist, especially if we rephrase Valla's denial of extreme dualism in terms slightly less abstract and describe it as a belief in the eternal harmony of created things and in an essentially serene world inhabited by a fallible but by no means hopelessly corrupted race of men, and in a God whose greatness is felt in his proximity to man rather than in his distance from him. In this form Valla's view was widely accepted at this time; it was shared by many popes and was not held to be outside the doctrines of the Church in any way.

Later, when Luther came to attack this amalgam of pagan, humanist and Catholic thought as Pelagian heresy, and to speak of an utterly corrupted race of men and of a God Who hates mankind and had done so even before the Creation, the matter was to become a major point of dissension during the Reformation. It cut deeply, dividing men into two mutually antagonistic camps: those who believed in free will, which is ultimately to say in human endeavour, and those who denied it.[3] It goes without saying that there could be no peace nor even compromise, between such adversaries, living or dead.

No survey of Erasmus's reading at Steyn, however brief, would be complete without mentioning his very special intellectual affinities with Aeneas Sylvius Piccolomini (1405–64), a writer of no small stature who had succeeded in scandalizing posterity with a love story, *Euryalus and Lucretia*. Aeneas's own contemporaries were perhaps even more scandalized when he went over from Italy to the anti-pope in Basle, 'over the Alps and, if necessary, through the gates of hell towards my career'. He became the legate of the anti-pope at the court of the emperor, was crowned poet laureate by Frederick III, became bishop of Trieste, then archbishop of Siena and, in 1459, Pope Pius II. He was anything but a saintly man, displaying far more interest in literature, erotic poetry and such matters as the reconquest of Constantinople from the Infidel. Yet he did in fact organize a crusade, out of purely ethical motives it might be said, and when its leaders, Charles the Bold and King Matthias of Hungary, failed to show up at Ancona, the port of

---

[3] As long as this remained at issue it made a common ground among such otherwise incompatible people as Savonarola, Calvin, Cranmer, Knox, Wesley and others, against such equally dissimilar figures as St Francis Dante and Erasmus.

embarkation, Aeneas Sylvius himself went to lead the armies, dying of heart failure as he arrived in Ancona on 14 August 1464.

His books, especially the *Commentarii* and *In Europam sui temporis*, mirror the early Renaissance in all its richness. Nothing escaped his notice, from statistics to chemistry, hunting, geography, folk-lore, dancing, boat-racing and archaeology; and precisely because of this there are no analogies to be drawn between his writings and those of Erasmus. His vivid imagination and far-flung interests were alien to Erasmus, who worked for humanism and for the world while Aeneas Sylvius was intent upon enjoying both to the hilt. Yet, with the possible exceptions of Socrates, St Paul, Origen and Christ himself, there was no one of whom Erasmus was to write so tenderly or with such awe. Unfortunately, however, he never tells us the real reasons for this intimate intellectual relationship in which Aeneas Sylvius seems to have been something between a paragon and a guardian angel to him – a paragon whose accession to the throne of St Peter had been a triumph of the humanist cause, in whose long career there had been no trace of fanaticism from beginning to end; and a guardian angel who had been a careerist with a taste for erotics and a lenient attitude towards human frailty. It was perhaps in some such terms that Erasmus thought of Aeneas Sylvius, who had been weak in small matters but adamant in important ones, who had longed for the same clarity, dignity and noble proportions in life which Erasmus was to seek. And when in later life Erasmus declared that he did not want to be admired or venerated, but merely loved as a frail Christian, he can hardly have failed to be aware that he was echoing Aeneas Sylvius's sentiments exactly.

As a result of Erasmus's six years at Steyn he left two short books, the first fruits of his literary career. A third, more important work was begun in his last years in the monastery, but its completion had to await a change of surroundings.

The first was a treatise entitled *De contemptu mundi* (*On Contempt of the World*), written during that early phase in which he either actually liked monastic life or else was trying to persuade himself that he did. It is a tract on the advantages of the monastery over the world, a favourite subject of edifying literature during the Middle Ages and for some time afterwards. Other than its admirable style the book has few merits, consisting for the most part of the repetition of well-known arguments.

More than 120 years before, in 1365, Petrarch had written a book of the same title. Well aware of the importance of true spirituality as opposed to scholastic dialectics and games of formal logic, Petrarch had hoped to attain the former by withdrawing from the world, by holding it in contempt. He had tried every means to achieve this. Being no ascetic, however, he constantly lost the struggle to do violence to his own nature, and inevitably returned to his basic concern with the world of men and action. It is a pity that Erasmus was not yet familiar with these beautiful and tormented pages, for they are a human document of the highest order.

Erasmus was not to publish his own *De contemptu mundi* for several decades, not, in fact until this was made necessary in the most painful manner. In all probability he had never intended to publish it at all. A copy of the manuscript remained at Steyn and, in 1521, the monks began circulating it throughout the Low Countries and Germany. It was no small triumph for them to demonstrate that Erasmus, then universally famous as the unyielding mocker of monasticism, had once been a humble monk who had written in favour of a life which he was now claiming to have always detested.

There are many pleasing lines in the second book, a thin volume of Latin verse. Erasmus, like many others, was able by dint of diligence, leisure and natural good taste to acquire the necessary skill to write Latin poetry which never quite sank to the mediocre. During the Renaissance and for some time after everyone was considered a poet who could versify conventional poetic subjects with some proficiency. By this standard Erasmus was indeed a poet. By more rigorous and realistic standards, however, a poet must be considered to be one who expresses his passions and visions in an entirely new way and conveys them permanently, and in mysterious fashion, to his reader. In this sense Erasmus falls far short of being a poet.

One wonders at how little has survived of that astonishing heap of neo-Latin poetry written between the fifteenth and nineteenth centuries. The humanists, in promoting classical Latin as an international language at the expense of dog-Latin, hoped by this means to bring about the intellectual and literary unity of Europe. They thought, with some reason, that the dis-integration of the Continent into chauvinistic national entities had been caused by the multiplicity of the vernaculars, and hoped fervently that classical Latin, the language of the learned classes, would slowly displace what they thought of as coarse country dialects. In a sense they were probably right: had they triumphed Europe would in all likelihood have become unified again in one way or another. But for all practical purposes they failed to realize that their plan was anachronistic, that the ver-naculars had already won the day and that the national literatures which rose out of them throbbed with the vitality of living speech.

Thus Poggio had once pitied Dante for having written his *Divine Comedy* not in Latin hexameters, as he had originally intended, but in Tuscan – thus depriving the work of eternal fame. Petrarch believed that his reputation was firmly anchored in his pedantic Latin epic *Africa*, not in his Italian sonnets, which he considered frivolous. The humanist Angelo Poliziano wrote in three languages: his best poems are those in Italian, followed by those in Greek; those in Latin are by far the weakest. The foremost poets of the entire era, those whose fame has survived to any real extent – Charles d'Orléans, François Villon, Lorenzo de' Medici, Pulci, Bojardo, Ariosto, Garcilaso de la Vega and, later, Tasso, Spenser, Ronsard, Camões, Balassi and Kochan-owski – all wrote in the vernacular. There are to be sure a few exceptions to the rule, for example the Dutch Ioannes Secundus and the Neapolitan Giovanni Pontano, both of whom restricted themselves to Latin and still have a secure place in the history of literature. But the muses have generally favoured those who write in the speech of their childhood. Although Erasmus continued to write poetry throughout his life, and in the beginning had hopes of making a career of it, he certainly did not consider himself a great poet, as indeed he was not.

On 25 April 1492, at the age of about twenty-two, Erasmus was ordained a priest at the hands of the bishop of Utrecht, David of Burgundy, on the occasion of the latter's visit to Steyn. The bishop was a great patron of learning and had formerly shielded the humanist Wessel (the same who had foretold that the scholastics would soon be 'drummed out of town') when he was accused of heresy by the witch-hunting Dominicans. It is probable that the prior of Steyn, Werner, told the visiting dignitary about the outstanding abilities of the young monk, and that the decision to find a more suitable background to his talents was taken jointly. In any event, it was about half a year later that a neighbour of the bishop, Bishop Henri of Cambray, was planning a journey to Rome in the hope of being created a cardinal, and thus found himself in need of a secretary with a perfect command of Latin. Some months later, we do not know exactly when, Erasmus, as an Augustinian canon, was granted leave from Steyn to enter the service of Bishop Henri. Thus it was his learning, or more specifically his knowledge of classical Latin, which provided as nothing else could a means of escaping the monastery.

Little is known about the two or three years which Erasmus spent in the service of the bishop of Cambray. Henri's hereditary residence was at Bergen-op-Zoom, but he was constantly on the move between Louvain, Brussels, Mechlin and his country house at Halsteren, skilfully coordinating his pastoral duties with avoiding the plague, both of which were likely to crop up at any point in his large diocese. He also travelled constantly because he loved good food, wine and festivities, and since most of his income was paid in kind he had to transfer his household and entourage frequently to maintain it in style. He seems to have been a kind-hearted and generous man. Being naïve and something of a dreamer as well, he always took for granted the gratification of his whims, and was perpetually making lavish promises which he could never hope to keep – an aspect of his personality which Erasmus never learned to appreciate.

Henri had chosen Erasmus as his secretary in order to have a first-rate Latinist at his side in Rome, where, once he became a cardinal, he would have only one more step to make in the career he had planned for himself. It is likely that this idea of being promoted in the hierarchy occurred to him during the events of 1492, when Lorenzo de' Medici, Pope Innocent VIII, and then Emperor Frederick III all died one after the other. His hopes can only have been increased when the former vice-chancellor of the Church, Rodrigo Cardinal Borgia, for many years an able administrator who had promised sweeping ecclesiastical reforms, acceded to the papal throne as Alexander VI.

It took Bishop Henri a long time to realize that any trip to Rome was destined to fail, and therefore that he had no need of a Latinist secretary. He probably learned the real state of affairs in Rome from his friend the archbishop of Rheims, who was in close touch with the new pope's arch-enemy, Giulio Cardinal della Rovere, who had fled Rome and taken refuge in France. The archbishop may have explained to Henri that he would not be able to become a cardinal without a considerable amount of money and, being poor, he should give up his hopes of advancement in the hierarchy, at least while Alexander VI was pope. Erasmus's hopes of seeing Italy collapsed with the frustration of Bishop Henri's dreams.

We know little about his duties as the bishop's secretary. It is even questionable that he had any duties as such. Henri of Bergen was not a man to dismiss someone from his colourful entourage simply because he had no apparent purpose there. It is not altogether clear just how Erasmus reacted to the situation, but when his friend William Hermans wrote him a moving letter from Steyn to say that his former friends, though missing him sorely, rejoiced that at least one of them had found his way back to freedom, Erasmus replied that he for his part envied them, for at least they could write in the privacy of their own cells and at their own pleasure. This was probably written out of tenderness, for Erasmus was determined not to return to the monastery. His interest in the bishop's court had vanished, however, and he did not know where to turn.

Although moving incessantly about the countryside and subjected after the fasting of Steyn to an equally disagreeable regimen of feasting, Erasmus managed to continue his studies in an environment in which piety and gluttony coexisted without complications. The bishop's company was more devoted to the pleasures of the table than to intellectual pursuits, and Erasmus had little in common with them to talk about. Besides a few Latin poems, he managed to complete two books during this time. One of these was the Platonistic dialogue *Antibarbari*, in which he attacked scholasticism in the usual manner, if with less demagoguery than was the custom, and raised for the first time some basic questions relating to the new pedagogy. This book, which had been begun at Steyn, was finished in the spring of 1494 at the bishop's country house at Halsteren where, once again, the company had taken refuge from an outbreak of plague. The second book was a less original work. It contained annotations to Valla's *Elegantiae* together with a commentary on the text.

The first book, *Antibarbari*, is in the form of a Platonic dialogue. It is full of youthful charm and ease, and is particularly revealing of Erasmus's development in its treatment of the problems of the age. The dialogue is set in the countryside surrounding Halsteren. The participants are William Hermans and a new friend, James Batt. While out strolling they encounter the burgomaster of the town and one Jodocus, a physician. The four begin a discussion of the essence of learning: does it consist in studying outdated grammars, memorizing the Psalms and lists of synonyms and knowing words but not their meanings? Or does learning mean history, literature and philosophy? Who represents true learning, the scholastic theologians and philosophers or the classical authors? Are the scholastics right in considering classical learning pernicious to faith and morals? Will boys be corrupted by reading

Plato rather than Aquinas, or Virgil, Horace and Terence rather than Scotus, Occam and Buridan? Had the teachings of scholastic theology achieved anything during the past centuries other than ensuring its own survival? And what would happen in the coming generations when the teaching of the classics would be widespread? Finally, and most important, they inquired into the connection between learning and morality. Does the former promote the latter, implying that the educated man is more ethical? Thus runs the dialogue, with Batt presenting strong arguments in favour of secular learning, taking the Erasmian point of view. This is countered by a carefully constructed, but not distorted presentation of the traditional stand as voiced by the burgomaster.

There are passages in *Antibarbari*, for example the lines concerning the 'saintly, irresistible, most subtle and seraphic teachers' who attribute to themselves an importance 'before which the very majesty of the Gospels is expected to yield'. which could be held up as harbingers of Erasmus's later advocacy of religious reform. Or the passages in which Batt-Erasmus skilfully alludes to the fact that the medieval Church, rather than concerning itself with the word of God, fostered nothing but theological quarrels. Yet if we attempt to do this we find at once that what we have done is to impose the thoughts of a later Erasmus upon the works of the young man. The tone of *Antibarbari* towards religious reform, and for that matter towards religion itself, is entirely negative. Erasmus was still rebelling here against the monastery, his environment and the influence of the Brethren; he attacked scholasticism as well as the practices of medieval piety, but, like his humanist predecessors, he had nothing to offer in their stead.

There is a central idea, however, or rather an implicit scheme, in *Antibarbari* which must be emphasized. With this book Erasmus had already found his method: to choose one of the chief issues of the day, expound its central problems in a book and then follow in the wake of the original idea with other books in which detailed explanation and clarification are given, rather than apodictic statement and rigid definition. For more than forty years he was to explore in this fashion the most crucial issues, including many which went all but unnoticed by his contemporaries. He was to examine these problems cautiously, using such words as 'probably', 'perhaps' and 'possibly' more frequently than had any writer since classical times. This sort of intellectual honesty led his enemies to call him a cynic and a sceptic, though the driving force of Erasmus was nothing if not unshakable optimism. He knew that every issue was many-sided, and did his best to detect and scrutinize each aspect of it. His adversaries clung stubbornly to the idea that all phenomena were possessed of that one face which they happened or wanted to see. This is one reason why everyone who presented himself as the repository of unalterable and eternal truth, from Aristotle to St Thomas, from Savonarola to Luther, necessarily aroused Erasmus's suspicion and antipathy.

In *Antibarbari* he chose to deal with what was in some respects the most important issue of the day: the substitution of one method of teaching for another, and the way in which the newer method, along with the book printing which accompanied it, was altering every aspect of human life from morals and ethics down to the very basis of the social order itself. Although the humanists had of course been much involved with matters of learning, no one had questioned its nature or essential purpose since antiquity. Erasmus agreed with the humanists, as far as they had gone, that learning would indeed benefit mankind. But he went on to devote the greater part of his life not only to the propagation of this idea but to explaining why it was true.

During this period Erasmus acquired a valuable friend in the previously-mentioned James Batt, the young secretary of the town council of Bergen-op-Zoom. Batt became an admirer of Erasmus, and he possessed, as his friend did not, a mind capable of dealing effectively with everyday affairs. Not knowing what to do with his life at this juncture, Erasmus turned to Batt for advice. Matters were particularly complicated by the fact that he had just finished his *Antibarbari*, which of course he hoped to publish. But such a book, a violent attack against scholasticism coming from the pen of a bishop's secretary, would have created a scandal.

Batt ingeniously suggested that Erasmus should persuade Bishop Henri to send him to the Sorbonne to acquire a doctorate in theology: in this way he could avoid returning to the monastery, escape the boredom of the bishop's court and, once in Paris, easily have his book published. Bishop Henri, when approached, raised no objections to the plan; on the contrary, he was delighted with the idea of playing Maecenas to a promising scholar, and offered him a lavish stipend. Thus Henri procured a place for his young secretary in the Collège de Montaigu, and then, in the autumn of 1495, sent him on his way to Paris.

II

The Collège de Montaigu

Arriving in Paris full of dreams of becoming a great humanist, a famous and independent champion of classical learning, Erasmus soon added loneliness to the list of his ills. With his usual lucidity of mind he almost certainly did not fail to realize that the odds were heavily against him. He was now nearly twenty-six and more than commonly aware that the majority of men did not live much past forty. Both his parents had died before reaching that age, and in the previous year Angelo Poliziano had died after his fortieth birthday. Pico had died at thirty-one. And he was still an Augustinian monk, subject to recall at any time by his prior. He longed for a fame much greater than any 'restricted to the Bishopric of Utrecht', and wanted to become 'a voluntary citizen of the world'; but he was forced to carry among all his other burdens that of his Dutch origin, the stigma of coming from a country considered to be the intellectual backwater of Europe.

In order not to come into conflict with Bishop Henri and Prior Werner he would have to study theology, which by now held no interest for him. To become a humanist, provided there was time left over from his theological studies to do so, he would still have to find a patron. Paris was not Florence (not that patrons were growing on trees in Florence now that Savonarola was ruling from his pulpit and proclaiming that the piety of old women counted for more than all the erudition of Plato), and it was anything but easy to find a patron in Paris if one was not already a well-known humanist; and to become a well-known humanist one first needed time and money, which is to say a patron.

His health had always been precarious at best. He suffered constantly from insomnia and therefore generally worked until long after midnight. Once awakened, no matter how briefly, he could not rest again. The result of this was that he spent many days in a state of groggy stupefaction. Nor was there anything promising in his very unprepossessing appearance: he wore a flat cap to hide his unusually low cranium, a physical peculiarity which, according to popular belief, indicated foolishness; his blond hair was sparse and straggling; he had watery blue eyes, thin lips, a pallid complexion and a nose so long and pointed that it was compared to the prow of a ship. In no sense could he have been described as handsome, although he seems to have attracted a certain type of woman who mistook the pallor and the long nose as indications of monkish lecherousness.

Against his ill-health, poverty, unpleasant mien and total lack of fame he was armed with formidable intelligence and humour, a remarkable clarity of thought, charm of speech and ease and fluency of literary style. He was industrious, and the tenacity of his mind could force his ailing body to do its bidding, except in the single matter of forcing it to sleep. By the time of his arrival in Paris he had already decided to make all the necessary compromises and sacrifices for a career, but, unlike his exemplar Aeneas Sylvius, he was far too shy and unsure of himself to go about finding an opportunity to do so. Moreover, his conscience reprimanded him sharply whenever he attempted anything not in line with his strict moral principles. But he was already an excellent Latinist, fairly well-versed in the *studia humanitatis* (though rather less so than he thought), and in his baggage he had the manuscripts of three completed books: *Antibarbari*, the annotations to Valla and the Latin poems.

It seems scarcely credible that such a man should ever have fulfilled his extravagant dreams; but humanism needed a leader, the printing-presses were still awaiting a universally popular contemporary author, and, as is so often the case when a name achieves immortality, the most unlikely of men arrived at the most opportune time.

*

The Collège de Montaigu in which Bishop Henri had procured a place for Erasmus was a very famous institution. Its rector, Jan Standonck van Mechlin, had also been educated by the Brethren of the Common Life. His spiritual ideal was St Francis of Paula, that ascetic who had been brought to Paris by King Louis XI and had subsisted on roots and never washed. Standonck maintained the atmosphere of the *devotio* at its harshest in his college, a regimen of abstinence and silence. Any student who displayed an interest in humanistic studies was automatically suspect, and the slightest infraction of the rules was punished by flogging.

Erasmus slept in the communal dormitory, which was dark, mouldy and malodorous. His colleagues, mostly young men between sixteen and twenty, were interested in little but scholastic theology and the mortification of their own flesh. Thus Erasmus found himself more than ever in the clutches of a system he had been trying to escape throughout his life.

The diet at the college seems to have consisted chiefly of eggs and herring. No meat was ever eaten. Twenty-five years later Erasmus was to describe something of this life in his dialogue *Ichthuophagia* (*On the Eating of Fish*). He spoke of the students drawing stagnant water each morning from the well in the courtyard, and the rotting walls of the ground floor dormitory, adjacent to a stinking privy.

> I shall say nothing of the merciless whippings, even of innocent persons . . . nor shall I take notice of the number of rotten eggs which were eaten . . . perhaps these things have been rectified by now. It is too late, however, for those who are already dead or are carrying infected carcasses about. Nor do I mention these things because I bear ill-will towards the Collège; I thought it worthwhile to give this account lest human severity disfigure those of callow and tender years under the pretext of religion.

Erasmus's judgement seems lenient compared with that of the Parisian populace, who had dubbed the Collège de Montaigu

'the very cleft between the buttocks of Mother Theology'; or
that of Rabelais, who in his time longed to burn the place to the
ground. Two of those who lived beneath its roof with Erasmus
were later numbered among his bitterest enemies: the Picard
Noel Beda, a member of the Inquisition, and Jean Major, a
Scotsman who was to become one of the last apologists of
scholasticism. Their names have survived primarily thanks to the
vitriolic ridicule heaped upon them by Rabelais, and, in the case
of Beda, thanks to a book Erasmus wrote against his calumnies.
It must be added, however, that the views of Erasmus and
Rabelais should not be taken for more than they were: the
natural antagonism of humanists against all such institutions.
The other students seem not to have minded the diet, the stench
or the filth; and the floggings, we know, were generally received
with humility or even satisfaction. Shortly after Erasmus's
time in the college two other students, whose names are remembered no less than his, entered those dank dormitories and were
to look back on the institution with nostalgia for the rest of their
lives: Ignatius Loyola and Jean Calvin.

Compared with the strength of the theological faculty of the
Sorbonne, the power of the humanists in France was quite small.
In pre-Reformation Paris it was not only the power structure
which counted, however, but the peculiarity of the situation as
well. The doctors of the Sorbonne were preoccupied with their
quarrels and did not fully realize the danger which humanism
meant to them. The royal court, superstitious rather than religious, and utterly medieval in character, was much attracted by
the historiographical abilities of the humanists; for eulogies were
very popular and the eloquence with which the humanists
flattered and entertained was unmatched. King Charles VIII,
who was little more than a half-wit, was at this time (1495) still
in Italy with his army, winning victory after victory. When he
came back home he brought with him among the spoils of war
the Italian humanist Ioannes Lascaris to adorn his court and to
lecture there, although the monarch himself understood scarcely
a word of Latin.

Humanism was becoming the fashion in Paris, as in most of

the cities of Europe. Even the Sorbonne was eager to have humanists as professors, ironically enough, and if possible genuine, viz. Italian, ones. They demanded only that they be eloquent beyond belief. It made little difference if like Erasmus's friend Andrelini, they had no professional ability. Humanists were paraded and displayed in the city as heroic and enigmatic figures, social adornments as it were. Those who really understood them, however, were by no means always as enthusiastic as those who did not.

The small circle of Parisian humanists lived in an atmosphere of almost triumphant optimism, certain that victory was at hand. It was easy to become acquainted with them as they were sociable and didactic in the extreme. The more successful a humanist became the more he needed disciples to help him in his work: to run to the printer's, to correct manuscripts and, not least of all, to sing his praise. To be allowed into the circle meant to be swept along out of personal interest as well as bound to the others by the common goal. The public was thirsting for more editions of classical literature, most of which had yet to be printed; and aside from this task the humanists were united by the fight against scholasticism and by smaller but incessant quarrels among themselves. It would be hard to say which they as intellectuals enjoyed more.

Since he was a priest Erasmus was probably not subjected to the full ferocity of the discipline at the Collège de Montaigu. In any case he displayed no fear of Standonck, and made contact with the humanists immediately after his arrival. The most important of those he met was Robert Gaguin, a man already over sixty, general of the Order of Trinitarians, dean of the Faculty of Law, diplomat, poet, writer, historian and translator. Gaguin had been educated in Italy and was a disciple of the neo-Platonist Ficino. In spite of his age he preserved a youthful enthusiasm for the new, and had established book printing at the Sorbonne and edited a number of books himself. He was to be mentioned with love and respect for many years after his death by Erasmus as well as by Reuchlin, who had studied law under him.

Erasmus sent some of his poems to Gaguin with a letter in which he introduced himself. The letter has been lost, but from Gaguin's reply ('my friendship is at your disposal . . . from your lyrical specimen I conclude that you are a scholar, but do not be too profuse in your praise . . .') we may surmise that Erasmus had gone farther in flattering the man than was the custom even in that age of overblown prose.

Gaguin seems nevertheless to have liked him from the beginning. Erasmus showed him the manuscript of *Antibarbari* and Gaguin advised him not to publish it unless he wanted to face the wrath of the Sorbonne, which could easily crush him. For his part Gaguin could afford to attack scholasticism with impunity, being in great favour at court, though when he did so it was with amused contempt rather than anger. It was his belief that medieval theology would soon slip quietly into oblivion and that there was no reason to expend much time or energy fighting it. For Erasmus, however, this meant that he had for the time being to shelve the manuscript on which he had pinned his hopes; and in fact he was to publish it only when, many years later, the ideas it contained had already been put to use in many of his other books – though seldom more skilfully than in *Antibarbari*.

He had no more luck with another manuscript, though for quite different reasons. Having become so enthusiastic about Valla in the rustic remoteness of Holland, he had almost come to think of him as his own discovery. But in Paris he found the *Elegantiae* on every bookshelf and in every shop. No printer could have been expected to publish it again with the annotations of an unknown Dutch monk.

Fortunately there were other possibilities for him. Thanks to the triumphant progress of the French forces in Italy, national feeling was running high in Paris. Since the time of St Louis French troops had always fought in defence of their own soil and could only dream of the luxury of foreign adventures. Under the impact of the new events Gaguin wrote a history of France, his

Compendium of the Origins and Deeds of the French. Being ill when
the proofs arrived from the printer's, he was unable to correct
them and so put Erasmus in charge of the task. When the setting
was completed it was discovered that the last two folio pages
remained blank, which was considered impermissible. Gaguin
filled one of the pages with a poem of his own and allowed
Erasmus to complete the other. Thus the history of France
appeared with a long and excellently written letter from
Erasmus to the author. A small matter, one would think, except
that the work happened to enjoy an enormous success. Four
years later when Erasmus met John Colet the latter was already
familiar with his name from page 136 of Gaguin's history of
France.

A few months later, probably in January 1496, a thin volume
of Erasmus's poems (most of them written at Steyn) was published. At this time young poets had little difficulty in having
their work printed. Most printers were happy to take new
manuscripts and to pay the authors off with a few copies of the
edition. The poems were printed in less than one hundred copies
and brought Erasmus some small measure of fame, though less
than the above-mentioned letter had already done. About a year
later he edited the poems of his friend William Hermans, the
manuscript of which he had brought with him from Steyn, and
added a verse of his own to them. From then on, however, he
was seldom to write poetry, and then only to commemorate
special occasions.

The conditions in which Erasmus was forced to live in the college made writing all but impossible. During the day he had to
attend lectures and debates in the Sorbonne, and he had to be
back within the gates by sunset, when they were locked. In the
evenings he was free to pray in the chapel or to sit in the common
room where, invariably, students were studying aloud, memorizing passages from St Thomas, Occam, Buridan, Gerson and
the rest.

During Lent in 1496 he became seriously ill and moved out of the college. He found a room on the Mont Ste Geneviève in which, he hoped, he would at least have his evenings free. His stipend, intended as pocket money only, arrived irregularly and even then did not begin to meet his expenses. After some months of semi-starvation he took in pupils – probably fewer than he wanted – in order to make ends meet.

In the meantime he began to display a certain fondness for Paris with its narrow streets, tall buildings and noisy, extrovert life, all quite new to a lowlander. He eavesdropped on bickering housewives, conversed with coachmen, soldiers and beggars, and strolled with his friends in the district of the Sorbonne, abounding with shops in which there were stacks of love stories, Latin classics, treatises on such subjects as the art of dying, prayer books, pamphlets on the first voyage of Columbus and the new Paris editions of Savonarola's apocalyptic prophecies.

His situation, however, remained painfully uncertain. He was expected to become a doctor of divinity at the Sorbonne, and he lived in fear that Prior Nicholas Werner would recall him or summon him at the bishop's behest should either of them become dissatisfied with his studies or behaviour. Thus he found it necessary to write long, ambiguous letters to both men, but especially to Werner, in which he rendered accounts of edifying conversations, important friends he had made and, in general, of his life as an eager and diligent student interested in nothing but theology and the affairs of the Augustinian order.

On one occasion, for example, he wrote to Werner describing the procession of 12 January 1497, in which the shrine of Ste Geneviève was carried down from its Abbey to Notre Dame. The abbot and monks of the Augustinian Order had escorted the shrine barefooted all the way to the cathedral, where all the clerics of the city, the whole theological faculty of the Sorbonne and the bishop of Paris met them to pray for the cessation of the rains and floods which had been devastating the countryside. 'And now,' concluded Erasmus sanctimoniously, 'we have a quite blue sky.' We know from others of his writings that he considered such theatrical displays unlikely to have much influence in heaven, and it is not hard to imagine what he who had such a weak constitution and a morbid fear of catching cold thought of going barefoot in January.

His relationship with the Sorbonne remained the worst of his problems. Those who knew his abilities, especially Prior Werner and Bishop Henri, expected him to earn his doctorate in record time. Erasmus knew quite well that the theological studies which he detested were at the same time his only means of pursuing his career as a humanist. Yet if he did take his doctorate in theology before becoming successful as a humanist then he would have little choice but to return to Steyn and, in all probability, to remain there the rest of his life.

The longer he stayed at the Sorbonne the more his initial aversion to scholasticism turned into outright loathing. As a humanist he felt humiliated even by being enrolled in the theological faculty, calling it 'a most hateful slavery'. 'It is said,' he wrote to his young English pupil Thomas Grey, 'that no one can understand the mysteries of this science who has had the least intercourse with the Muses or Graces. All that you have learned of good literature must first be unlearned. If you have drunk of Helicon you must first vomit up the draught.'

It would be a mistake to assume that the rejection of scholastic theology and philosophy was restricted to Erasmus and his humanist colleagues. It was by this time clearly recognizable as a major trend throughout Europe. Those who had already led the way in this revolt included Jan Hus, who had been burned at the stake for heresy in 1415; Tomaso Parentucelli, who became Pope Nicholas V and was the founder of the Vatican Library; and Cardinal Cusanus, a follower of the *devotio moderna* who proclaimed long before Galileo that the earth revolved around the sun. Thomas à Kempis, another adherent of the *devotio*, had been among the first important enemies of scholasticism.

The rejection was shared by a majority of the cardinals during the reign of Leo X, as it was in turn by their foes Luther and Zwingli. When reading the most characteristic works of the period, such books as Pulci's *Morgante*, Brant's *Ship of Fools*,

Rabelais's *Gargantua* and the various Italian novellas, one soon
realizes that the two favourite targets of the writers' malice and
contempt were the morality of monks and the mentality of
scholastics.

Not a few historians have condemned the humanists for having destroyed the 'great cathedrals of ideas', i.e. the logico-
theological systems of the Middle Ages. There is, however,
much evidence to show that by the end of the fourteenth century
these structures were already well on the way to collapsing by
themselves. Dissent was in the air long before the humanists
began their attack.

The adherents of the *devotio* thought, with good reason, that
it was a disastrous failing on the part of the Church that it
permitted the most important questions to be decided by scholastic quibbling; all the more so since, whatever the result might
be, it was sure to be understood only by a few men.

Apart from the essential hope of redemption, the Church had
nothing but ritual to offer the layman, who not unnaturally
regarded the theologian with apathy and disgust. The higher
clergy, who for the most part knew well enough that the intellectual and spiritual sources of scholasticism had withered some
time before, generally tried to dissociate themselves from the
theologians. The various systems had successfully sealed themselves off from reality and fresh ideas. This is perhaps shown most
clearly in the most important scholastic work of the age, the
forty-one volume *Opera Omnia* of Denis the Carthusian, a magnificent compendium of the past which nevertheless contains no
trace of original thought on any of its thousands of pages.

The situation was nowhere more confused than in the Sorbonne, a bastion of scholastic theology, a state within a state
which very often defied papal authority but did not hesitate to
crush anyone else who dared to do so. All three great systems,
Thomism, Scotism and Nominalism were represented within its
walls in one form or another. The system of the Thomists consisted, roughly speaking, of a coherent and fairly logical explanation of man, religion, the structure of the universe and all its
phenomena, including even the hierarchical order prevailing

amongst angels and the topography of hell; the system's logic, however, began with the superstructure, the foundation being an unquestioning acceptance of a host of priorities based on Revelation.

While the system of Thomas Aquinas relied heavily upon the logic of Aristotle, that of Duns Scotus was developed upon similarly universal lines but was based, in part, on the neo-Platonistic views of Dionysius the Areopagite, believed to have been a disciple of St Paul.

The newest system, that of the Englishman Occam (and of Buridan, a Frenchman), was to a great extent a negation of Aquinas and Duns Scotus. Occam asserted the 'complete dialectical impotence of reason in exploring reality'. Consequently he denied the value of theological speculation, except presumably his own, and insisted on man's inability to understand God, to explain religion or to comprehend even the reasons for necessary dogma. With his back to the wall, dialectically speaking, he recommended blind faith and unconditional submission to the teachings of the Church. Thus, having begun with the wholesale abandonment of metaphysics he returned inevitably to a whole-hearted acceptance of it.

From 1350 onwards Nominalism, the doctrine which undermined all doctrine, had become the official view of the Sorbonne, although by 1495 the majority of the theological faculty were Scotists and were trying to reverse the 150-year-old trend. To make the intellectual disorder even worse, the Thomists could refer to the still valid decree of King Louis XI, dating from 1473, which laid down that the doctrine of Aristotle and his commentator Averroes should be 'acknowledged, as of yore, as healthy and safe'.

Thus three rival factions fought inside the Sorbonne with every means at their disposal, and were united only in so far as they were all at odds with the bishop of Paris, the secular clergy, the mendicant orders, the civil authorities and, not least of all, with the populace. It was far from forgotten in France that little more than half a century earlier the Sorbonne had sided with the English during the occupation of Paris under Henry V; and at the time of the trial of Joan of Arc the faculty had dispatched a theologian to Rouen to insist that she should be tortured. At the time Erasmus arrived in Paris the faculty was loud in support of the Orleans dynasty and was advocating – in spite of the growing military and naval power of the Turks – the suicidal dream of liberating Constantinople.

Because of the irascibility of the scholastic mind and the bitterness fanned by decades of quarrelling, the public debates of the theological factions not infrequently ended in violence. Unfortunately we do not possess records of those debates which were conducted while Erasmus was in Paris, but we do have detailed accounts of similar, if probably less subtle, debates held at the University of Louvain while he was visiting that city with Bishop Henri in 1493, and again nine years later when he was living there. It is unlikely that Erasmus attended any of these, but no doubt he heard much about them.

One of these debates was on the following crucial issues: Do four five-minute prayers said on consecutive days stand a better chance of being heard by the Almighty than one twenty-minute prayer? Is a prayer of ten minutes, said on behalf of ten people, as efficacious as ten one-minute prayers? The issue was settled after eight weeks of speeches – slightly longer than it had taken Columbus to sail to America the previous year.

Another point being argued was the matter of running public lotteries: was it immoral to earn money in this fashion? One might guess that the theologians would have condemned such a source of income, but no: while maintaining that it was indeed immoral to acquire money without working for it, they insisted that winning a lottery was outside the question since it was a matter of being favoured by fortune. As it happened, the city of Louvain was running a lottery that year and had promised the clergy a portion of the net gain in return for their support.

It is scarcely necessary to add that the debates seldom had anything to do with practical–or even theoretical–Christianity. They were often followed by brawling in the classrooms, in the university corridors and in the city streets. Arson and murder frequently resulted, and more than once the university had had to be closed for a year by the civil authorities. At such times the students and those of the *magistri* who had no outside income made their living by such pursuits as cheating at cards and petty theft (François Villon provides a famous and typical example); but even in more normal times the intrigues and battles of the professors and students kept the population outraged.

The people of Paris, deeply pious for the most part, had long since acquired the habit of distinguishing between the clergy and the Church itself, a minimal feat of mental gymnastics and one often recommended through the centuries by 'Holy Mother Church herself, in her wisdom', as it is said.

There is nothing surprising in the fact that Erasmus revolted against submission to the regimen of the doctors with 'wrinkled brows, bulging eyes and puzzled faces', and eventually refused to attend any more lectures at the Sorbonne. Nor is it surprising that, having a bad conscience at cheating his well-meaning bene-factors in Holland and at having made little progress towards fame as a humanist, he soon returned to the classroom. It could not last, of course, and before long he abandoned the Sorbonne once again. This vicious circle of duty versus vocation was to continue for many years, far beyond the Sorbonne. Thirty years later Erasmus was to write that he was suffering bad dreams about this time of his life. Perhaps it is not too far-fetched to imagine that he was having nightmares about being compelled, as a white-haired old man, to attend once more those lectures in theology while outside his books were being burned in the courtyard – as in fact they were to be in 1527.

During the summer of 1496 he left Paris to return to Bergen. He had resolved, evidently in despair, to abandon his studies once and for all and to return to the service of Bishop Henri or, should that prove impossible, to go back to Steyn. Fortunately Prior Nicholas Werner, Bishop Henri, Batt and Hermans all stood by him during this mental crisis and persuaded him that it was madness to give up so promising a career. Thus by the autumn of the same year he was back in Paris.

This time he made new acquaintances among the humanists, and took on new pupils. Two of these were the brothers Northoff, Christian and Heinrich, sons of a wealthy Lübeck merchant. Others were the young Englishmen Robert Fisher, nephew of the man who later became bishop of Rochester, and Thomas Grey. Erasmus so doted upon young Grey that it drew protests from the latter's guardian in the form of letters addressed to 'Reverend Father Herasmus of Rotterdam'. In these letters Erasmus was compared, down to his humble origins and the state of his morals, with Pierre Abélard, who had also been tutor to a young aristocrat and had been unable to resist seducing his charge. Until now, the guardian wrote, one had to shield only one's daughters against priests and monks. Had it become necessary in modern times to defend one's sons as well? We might expect Erasmus, hypersensitive as he was, to have been greatly upset by these letters, but there is no evidence that he was. The friendship he felt for Grey was obviously reciprocated, for their relationship endured until Grey was summoned back to England a year later.

Gaguin, who remained Erasmus's staunchest friend in Paris, continued to advise him in literary and philosophical matters. It was about this time that he also met Jacques Lefèvre d'Étaples, a distinguished humanist and neo-Platonist with whom he was to be at odds for the rest of his life, although they made a point of exchanging friendly greetings every decade or so.

Another acquaintance was Filippo Beroaldo of Bologna, who arrived in the spring of 1497 to teach philosophy. He remained in Paris for two years, and during that time published editions of Virgil, Sallust and Cicero, all with excellent commentaries. His students were enchanted with Beroaldo's lectures, which were based upon 'a philosophy at once classical, modern and Christian'. Gaguin, although suffering from old age and illness, attended the lectures of the twenty-three-year-old professor with Erasmus, expressing to Beroaldo his hope that 'Platonism would enlighten our modern times and save them from barbarism'.

The man who eventually became Erasmus's closest friend in

Paris was Fausto Andrelini. Andrelini had been born nine years before Erasmus, in Forlì, and was a disciple of Francesco Filelfo, previously mentioned as the loquacious gossip-columnist of the humanist movement. Before coming to Paris in 1488 Andrelini had been crowned poet laureate in Rome and had spent some time at the art-loving court of Mantua, where he met Pico della Mirandola on the occasion of the marriage of the latter's sister to Duke Ridolfo Gonzaga. In Florence he had attended the meetings of the Platonic Academy and continued to correspond regularly with humanists throughout Italy. In Paris he attracted the attention of Charles VIII with a poem on his Italian campaign, a eulogy which was all the more welcome for coming from the pen of an Italian.

Charles VIII made him court poet and provided him with a handsome salary. He also lectured in the Sorbonne on classical poetry, of which he knew practically nothing. He was witty, deft, amusing and frivolous, and with his refined but empty eloquence and his habit of tossing back the jet-black locks from his redoubtable forehead and accompanying the gestures of his right arm with smaller, most Ciceronian movements of his left foot, he could captivate any audience.

Andrelini found himself rivalled in the Sorbonne by another Italian, Girolamo Balbi, but soon managed to force him back to Italy after a slanderous campaign. One wonders how this man, who was certainly incapable of understanding Erasmus, nevertheless was so drawn to the poor and struggling monk that he became his friend immediately. Erasmus for his part took their friendship very seriously and permitted it to become intimate.

They spent many afternoons and evenings together in the public-houses around 'la grande rue St Jacques', or strolled through the vineyards on Montmartre, where, quite in the Italian style, young wine was sold with chickens roasted in herbs over a spit before the entrances of the cellars. We know that Fausto was an extremely garrulous man and that he liked to boast of his connections with famous people, above all his relationships with the neo-Platonists of Florence who, being dead by now, were more

useful than ever in his social climbing. It may be assumed that
Erasmus was a good listener and that Fausto paid the bills. If
neither Gaguin and Andrelini nor any of the others possessed
the first-rate mind which Erasmus needed to help him progress,
it can be said at least that Andrelini provided him with a measure
of much-needed diversion and consolation.

During the summer of 1497 Erasmus visited Bishop Henri and
went again the following year for a third time. The last of these
encounters was very unpleasant. The bishop, in the midst of
preparations for a trip to England, was nervous and irritable.
He probably reproached Erasmus for having abused his trust
and for having accomplished so little in three years of study. In
any case, he ended their relationship summarily.

Thus Erasmus was faced with the urgent necessity of finding
another patron, and once again it was James Batt who provided
a solution. At this time Batt was no longer secretary of Bergen's
town council but was living at the Tournehem castle of Anna
Borselen, Lady van Veere, as tutor to her son. Erasmus, recommended to the ageing widow by Batt, was promptly invited for
a visit. Anna Borselen was a stupid woman, both bigoted and
miserly. She was also wealthy, proud, beautiful and profligate.
We know that she received Erasmus condescendingly, but
promised him her help. The money which she dispatched to
Paris afterwards was, however, by no means enough for him to
live on, even when added to the pittance which Bishop Henri,
having had a change of heart, began to send once more.

Erasmus tried to set aside a small amount for a long-desired
trip to Italy, but was unable to save anything. Thomas Grey
had hoped to take him to Italy, but unfortunately he had been
summoned home to England. It was probably during this
autumn of 1498 that Erasmus made the acquaintance of William
Blount, Lord Mountjoy, who became his next patron, or as
Erasmus put it, 'a friend more than a benefactor'.

In January 1499 Batt invited him to pay another visit to
Tournehem, but Erasmus refused, afraid of offending Mountjoy

who had asked him to move into his house. In March he went to live with Mountjoy, then made a brief journey to Holland, stopping off at Tournehem. Still afraid of losing Mountjoy's friendship, he quickly returned before he could accomplish anything and, back in Paris, accepted the latter's invitation to a holiday in England.

The fruits of Erasmus's literary activity during these first years in Paris were meagre. He wrote only four short treatises during the whole time. One of these is a rhetorical exercise entitled *In Praise of Matrimony*. It is a skilfully compiled collection of commonplaces, written for Mountjoy's amusement. The others were also intended as exercises for his pupils, including a little handbook on polite conversation for the Northoff brothers and a treatise on letter-writing, probably for Thomas Grey. It is possible to contend, as many writers on Erasmus have, that these treatises already contained the nuclei of three later books, the first published in 1512 and the other two in 1522, which were to add enormously to his reputation. But the treatises written in Paris were the works of a grammarian, not those of a man much advanced in the other disciplines of humanism.

The only evidently significant event in Erasmus's intellectual development during his first years in Paris was his belated acquaintance with Florentine neo-Platonism. Ficino, Poliziano and Pico were all his contemporaries, the last only six years his senior; yet none of them was still living when he set out for England with Mountjoy in 1499. His mentors and friends, both past and yet to be, from Agricola, Gaguin and Andrelini to John Colet, Pietro Bembo and Johannes Reuchlin, had either known personally or corresponded with the Florentines, and had remained under their influence to one degree or another throughout their lives. There can be no doubt that Erasmus heard more about them than about anyone else.

His acquaintance with their works, however, as with the works of their predecessors, did not progress according to any logical system. Although he had been familiar with their names since his schooldays, it appears that he did not read any of the books of Pico or Poliziano, for example, until he reached Paris. A few years later in London Thomas More was to lend him a copy of the biography of Pico written by the latter's nephew, Gianfrancesco, and this had an enormous impact on Erasmus as indeed it had had on many before him. In the years between 1500 and 1510 he was to buy the collected works of Poliziano and Pico in the beautiful Aldine editions of 1499 and 1501 respectively, and we know that he read them through carefully from beginning to end. After this he never ceased referring to the 'angelic nature' of Angelo Poliziano or the 'admirable person' of the prince of Mirandola, calling both 'the glories of their century'.

Erasmus's relation to the neo-Platonists, however, was of a less direct, less obvious and altogether more complex nature than were his affinities with Valla or Poggio; and neither his punning references to them nor his sincere if somewhat flatulent eulogies of the men themselves are of much help in understanding it. As far as that goes, any explanation of neo-Platonism itself runs up against similar difficulties: it remains too elusive to allow for broad general statements or definitions. Yet its influence on the Renaissance was of such depth and importance that some effort must be made to characterize it, however briefly and inadequately.

The humanists were generally known for their preference of Plato to Aristotle. Since the second decade of the fifteenth century they had been translating Plato, of whose works only three of the less important dialogues were known by the end of the Middle Ages. Long before this, however, Petrarch had called Padua, dominated by Aristotelian philosophy, the 'city of sadness and the mother of error'; and in his time Ficino was wont to refer to Aristotle as 'the beast'. Cosimo de' Medici, an enthusiastic Platonist, founded the Academy in order 'to establish in Florence a Republic of the Learned', and until the death of his grandson in 1492 the body met regularly in the garden of Lorenzo's villa at Careggi. The members of the Academy addressed one another as 'Brother in Plato', celebrated their philosopher's birthday each November with a symposium and regularly bombarded Rome with petitions for his canonization.

This lionizing of Plato was the rallying-point of the humanists' rebellion, their rejection of Aristotle, the Middle Ages and, for that matter, everything else they happened to dislike. More specifically, their love of Plato lay in his view of the world as unrestricted and filled with contradictions which resist all attempts at systematization; a fluid philosophy which can absorb many systems within itself and feel no compulsion to weld them together beneath the massive force of static logic.

The humanists were, like Plato, naturally inclined to start from general, preconceived notions and to work through them down to particulars, quite the contrary of the Aristotelian method. They also felt kinship with Plato because he had shown interest in the 'nuances of life', in all things human and divine, and because this attitude was displayed throughout his works. They shared with him a tendency to embrace simultaneously the world of dreams and myths and that of sensible reality, and because of this they rejected Aristotle's 'supreme and altogether intolerable' order, in which contradictions were either denied or else played down for the sake of a tyrannical discipline.

Thus the neo-Platonists of the Renaissance saw themselves as happy fugitives from the Aristotelian monastery, free at last to roam the gardens of Plato's republic in which, as they saw it, poetry, music, love, good company and general *joie de vivre* were nicely balanced by a necessary amount of melancholy. Botticelli captured this view, far better than any amount of explanation, in his *Primavera*.[1]

Botticelli's painting was in all probability executed according to the specifications of Marsilio Ficino, and was intended to be an allegorical representation of neo-Platonism – which in any serious analysis is bound to be seen as having little to do with Platonism itself. Nevertheless, unhampered by such considerations, the humanists could be found gathered in the court of Lorenzo the Magnificent reading Plato in the original, examining his text with the best philological methods of the day,

[1] Now in Uffizi Museum, Florence.

continuing blithely not to distinguish between his ideas and their own whimsical cosmologies, scientific speculations and romantic fantasies.

This phenomenon was the result of the circumstances attendant upon the rebirth of neo-Platonism in Italy after 1440. A Greek scholar, Gemisthos Pletho (1355–1450), who came to Florence to participate in the Council of 1440, wanted to teach his Italian friends something of Plato. But what he actually offered them was a mixture of neo-Platonism and his own prophetic theories. He predicted the imminent collapse of the three monotheistic religions – Christianity, Judaism and Islam – and the birth of a Platonistic state in which neo-Platonism would assume the functions of a supreme ideology and in which, after far-reaching religious, moral and political reforms, mankind would finally enjoy justice and prosperity under a republican world-government.

It was Pletho who convinced Cosimo de' Medici to promote within his court a renascence of Plato's school and to invite the son of his physician, Ficino, to translate and expound Plato there. Pletho's work, the *Laws*, has survived only in fragments, published 400 years after the author's death. Yet his fantastic prophecies, his highly arbitrary adaptations of ancient myths, and his poetical visions all survived in the works of his friends and pupils, especially in those of Cardinal Bessarion and the Florentine humanists. In spite of their confusion and capriciousness, the Florentine Platonists provided a point of departure for some of the highest speculative work of the Renaissance and after. They had also profound impact on Erasmus, More, Bruno and Campanella, to mention only a few.

The first neo-Platonist among the Florentines was Cristoforo Landino (1424–1504), who discussed the relationship between the active and contemplative ways of life and the relative value of each. This was to become a favourite topic of conversation at the court of Lorenzo, who, when his guests deplored their patron's preoccupation with affairs of state, used to retort that it was his deplorable activities which made their contemplative existence possible.

The leader of the Florentine neo-Platonists was Marsilio Ficino (1433–99), head of the Academy, canon of Santa Maria dei Fiori and favourite of both Cosimo and Lorenzo de' Medici. With his unlimited imagination, Socratic leanings and strict sense of duty, combined with a lenient attitude towards the failings of others, Ficino was a unique amalgam of poet, philosopher, humanist and dreamer. He set himself the goal of developing a new and pious philosophy which would serve at the same time as a theology. He attempted to continue the work of Plotinus, Origen, Dionysius the Aeropagite and Pletho all at once, and to reconcile Plato with Christ. It might be said that his ultimate aim was to substitute his neo-Platonistic theology for scholasticism and to purify the medieval Church of its undergrowth of superstition by means of a Platonistic hyperidealization of faith and human love.

The enraptured pages of his *Theologia Platonica* of 1482 can no longer be read without some amusement. According to Ficino, we live in a universe filled with poetry, harmony, beauty and love. There are male and female flowers, bound to immobility yet, when the wind blows, inclined to make wistful bows towards one another. Nature works from without, God from within, all phenomena: in every tree there is hidden a divine carpenter who shapes the wood from within. Ficino likens creeks to silver-skinned boys with wriggling hips. They lie on Mother Earth and make love to her. Providence keeps vigil over us and incessantly renews the universe. One has only to watch the sky at night to see that radiantly naked stars are born every instant. The Milky Way is an enormous store of semen: when the earth becomes old this reservoir will empty itself to rejuvenate mankind.

Alongside these fanciful speculations and daydreams, Ficino developed subtler and more important ideas. He maintained that beyond the beauties of nature, beyond all sensual manifestations and mathematical harmonies, there is only one artist, the Logos, i.e. the metaphysical Christ. There is only one Truth, and in it all the manifestations of the universe converge. Elements of truth are present even in the most primitive cults, he maintained,

since God is adored, however ineptly, in every part of the world
– while the philosophers of antiquity, such as Zoroaster, the
Egyptian mystics and Pythagoras lead straight to the divine
Plato, i.e. to the Logos.

There was little new in these woolly neo-Platonistic views, but
Ficino, honest as he was, did not neglect to draw all the obvious
conclusions from them. From the 'spiritual unity of mankind',
for instance, he concluded that war was against nature and thus
to be condemned. From the same source he derived a sympathy
for the Jews, and considered the Moslems to be slightly heretical
Christians whose error was more the product of geographical
accident than of intention. Thus after many centuries in which
war had been considered both logical and just, and intolerance
had been the order of the day, pacifism and tolerance were
voiced, albeit almost inaudibly, within the pages of his philosophy.

The poet Angelo Poliziano (1454–94) is generally listed among
the leaders of Florentine neo-Platonism, though his influence on
Erasmus and others was in aesthetics, stylistics and philology
rather than in anything resembling Ficino's cosmology. Giovanni Pico della Mirandola (1463–94) drew the attention of
Europe in a way none of his predecessors had managed to do.
Although the leading of an uneventful life had become something of a tradition among humanists, Pico broke all the rules
by having to flee to France from the Roman Inquisition in 1488,
and he was imprisoned briefly at Vincennes. He was saved from
the stake by the intercession of the Franciscan doctors of the
Sorbonne, who hated him but hated the Dominican papal
Inquisitor who asked for his extradition even more. Two years
before this he had been saved only by the speed of his horse
when the *podestà* of Arezzo and 200 riders had chased him across
the countryside because a noble lady of the town had run off
with him.

When he was twenty-five, it is reported, Pico 'knew everything which man can know'. It is at any rate certain that he knew
the classics, scholastic theology, philosophy, astronomy, optics,
literature and was even familiar with various forms of magic and

the Kabbala. He is said to have been incredibly handsome, but after the incident at Arezzo he evidently gave up his life of sexual exploits and devoted himself entirely to his studies. Extremely wealthy, he eventually distributed his money among the poor with the intention of becoming a wandering monk. He planned to preach peace and tolerance beneath the porticoes of churches, in universities and in the field between warring armies, but his untimely death at the age of thirty-one intervened.

In 1487 the prince of Mirandola attempted to assemble philosophers and theologians from all over the world for the purpose of establishing peace among them – which experiment, as might have been expected, met with resistance from Pope Innocent VIII and the Inquisition. To introduce the discussion Pico wrote *On Human Dignity*. Elaborating on the views of his master Ficino, he discussed in this essay the central position of man in the universe, contending that, while a dog will always behave like a dog and a lion like a lion, man alone is capable of determining his own behaviour. 'The only condition [man] is subjected to on earth is that there are no conditions for him.' He is, proclaimed Pico, his own means and his own end.

Since man is a free agent, Pico continued, he is able to control his fate and to solve such discords as those between philosophical and theological schools, political systems and states. Insisting on Ficino's thesis of the essential unity of human thought and the ultimate harmony of the universe, he held that the antitheses between Plato and Aristotle, St Thomas and Scotus, Bernard and Abélard, Avicenna and Averroes were only illusions. Human thought dwells now on one aspect of an issue and now on another. At first sight they may appear irreconcilable, but in reality they complement or imply one another: they are but different levels of reality which can be made to converge in man, the meeting-point of the visible universe.

Pico hoped that he would be able to convince the leaders of the different philosophical and theological schools to make peace. He also hoped that this *pax philosophica* would anticipate and prepare the way for an eventual unification of the three monotheistic religions, just as Pletho had prophesied. This in turn was to pave the way for the unification of nations, world government and eternal peace. He hoped as well that these changes would take place in the following decades, and when he decided to become an itinerant monk it was the propagation of this goal that he had in mind.

These short and necessarily incomplete remarks on neo-Platonism have of course been given from a distance of 500 years. Erasmus's view must have been considerably different. Nevertheless, humanist scholarship, Florentine neo-Platonism and the programme of religious and social reform, however viewed, were the three leading trends of the day, and Erasmus was to be the man who united them more effectively than anyone else had been able to do. Although learning everything he could about humanism and neo-Platonism, it was to be some time before he realized to what degree the programe of reform would be a direct consequence of these studies.

Erasmus needed more time, and he still lacked the experience and stimulation which England was soon to provide for him. As strange as it may sound, meditation seems to have played little part in the development of his thought. The impressions he gathered and the ideas he gleaned from books tended to remain dormant within him; after some time his own synthesis of these things would emerge almost automatically, as if his brain had arrived at its solutions without his knowledge. The results were sober, practical and realistic from our point of view, but to his contemporaries they were nearly always enigmatic. Erasmus worked ultimately for the future; he quietly dismissed the fantastic cosmologies, the theological and philosophical speculations of the neo-Platonists, but from their Utopian day-dreams, those naïvely-worded intellectual baubles, he extracted that which was worth saving, viz. the concepts of tolerance and pacifism. And he championed both with farther-reaching, if ultimately unsuccessful, results than anyone else. He extracted the concepts of tolerance, pacifism, Socratic pedagogy, liberalism, research and independent thinking, all of which played such an important role in the intellectual history of Europe from the Renaissance on.

III

The English Influence

The conditions prevailing in England when Erasmus arrived there in 1499 as the guest of Lord Mountjoy could scarcely have been more favourable. The new learning had become deeply entrenched during the final decades of the fifteenth century, although this meant, as it did in most of Europe outside Northern Italy, that it flourished in small enclaves within the universities. English book printing was still in its infancy compared to that of most of the Continent, but this disadvantage was offset by other factors. Most important of these was the presence of original and first-rate minds, such men as More, Colet, Linacre and Grocyn. Behind them stood such powerful patrons as John Fisher, later bishop of Rochester, and Richard Fox, bishop of Winchester, who grasped the fact that learning need not and should not be the private preserve of the universities. They were joined by Lady Margaret Beaufort, mother of Henry VII, William Warham, archbishop of Canterbury, and later by Catherine of Aragon and Princess Mary.

Although the British Isles had been the birthplace of a host of scholastics, from Duns Scotus and Alexander of Hales to William Occam, and its Catholicism was strict and orthodox, there was nothing there to match that power and reaction which in the Sorbonne resorted to any means to prevent a non-scholastical interpretation of the faith. Scholasticism seemed to be yielding slowly and peacefully to humanism, as had happened in Ferrara, Urbino, Siena and many Italian city-states. The English humanists formed a fraternal, though by no means homogeneous, community much like that of the Florentine neo-Platonists. They received the nearly unknown Dutch monk, by whose wit and intelligence they were charmed, with genuine friendship. And in this atmosphere of intellectual freedom he immediately felt at home.

At first, in the summer of 1499, Lord Mountjoy took him to Bedwell in Hertfordshire, his father-in-law's estate, where they spent some weeks. Erasmus was delighted with his new surroundings and described his reactions in a letter to Fausto Andrelini:

> I too have made progress in England. The Erasmus you used to know is on the verge of becoming a sportsman, is not a bad rider, and has gained some experience as a courtier. I bow politely, smile gracefully and do all this in spite of myself. . . . To mention only one attraction among many: there are nymphs here with divine features, so gentle and kind that they may be preferred to the Muses. Moreover, there is a custom here which cannot be commended enough. Wherever one goes one is received on all sides with kisses; when one takes leave one is dismissed with kisses . . . wherever a meeting takes place there is abundant kissing. In fact, whichever way one turns one is never without this. Oh Fausto, if you could once taste the fragrance and sweetness of these kisses you would indeed wish to be a traveller, not for ten years, like Solon, but for the rest of your life – in England.

From Bedwell he moved with Mountjoy to the latter's house at Greenwich, and then to his town house in Knightrider Street near St Paul's. They visited Eltham Palace, where Erasmus was presented to three of Henry VII's four children, Prince Arthur being absent. Prince Henry, a boy of eight, during supper sent him a note in which he requested something from his pen. Erasmus was embarrassed at having nothing at hand. Within three days, however, he composed a poem in praise of England and the Tudors, neatly phrased and very elaborate in the manner of the time.

At Greenwich he had met Thomas More, and it would be hard to say which of them was more captivated by the other. More was twenty-one at this time. He had studied at Oxford and was thinking about becoming a Carthusian. Erasmus was of course familiar with the problems such a decision entailed, though not in the same context. He had never enjoyed wealth nor had he, like More, ever been free to chart his life along any course he might choose. More was a man of ascetic habits: he slept only a few hours each night, and even then on wooden planks and wrapped in a frieze cowl. Rather to Erasmus's surprise, he considered Aquinas to be 'the very flower of theology'. All this would have soured Erasmus on anyone else, but in the case of More there were too many other things they had in common. They shared, for example, the same happy propensity for humour and satire. Each of them was still searching for his path in life and felt the need of a friend who was at once congenial in his learning and firm in his moral values.

Unfortunately we know comparatively little about what More and Erasmus discussed when they were together. At this point, we may assume, More was preoccupied with the question of entering a monastery, and Erasmus may well have spent his time conjuring up for his benefit the ideal of a humanist layman who best served the Church, the world and himself by remaining just that – which ideal More was in fact later to embody. In any case it was only during Erasmus's later visits to England that their relationship became important and both men joined efforts to create those changes in society from which they expected to see a new spring in Europe and which, they fondly believed, depended largely on their own participation.

In October 1499 Erasmus left London for Oxford with a letter of introduction to Colet. Actually there seems to have been little need of the letter as Colet was already familiar with Erasmus's name and received him with enthusiasm.

That winter Colet was lecturing on the Epistles of St Paul before large audiences. Erasmus's senior by two years, he came from a well-to-do family, had studied at Oxford and, probably, at the theological seminary in Rome (but not, as some historians have maintained, at the University of Florence – which had been moved to Pisa some twenty years earlier). He had heard the sermons of Savonarola in Florence in 1494 and had exchanged letters with Ficino. He was well trained in history, law, mathematics and scholastic theology, and had read extensively of the Church fathers, Plato, Plotinus and the writers of the *devotio*. Having no literary ambitions and being primarily a pedagogue and theologian, he had found his way earlier than Erasmus and much more easily.

Erasmus did not care for Oxford at first. He had come to England as a man of letters and had presented himself to his English friends as a poet. In the midst of his worldly preoccupations he now found himself surrounded by scholars who were passionately discussing theological subjects. Their company, however, was good, their kitchen adequate and the wine excellent. In the face of all this he quickly permitted himself to share their interests.

Among the letters from this period there is a description of a dinner party written by Erasmus to John Sixtin who, though invited, had been unable to attend. Erasmus began with a list of the guests. Colet presided, and on his right sat William Charnock, prior of St Mary's. On his left sat a divine, an advocate of scholasticism, and beside this worthy sat Erasmus, 'so that a poet should not be wanting at the banquet'. The discussion during the meal was about Cain, 'whose sacrifice displeaseth the Lord'. Colet produced the theory that Cain had offended God inasmuch as he, in tilling the soil, had seemed to doubt the Creator's goodness, i.e. had believed too much in his own industry. Abel tended his sheep and was content with what grew by the mercy of God. The divine contended with scholastic syllogisms, Erasmus put forward rhetorical arguments and Colet grew increasingly annoyed with the whole matter. Erasmus, ever the good guest, lightened the mood 'in order to play my part, that is, the poet's . . . and at the same time to cheer the meal with a tale'. The tale was rather frivolous: Cain's real crime, according to Erasmus, had been to bribe the angel at the gates of Eden in order to get some of the seed, so much finer than earthly grain, which mankind had lost after the Fall.

Erasmus attended Colet's lectures on the Epistles of St Paul. He had never heard anything like them. At the Sorbonne he

had been compelled to listen to the so-called 'quadruple interpretation' of the Bible which, in reality, amounted to the reading
of superannuated commentators such as Petrus Lombardus and
Alexander of Hales. Colet on the other hand offered an entirely
new approach. He explained the background of the birth of
Christianity in a historico-humanistic manner, at once modern
and orthodox. He maintained that the scholastics, with all their
gymnastics, were doomed to failure when trying to deal with
the infinite. The real face of God and its symbols, he asserted,
could be recognized only in the study of the New Testament.
He was as well a Pauline who placed the redemptive power of
Christ's sacrifice above the overemphasized role of sacraments
and ritual. As a pedagogue he did his best to see that theology
reached the educated layman rather than a limited number of
the clergy, and he stressed in his lectures the 'essential unity of
divine truth' as well as the simplicity of the 'truly spiritual',
certain that it would by its very nature always be easy to understand.

Thus far the opinions of Colet are those which Erasmus either
shared with him or accepted from him as extensions of his own
thought. As for some of Colet's remaining views, they are of a
highly complex nature, and any attempt to summarize them
would be fraught with hazard. His historically-oriented exegesis
of the New Testament may be safely labelled a humanistic
enterprise. But his theology, though purportedly based on a
study of the Gospels, was largely derived from Origen, Dionysius the Areopagite and Marsilio Ficino. According to neo-
Platonist theology God is light, and reality is the 'ninefold chain
of Being' ranged in concentric circles around the Centre. Every
appearance reflects, more or less brightly depending upon its
spiritual distance from the God-head, the eternal light. Man holds
a high position in this God-centred 'flower of a universe', and
this is because his soul is able – is even inclined or forced – to
become the earthly tenure of the Infinite.

Nevertheless Colet deviated in a very basic way from the neo-
Platonists' view of a harmonious universe perfectible by divine
grace. He maintained that created matter is evil, and that divine

grace must finally destroy nature – a thought he shared with
some of the fathers and one which would be advanced by Luther
twenty-five years later.

Breaking away from one of the basic axioms of humanism,
namely that learning leads to understanding, perfection and
ultimately to God, Colet saw both learning and reason as contradictions of, or at least obstacles to, divine truth. Thus,
curiously, the founder of St Paul's School, the man who introduced humanism into England's institutions of lower learning
(although he banned Horace, Ovid, Catullus, Tibullus, Lucretius, Lucan, Propertius and Juvenal at St Paul's) was, for all his
merits, a grim sort of humanist, full of unresolvable conflicts
in his combination of a straightforwardly Pauline faith with a
neo-Platonist theology, and hopelessly attempting to combine
humanist pedagogy with a mistrust of philosophy and classical
literature, and unbending Roman orthodoxy with what was in
fact an anticipation of Lutheranism. It is significant that Erasmus,
who so wholeheartedly approved of those of Colet's views
concerning historically-orientated biblical exegesis, ignored these
others almost as if he had been unaware of them.

Though he saw Colet every day, Erasmus found it important
to write his friend a letter praising his efforts to restore 'the
pristine beauty and the dignity of the old and true Theology'.
A few days later he received a reply from Colet inviting him to
lecture on poetry in his college. A month earlier he would no
doubt have accepted with alacrity, but by now he had played
the part of the poet to the point that it was becoming tiresome
to him and he declined the offer. After this Colet urged him to
expound the Pentateuch or Isaiah in the same manner in which
he himself had dealt with the Epistles of St Paul. Again Erasmus
declined.

> You deceive yourself [he replied to Colet] when refusing to
> believe that which I told you about myself. I did not come here
> to teach rhetoric and poetry, which have ceased to be sweet to me
> as far as they have ceased to be necessities to me. I declined the first
> task because it did not meet the aims of my life, the other because
> it is beyond my strength. . . . One day, when I should be conscious

of the necessary power within me, I too shall choose your part and devote to assertions of divinity if not excellent, at least sincere labour.

These cautious words signify simply that his conscience did not permit him to lecture on the Bible without being truly familiar with it, i.e. with the original texts. 'Necessary power' means here nothing more than a knowledge of Greek, which Erasmus hoped to master in order to play the same role in theology that his friend was playing. This polite evasion was necessary if he was not to offend Colet, who himself lectured on the Epistles of St Paul without knowing Greek.

In the course of two months or so Erasmus had changed from a humanist who was interested in nothing but poetry, literature and classical learning to a scholar interested in nothing so much as the 'new' Biblical theology, ready to sacrifice all his energies in this pursuit and already saving money to be able, once back in Paris, to spend an entire year acquiring a knowledge of Greek. No doubt he did not suspect that this new plan could not be altogether successful: by now he could not have abandoned classical scholarship even if, as is possible, he was tempted to do so; for this 'new' theology was born of, and dependent upon, its methods.

Indeed, it was hardly possible to study Greek and at the same time remain entirely aloof from classical studies. Moreover he was by now already too strongly tied to humanism, and was soon to face the irony of earning a living from it just at the time when, otherwise, he might have left it. He underestimated his own abilities and the 'inexhaustible resources of the human spirit'. During the remaining thirty-six years of his life he proved that with certain limitations he could expand both his interests and his energy to enjoy the best of both worlds. He did not yet realize that, since he had mastered classical scholarship and extracted the best neo-Platonism had to offer, learning Greek in order to read the New Testament in the original would in no way cut him off from humanism; on the contrary, it would of necessity lead him, through criticism of the Biblically-unsupported aspects of the Church, towards a programme of religious, moral and social reform – would in fact open the gates to his career as a humanist and thus to his greatness.

Shortly before Christmas 1499 Erasmus left Oxford to go to London, where he spent the holidays in the company of More and Mountjoy. His spirits were high: the visit to England was proving a success in every way. His plans for the future, still uncertain and unpromising only six months before, had taken a specific shape. He had found the sort of friends he had for a long time needed, kindred and congenial souls who, intent upon their own individuality, nevertheless displayed a gracious tolerance for the ideas of one another. He had had the heady experience of seeing them charmed by his knowledge, intelligence and wit. And, finally, he could view the state of his finances without panic for the first time in his life. Thanks to the hospitality of his friends and the moderate munificence of Mountjoy, he had succeeded in saving twenty pounds. This sum would enable him, so he hoped, to spend an entire year studying Greek without being forced to lose time tutoring and writing stylistic exercises for the sons of the rich. This at least was his hope.

The decree of Edward III prohibiting the export of more than two pounds from the country had been renewed by Henry VII. Mountjoy, who had often been in France, was only vaguely aware of this fact – such laws scarcely applying in any real way to the rich. Nevertheless he advised Erasmus to take his money in foreign currency, assuming this to be unaffected by the decree. As Erasmus left England, however, the customs officers at Dover relieved him of eighteen pounds, leaving him with 'six angels'.

On the highway from Calais to Paris he was haunted by nightmares, imagining highwaymen lying in wait for him in the misty fields. At the inn at St Just-en-Chausée he thought the man who was sharing his room was planning to rob and murder him. He arrived in Paris nearly destitute and not knowing where to turn. Some of his friends, probably including Andrelini, advised him to take the revenge best suited to a humanist: to write a vicious satire on the Tudors, English greed and the general corruption of the country. Erasmus had ethical compunctions against attacking a king and a country he had only recently praised with justified sincerity in a poem, and in any case he had no wish to embarrass his friends. We might add to this the obvious foolishness of losing a potentially splendid patron just for the brief pleasures of revenge.

In the end he wrote to Mountjoy, saying that he had no intention of revenging himself on England for what was, after all, a private wrong. Mountjoy may well have sighed with relief when reading this, for he had just been appointed one of Prince Henry's tutors, and could easily have fallen from favour over a satire from the pen of his protégé. Nevertheless he did not make good to Erasmus the sum which had been taken from him, which perhaps casts a new light on the latter's statement that Mountjoy was 'more a friend than a benefactor'.

He arrived in Paris on 2 February 1500 during carnival, 'which turned out to be Lent for me'. Once more he entered the theological faculty and was immediately forced to look for a patron, to fall back upon the sycophant's life. His greatest fear now was not to be able to pursue the study of Greek. 'I decided,' he wrote to Prior Werner, 'to learn [Greek] rather late in my life than not at all, since it is of the utmost importance. . . . Latin erudition, however great, is lame and imperfect without Greek. . . . If there is any fresh Greek work at the bookseller's I prefer to pawn my coat than go without it.'

In order to get some money quickly he compiled in a period of a few days a random selection of 818 Latin adages, accompanying each with a commentary. This slim volume, generally known as *Adagia* (its complete title being *Adagiorum collectanae*) was published in June 1500. The printer intended to arrange for discussions of the book in the Sorbonne, a not uncommon method of advertising books and their authors. However, an outbreak of the plague prevented this. The gates of the university were closed, and Erasmus took refuge both from the plague and from the problems of publication by travelling with a little-known humanist by the name of Caminade to Orleans. He left Paris with little hope of seeing his book sold.

To the surprise of everyone, however, the book was a great

success. In the dedication to Mountjoy Erasmus stated that the work had been compiled for the purpose of helping the reader to refine his style and to provide arguments and ideas from the inexhaustible storehouse of antique wisdom. He had insisted to the publisher that the edition should be inexpensive enough to be within the reach of everyone who might want it.

To us it may seem odd to attach so much importance to a book which, today, would probably be compiled by a literary hack. But in its own day the book performed a great service, for there was need of a conspectus, however incomplete, of classical wisdom. The students Erasmus intended to reach were in their overwhelming majority the sons of burghers and, at least in northern Europe, the first generation to share in what had been the clergy's exclusive right to learning. It was as well a generation seeking positions in national administration and forming the framework of a modern intelligentsia utterly unknown in the Middle Ages. Its need of learning was to be satisfied by no other single man so much as by Erasmus, and the *Adagia* was his first step in this direction. It was also the first and one of the most enduring proofs of his concern for the burgher class, a spiritual alliance which he maintained for the rest of his life.

All this was immediately noted with alarm by the minor humanists. It was their custom to guard jealously such knowledge as they had, and publication was for them nothing but a stepping-stone in their career. They saw knowledge as a commodity, not as public property. We learn from Beatus Rhenanus that not a few of the Parisian humanists were soon up in arms against Erasmus 'for having sold out the tricks of the trade'. The success of the book soon quashed the opposition, however; and Erasmus, realizing the inadequacy of his work, began its revision and enlargement into a book of major importance.

He remained in Orleans with Caminade until the end of 1500, occupying himself there mainly with the study of Greek. At first he intended to master Hebrew simultaneously, but after a year or so he gave it up. In any case he did not much care for the Old Testament, considering its impact upon Christianity much too 'shadowy'. The stories of Jewish history struck the budding humanist as 'barbarous and savage', and the ritual of Judaism repelled him, not because of any antisemitism on his part, but merely because its form reminded him of nothing so much as the ritual of the medieval Church. Indeed, he once confessed that he would not have minded if the whole of the Old Testament had been lost to posterity.

Greek was causing him the greatest difficulties. 'It is nearly killing me,' he wrote in March 1500 while still in Paris, 'but I have no time, no money and no teacher.' In Orleans no Greek books were available, though Caminade lent him his Homer. When he later asked to have it back Erasmus wrote to him: 'You deprive me of my sole consolation. For I burn with love for this author, though I cannot understand him . . . I feast my eyes [on the book] and recreate [Homer] in my mind by looking at it.'

But Erasmus was persistent and indefatigable. He wanted not only to learn Greek but to master it as thoroughly as Latin, which was for all practical purposes his mother tongue. The uses to which he hoped to put his new language had already been planned while he was in England: first of all an edition of St Jerome, the manuscripts of whose works were in a deplorable state. Secondly to examine the Greek texts of the New Testament and to apply Colet's method of research – augmented in this case by a knowledge of the language – on the Holy Scriptures. Considering the state of historical knowledge, and especially that of linguistics at this time, it was a primitive method; but it was nonetheless a great stride forward, and not significantly different in its fundamentals from modern exegesis.

He hoped with his new-found knowledge of Greek to find the original, unspoiled sources of Christianity, the evangelical truth itself. He was certain that the *Vulgate*, the Church's authorized version of the Bible, had been corrupted by translators and copyists, thus casting shadows over and sometimes completely obscuring the mirror of faith. As Lorenzo di Valla had embarked seventy years earlier to find the original and unspoiled meanings

of words, so Erasmus now hoped to find somewhere an auth-
entic Greek text of the New Testament, one still fragrant from
the touch of the apostles.

In December 1500 he returned to Paris, the plague having
spread to Orleans. He was still in desperate straits financially,
and although he seems now to have been somewhat optimistic
about his future, he was nevertheless nervous, irritable and often
high-handed with his friends. The *Adagia* had made his name
well known, but the fifty to one hundred copies with which
the printer had paid him off were quickly sold and, since he
himself had stipulated that the edition be inexpensive, the money
he received for them lasted no more than a month or two.

Writing to Batt during this period, he tells how he was
yearning to have finished with 'all his works', meaning by this
the literary works which had now become a source of livelihood
(he was already at work on an edition of Cicero's *De officiis*),
and to spend his time on theology. 'I am in fairly good health,
so I shall have to strain every nerve this year to complete the
work which I have given to the printer . . . if three or more
years of life are granted me I shall be beyond the reach of envy.'

From this time on Erasmus's letters begin to be studded with
Greek quotations, a gratuitous bit of egotism on his part since
the recipients did not know the language. But perhaps he was
proselytizing: when he visited his friend William Hermans
during the summer he brought him a whole sack of Greek books,
and tried to convince him to learn the language. He was dejected
when William failed to show any enthusiasm.

Erasmus now had three patrons, none of whom, in all probability, knew of the others' existence: Bishop Henri, Lord
Mountjoy and Lady van Veere. They did not make any sort of
financial sacrifice for Erasmus, though all of them could certainly have helped him more – except possibly the bishop, who
was notoriously short of cash. Erasmus was now calling Bishop
Henri his anti-Maecenas, and even suspected that he had encouraged Standonck to spy on him in college to find a pretext
for withdrawing his support altogether. Mountjoy, 'more
friend than benefactor', was also to come in for his share of

complaints: 'Some yearly allowance was promised, nothing sent: such is the custom of princes.'

His chief demands, however, were addressed to Batt, still tutor to Lady van Veere's son, Adolphe, at the castle of Tournehem. Anna Borselen was ageing, and spent large sums on perfumes, clothing and young lovers. Erasmus seems to have taken this as a personal affront. He wrote to Batt instructing him as to how to get more money out of the woman, adding that it would be idiotic to spare someone like her. In another letter he promised Batt that he would immortalize him if only he would extract more money from Anna. Knowing well that lust and pride combined in her with the worst sort of formalistic piety, he sent her some prayers he had written, adding: 'Herewith I enclose a few prayers by means of which you can, as by incantation, call down from Heaven even against her will not the moon but her who gave birth to the Sun of Justice.'

Because of these letters some of Erasmus's biographers have set about 'unmasking' their subject as a shameless sycophant. The Erasmian writers of the eighteenth century were less coyly moralistic in the matter, realizing that a young humanist, if his father happened not to be wealthy, had a difficult time even finishing his studies. Those twentieth-century authors who have taken a dim view of Erasmus's dealings with his patrons find themselves in the untenable position of applying what is, in effect, a survival of nineteenth-century morality to the utterly different situation of the sixteenth century. Leaving moral pronunciamentos aside, let it be said that Erasmus was unhappy with his mode of existence, and excused his conniving on the grounds that his activities would be more beneficial to mankind than those of Anna Borselen and her lovers.

In April 1501, having edited Cicero's *De officiis* to earn money for the journey, Erasmus again left Paris for Holland. He went first to Antwerp, then to Gouda and finally to Steyn, where he received Werner's permission to stay out in the world another year – although his friends there, including Hermans, Servatius and Werner himself, were embarrassed that his studies in divinity had gone on for six years and were still uncompleted.

Erasmus was no less embarrassed. 'In Holland the air is good for me,' he later wrote to Servatius, 'but the extravagant carousing annoys me; to this may be added the vulgar, uncultured character of the people, their violent contempt for studying, the lack of any fruits of learning and the most egregious envy.' In later years this disgust for his homeland abated somewhat, and he relented to the extent of praising the Dutch for their cleanliness and general good-heartedness, adding that there was no other country in which such a large number of moderately learned people might be found, although people of extraordinary learning were rare. But this attitude developed in him only after he himself had become the first Dutchman 'of extraordinary learning' and no longer needed to defend himself on this score. In any case, the trip of 1501 was the last he was ever to make to Holland.

From Steyn he went to Cambray to see Bishop Henri, and then on to Tournehem to visit Batt and Anna Borselen. He stayed there, probably for some weeks, during the summer and became friendly with the Minorite Jean Vitrier, warden of the Franciscan monastery of St Bertin in nearby Courtebourne. He spent a few days in the monastery and has left us excellent descriptions of his host and their conversations.

Vitrier had been condemned for heresy by the Sorbonne in 1498, but was not much bothered by the fact. His dream was to get permission from his superiors to become a missionary among the pagans. He was an extremely intelligent man, enthusiastic about his faith to the point of exaltation, and in a way which was at once honest and extremely confused. As a disciple of Scotus he was of course excellently versed in all the subtleties of scholastic theology. He also knew Jerome, Ambrose and, above all, Origen. Erasmus questioned him about his devotion to Origen, asking how it was possible, since Origen had been a heretic. Vitrier replied with a smile that works of such depth and inner fire as those of the divine Origen could not have been written without the inspiration of the Holy Ghost.[1]

---

[1] Origen (?185–?254), a neo-Platonist Church father, was beloved of all those humanists who hoped for the reconciliation of Christianity and Greek philosophy,

A few weeks later Erasmus began work on a book in which he placed Origen immediately after St Paul and Jerome as the greatest witness of Christ and as the ideal Christian. Thirty-three years later, at the end of his life, he was to occupy himself translating, editing and annotating the works of Origen. Thus the question he raised at the table of Jean Vitrier was in all probability a rhetorical one.

In the monastery of St Bertin no food was eaten before noon. This custom, as was said sarcastically among the clergy, was established to make up for the money lost ever since Pope Alexander VI had doubled the tithes paid into his treasury by the monasteries during the jubilee year 1500. Erasmus, as we have already noted, had no stomach for fasting in either sense of the phrase, and he complained to the warden. 'You would sin,' Vitrier replied, 'if, persisting obstinately to fast, you jeopardized your sacred studies over the trifle of nourishing your body.'

When pressed by Erasmus on the subject of monasticism, the warden admitted that monastic life with its regulation of each hour of the day used up and eventually wore out even the best minds by its monotony. He added, nevertheless, that he did not approve of breaking a solemn vow, and that he would never turn his back on the faith of the humble, and would continue to fulfil his pastoral duties – though working at the same time for a thorough reform of the monastic orders. He spoke plainly and with deep conviction, quoting from the Gospels rather than from Thomas or Scotus, as was the custom. He told Erasmus how the theologians and priests and the monks and nuns all hated him, and how he had been transferred to St Bertin a few months earlier because he had condemned indulgences and tithing. Since his enemies were bent on destroying him, he lived in hourly expectation of official condemnation and ostracization.

especially Platonism, or who hoped for ecclesiastical reform through a Platonistic hyperidealization of the chief doctrines of the Church and a liberal attitude towards the minor ones. The Church itself sometimes considered Origen as one of the fathers whose apologetics were deserving of praise, and sometimes as a heretic. It is worth noting that Pico was accused of heresy in 1488 for thirteen of his nine hundred theses, one of which included the statement, 'It is more reasonable to believe that Origen was saved than to believe that he was damned'.

Erasmus seems to have been dismayed by Vitrier's overly passionate character and his overbearing attitude, so typical of the times but so far from Erasmus himself. Yet in the end they became good friends and spent evenings reading St Paul and Origen aloud to one another. Although Erasmus does not say so definitely, he implies that they discussed the details of the reforms Vitrier proposed to reestablish an acceptable ethical and moral standard in the monastic orders and in the rest of the Church.

It is likely that Colet's lectures in Oxford, Erasmus's own new theological aspirations and the visit to St Bertin all worked hand-in-hand in bringing him to write his next book. The final impulse, however, came quite by chance. Back at Tournehem he was to meet two friends of Batt, an officer and his wife. The man was a rude and truculent soldier, boorish and cruel to his pious and gently-bred wife. This lady pleaded with Batt to prevail upon Erasmus to write a few pages which might bring her husband to his senses. Erasmus accepted, and after conferring with Vitrier in the matter he quickly produced a short book entitled *Enchiridion militis christiani*, which may be translated either as *The Handbook of the Christian Soldier* or, more usually if less satisfactorily, *The Dagger of the Christian Knight*. He was to revise it during a stay at Louvain the following year, but it was published only the winter after that. In all probability he had difficulty finding a publisher.

The *Enchiridion* is a guide to practical piety, but contains as well a precise and thorough programme of moral reform. The book was presented not in the usual form of a thesis but as a straightforward narrative of the prerequisites of real piety. It was written with the most heartfelt sincerity and with an audacity which repudiates the claims of those who have seen in Erasmus nothing but a timorous scholar and bookworm. It was far from the first, but certainly the last attempt anyone was to make in this manner to reform the Church from within. It contained some of the most important messages Erasmus has for his contemporaries, and throughout his life he was to advance them again and again with ever new arguments.

The *Enchiridion* begins with an enthusiastic declaration of faith in which the author calls St Paul the standard-bearer of Captain Christ. A Christian, he asserts, has but two weapons: prayer and knowledge. Knowledge comes especially from the study of Holy Scripture, the very basis of faith. Such study, however, should be preceded by a sojourn among the classical poets, rhetoricians and philosophers. Of these last the Platonists are to be preferred as they were the temporal and spiritual neighbours of the prophets and evangelists; they should be read for their ethics and their science, and for an understanding of the historical background of Christianity. One must become familiar with all the ways of classical thought, but must take care that this should lead not to paganism but to an appreciation and understanding of the Bible.

The book continues to the effect that one should keep away from medieval theologians, particularly the Scotists, who 'never opened the Gospels' but 'read only the commentaries'. If additional clarification of the New Testament is required, one should consult the early doctors for help, those who were near the cradle of the faith. After St Paul these were Origen, Jerome, Ambrose and Augustine. The Gospels have not only literal meaning, but are full of myths and symbols. In order to understand these one must go below the surface of the letter to the inner meaning of the Word. That instruction which restricts itself to relating the stories of the Bible is sterile.

In the following chapters Erasmus analyses the conflict between the body and the spirit in the manner of a Platonic allegory, and closely follows the ideas of Origen in explaining the dual nature of the soul. Then, turning to the present state of the Church, he maintains that religion should not be confused with the mere observance of ritual; this is a betrayal of the faith. He does not, however, wish to offend the feelings of humble people: it may be that ritual is helpful to the young and the ignorant. But to offer Christ nothing but outward devotion is to break the bond of spiritual allegiance to the Gospels and to

return to the valueless ritualism of Judaism. He warned the
Christian reader not to expect any help from the sacraments
without first having true inner piety. The sacrament of penance,
for example, is nothing but an empty ritual if one does not
accuse oneself before God and not merely before the priest.

After this he went on to paint a neo-Platonistic portrait of
the universe, in which every visible thing is but a symbol of the
invisible. Only the Eternal illuminates with its beauty the mirror
of the earth, empty in itself. Possessed of a two-fold nature, man
must choose between the visible and the invisible, between flesh
and spirit, and it is only the latter which will profit him. The
apostles, though having the privilege of actual contact with
Christ, were weak and fallible until the Spirit descended upon
them. 'The corporeal presence of Christ,' he maintained in open
refutation of some popular superstitions concerning the Eucharist, 'is not profitable to health.'

Needless to say, all this was daring at the beginning of the
sixteenth century, and not at all the sort of view fostered by the
Church.

The salt of the earth [Erasmus went on] has lost its savour. I am
ashamed to say how superstitiously the majority of religious
observe ceremonies of completely human origin, how hatefully
they expect others to conform to them, how implicitly they trust
in them, how boldly they condemn others and how cock-sure they
are in their expectation of heavenly reward.

They lack, he insisted, even the simple virtues of the pagans,
which are the gift of nature herself. They are ineducable,
avaricious, unsociable, lecherous, mistrustful and vain. They
venerate St Augustine as their model, but should he descend to
earth he would protest against having anything to do with them.

Empty practices, he continued, are worthless and do not save
the soul. What is the value of endless praying in which the mind
and heart play no part? People are pleased to touch relics of the
saints with their hands, but they have no wish to follow the
saints' example. Some busy themselves with pilgrimages: 'Do
you want to gain the favour of SS Peter and Paul? Imitate their
faith and goodness and you will have accomplished much more

than in running ten times down to Rome.' And further: 'You probably believe that all your sins and offences will be washed away at once with a little paper or parchment sealed with wax, with a little money, waxen images offered up or with a little pilgrimage. You are utterly deceived.'

At the end of the book he quotes St Paul: 'Stand fast therefore in the liberty wherewith Christ had made thee free, and be not entangled again with the yoke of bondage', which passage was to resound a few years later in the sermons and writings of the reformers. In the last lines his style suddenly changes and takes on a curious resemblance to the mystic Ruysbroeck and to Gerard Zerbold of Zutphen, both of whom he had left far behind by now:

> Lift up yourself, as it were, with sure steps on the ladder of Jacob from the body of the spirit, from the visible word to the invisible, from the letter to the mystery, from the things of the senses to the things of the mind, from things gross and compound to things single and pure. Whoever will approach after this manner and draw near to the Lord, the Lord on His part will as well approach and come to him. And if you on your part shall endeavour to rise out of the darkness and troubles of the powers of sensuality, He will come to you pleasantly and for your profit, out of this light inaccessible and out of that silence unthinkable in which not only all tumult of the senses but also all imagination of the intelligence ceases and keeps silence.

It has been repeated far too often that the *Enchiridion* was the book which made the Reformation and that it was Erasmus who laid the egg that Luther hatched – which assertions Ulrich Zwingli accepted, Erasmus and Luther vigorously denied and Calvin deemed unworthy of refutation. It would be futile to raise this question again here, as to do so would be to embroil ourselves in an unconscionable amount of previous academic and religious contention in which both points of view are inevitably 'proved'. It seems more useful to look again into the *Enchiridion* and draw some simple conclusions from it.

Many of the book's ideas had been previously voiced by Clemenges, Wycliffe, Hus, Poggio, Valla, Pletho, Ficino, Pico, Colet, and the followers of the *devotio*. Some of the ideas had been in the air ever since the Councils of Constance and Florence. Hus and Wycliffe had sought to simplify the doctrines of the Church; the Brethren of the Common Life had yearned for the simplicity of the primitive Christians; criticism of the monastic orders and of clerical depravity were common to the point of having become every writer's stock-in-trade; and neo-Platonism was at the zenith of its popularity. As for the *Enchiridion*'s insistence on an historical explanation of the Bible, this seems to have been taken directly from Colet, as some of the ideas for reform were from Vitrier.

It must be added, however, that the *Enchiridion*, which summarized the essence of all these trends coherently for the first time, and generally more clearly than ever before, nevertheless excluded all those proposals which the author deemed far-fetched, exorbitant or tending to lead to futile theological disputation. Writing a matter-of-fact *vade-mecum* of practical piety with his own unique brand of moderation, Erasmus superimposed on the reforms of his predecessors new ones of his own, more radical and revolutionary in their way than those of Hus, Wycliffe or the *devotio* had ever been.

Tacitly ignoring hierarchical authority, the *Enchiridion* presupposed the existence of a layman's Church in which everyone was in a sense his own priest. With the emphasis deftly removed from the sacraments and placed on Pauline liberty, Erasmus suggested the simplification of the faith to its very essentials, and the outright abolition of scholastic theology. He rejected ceremonies, fasting and pilgrimages as absolutely worthless; he refuted the ecclesiastical contention that the life of a priest or monk is necessarily dearer to God than that of other men; and he advocated a secularly-orientated and humanistic education in all subjects, including even religion. This programme of reforms was more audacious and farther-reaching than that Luther was to demand in his ninety-five theses in 1517. All things considered, it went farther as reform than Luther ever dreamed of doing.

The *Enchiridion* was the first formulation of that which Erasmus called his 'philosophy of Christ'. Thus he became the first humanist to attempt to meet this particular need of the time, the longing of the educated classes for a more humane and more helpful Church, nearer to the spiritual needs of man and less rigidly hierarchical, dogmatic and ridden with superstition.

However paradoxical it may sound, Erasmus had not abandoned the broad basis of Latin Catholicism. Unlike Luther, he insisted on 'pruning the tree of Christianity rather than cutting it down', and every sentence of the *Enchiridion* was carefully constructed to soothe any possible misapprehensions. As opposed to Hus, whose chief efforts were directed towards a new interpretation of the doctrine of the Eucharist, and Luther, Zwingli and Calvin, who all brought new schools of theology in their wake, Erasmus was determined to reduce the theological mountain of Christianity to the molehill he thought it ought to be.

He left the chief mysteries of the faith untouched, knowing full well that any new interpretation of them could easily result in schism – but aware also that defining and codifying the unknown is at best a futile pursuit. Much later, when the Spanish Inquisition condemned the *Enchiridion*, it did so only with the greatest difficulty, finding at last only two 'dubious passages', which even then served only briefly to sustain a charge of heresy.

Erasmus intended the book to become a rallying-point of reform within the Church. And indeed he did succeed in impressing upon the learned, including sovereigns and cardinals alike, the necessity of carrying out this programme of reform before it was too late. That he did not wholly succeed was scarcely his own fault: the Church refused to change until it was too late to do so without schism – or, if one prefers, Luther came too soon, bringing schism with him. Protestantism adopted many of Erasmus's ideas when it arrived, but in general it disregarded his fundamental thoughts.[2]

---

[2] It must be added, however, that he had many followers among the Protestants, and his influence was to make itself felt in the Henrician Church as well as among the Lutherans and Calvinists, and even more so among the Anabaptists and Unitarians. Though the Erasmian minority lost the battle at the Council of Trent, many movements within the Catholic Church, especially those we are witnessing in our own time, resemble nothing so much as the proposals voiced by Erasmus in the *Enchiridion*.

The book's weakness lay in Erasmus's lack of sympathy for, or understanding of, metaphysics. In the beginning this was probably a greater help than hindrance in the simplification of doctrine; but once he had arrived at this point the deficiency began to cause him difficulties. In the *Enchiridion* he had followed Colet's method of interpreting the Gospels historically, but at a certain point, namely when he arrived at 'the symbols behind the words, which cannot be understood by reason', where rational interpretation was of little use, then he was at a loss. Being pious, rational and inclined at once to be anti-mystical and anti-metaphysical, he took refuge in the allegories of the Fathers, those which the scholastics had squabbled over for so long – and found himself trespassing dangerously on the boggy ground of his adversaries.

The other refuge open to him was that provided by Origen and the Florentine neo-Platonists, the homeopathic treatment of swallowing metaphysics to rid himself of it. Among his Catholic friends, and even enemies, he was reasonably safe since he simply accepted outright the heart of Catholic metaphysical thinking. But when Luther arrived with his totally different system of metaphysics the *Enchiridion* and its author were helpless against him, i.e. against his metaphysics, for Luther was fighting a different battle and with different weapons.

Quite apart from the influence it was to have, the *Enchiridion* was at the very least a good book, and possibly a great one. If it lacked anything at all it was passion. Loyola, for example, complained that reading it decreased his religious fervour – but then Loyola saw the Christian soldier in glowing colours and permanently engaged in combat, while Erasmus's idea of him was altogether less spectacular. His world was less complicated than Loyola's, and he was haunted by no chimeras. Instead of the hierarchy of angels and saints which accompanied Loyola, Erasmus followed St Paul, Origen, Jerome and the shadow he knew as St Socrates.

The book was published a year and a half after it was written, and at first did not enjoy the success of the *Adagia*. For the time being there were few who grasped its real significance. Exceptions were young Guillaume Budé, who later became Erasmus's lifelong friend and the leader of French humanism, and Beatus Rhenanus, an equally faithful friend.

After the initial printing it reappeared in 1509 and again in 1515. By then it had become so famous all over Europe that its contents were academic subject matter in many universities. In 1513 Dürer did his famous woodcut *Knight, Death and the Devil* which, according to the artist, was inspired by the *Enchiridion* (although it must be said that Satan had no place in Erasmus's thought). A famous preacher in Antwerp based all his sermons during the years 1514–16 on passages from the book; and the sermons and letters of Luther during the year 1516, when he read it, echo it as well. It was discussed in the circles of the Spanish *Illuminati* (a religious movement somewhat resembling the *devotio*), at the court of the Gonzagas at Mantua and that of the Estes at Ferrara, and in the Roman salon of Vittoria Colonna; and it was read aloud chapter by chapter at the Buda court of Queen Mary of Hungary, Charles V's sister who later became regent of the Lowlands by the Sea and one of Erasmus' smost ardent admirers.

After 1515 new editions were brought out nearly every year until the author's death, and during the next hundred and sixty years some forty more editions appeared. The book was translated into Czech in 1519, into German in 1520 and into English some time between 1518 and 1533. The following years saw it translated into French, Spanish, Italian, Portuguese and Polish. The Spanish edition alone was reprinted eight times between 1526 and 1556, and many times thereafter, the most recent occasion being in 1932. Even Orthodox Russia received it in 1783; and it is interesting to note that excerpts from it are among the only specimens we possess of the now-extinct Baltic language Old Prussian.

For the time being, however, Erasmus had little reason to rejoice. In autumn 1501 he returned from Tournehem to Paris to find that Gaguin had died during his absence. He continued his Greek studies and his struggle to make a living, comforting himself with new and romantic plans to visit Italy. He had the manuscript of the *Enchiridion* with him, but neither showed it to anyone nor mentioned it in any letters to England. Either he had no time to correct the first draft or no inclination to do so.

During the following year his luck changed little. 'Fortune raged truly violently against him in 1502', as he wrote. His friend Batt died quite unexpectedly at Tournehem; Anna Borselen remarried, and no longer wished to hear from him. At the end of the summer he moved to Louvain.

The University of Louvain was known as a stronghold of medieval tradition. Less powerful than the Sorbonne, it was no less reactionary. Hadrian of Utrecht, dean of St Peter's and professor of theology (later archbishop of Utrecht and Pope Hadrian VI), offered Erasmus a professorship, which he declined. Concerning this matter we possess an enigmatic letter, from which it is not clear whether he refused the offer because he was afraid of getting into trouble with the scholastics or because he wanted all his time free for study. In any case it is hard to understand why he nevertheless moved to Louvain, where, by his own account, he had no friends and where life was much more expensive than in Paris.

In October 1502 he lost his second patron, Bishop Henri of Bergen. 'I commemorated the bishop of Cambray in three Latin epitaphs and a Greek one,' he wrote. 'They sent me but six guilders, that he should remain true to himself in death as well.' At this time he began revising the *Enchiridion*, which was published in Antwerp in February, and busied himself during the winter studying Origen and St Jerome. As we have mentioned, he intended to publish the works of the latter, and he explored those of the former for use in his studies of the New Testament. Probably in the early part of 1503, he translated Libanus, a fourth-century Greek rhetorician, perhaps merely to earn money to live on. It was his first translation from Greek and the *editio princeps* of Libanus. The book was published a few months later and bore a dedication to the bishop of Arras, 'who sent me ten guilder and as many promises'.

Although he still lived in near-poverty, his name had become sufficiently well known to prompt the civil authorities to request a gratulatory address to the sovereign, Philip the Handsome, archduke of Austria, on the occasion of his arrival home from a voyage. Erasmus accepted, but seems to have been less than enthusiastic about the commission. Even in the preface of the *Panegyric for Philip, Duke of Burgundy* he could not resist mentioning that such eulogies were not at all to his taste. He kept flattery to a minimum in it, listing instead what he held to be the virtues required of monarchs: the maintenance of peace, the increase of clemency, moderation and benignancy.

Erasmus wrote with great speed and ease, occasionally completing thirty to forty pages a day, and even more when writing a polemic. He worked standing behind a lectern to stay alert, and seems to have enjoyed the act of writing, adapting himself in it from this period until the end of his life to the speed of the printing presses. When questioned about the large number of books he was turning out, he replied that they were to be attributed to his insomnia. Half seriously he called himself a polygraph, pronouncing his books miscarriages, delivered too early and too quickly. But about the writing of the *Panegyric* he complained bitterly: 'It occupies me day and night . . . I never wrote anything with such aversion; and what is more fruitless than writing something through which one unlearns writing?' The address was finally presented in book form, excerpts from it being read aloud at Brussels on 5 January 1504, to Philip the Handsome, who bestowed upon its author the sum of fifty *livres*.

Erasmus continued to live at Louvain throughout the year 1504, and received some small subsidy from the government, probably because of the *Panegyric*. The only important event of the period was his visit, during the summer of 1504, to the Premonstratensian monastery of Parc, near Louvain, where he went to hunt for manuscripts. There he came across a handwritten copy of Valla's *Annotations to the New Testament*. It was an incredible find, the very sort of book he had dreamed of but the existence of which he had not even suspected. Valla was the only man to have applied textual criticism on the New Testament, at least in any systematic or thoroughgoing way, during the past thousand years. Written in Rome half a century before, the work had never been published. No one seemed to know how it had found its way to Parc. Erasmus tells us that when he found the book he stood there trembling with joy and excitement; he did not fully believe in his good fortune until he had actually read the book through for the first time. He decided to publish it at once.

At the end of 1504 he returned to Paris, the reason for his departure from Louvain as mysterious as his arrival had been, except for a letter to Colet:

> I cannot tell you, my dear Colet . . . how much I dislike every-thing which keeps me from sacred literature. But fate always looks on me with the same face of disfavour . . . So I returned to France for the purpose, if not of solving [my problems], at least of ridding myself of them in one way or another. After that . . . I shall devote the rest of my life to sacred literature.

Although he was evidently bracing himself to face new difficulties, his situation soon improved. The *Adagia* had sold out its first edition and a new one was in preparation. Looking again at the book which had made his reputation, he found it wanting. For the most part the Greeks were not represented in it, and the Latin selections were haphazardly arranged. The commentary was hastily written, yet it earned him continuous praise. It was already being said that while other humanists merely paraded their knowledge Erasmus cared for the education of others. His editions of Cicero and Libanus were also widely known and appreciated by now. The *Enchiridion*, though selling slowly and comprehended by few, had nonetheless gained him wide acceptance as a distinguished theologian, one interested in the souls of his fellow men rather than in scholastic disputation.

There is little doubt that he was deriving at least some income from his books at this point, although we know that he did give Greek lessons to the Swiss Wilhelm Cop during that winter of 1504-5. Cop was 'physician to the German nation at the

University of Paris'. Often consulted by the humanists, he enjoyed a great reputation. He was later to translate Hippocrates and Galen. In 1496 he had cured Erasmus of a severe attack of fever, that which had induced him to leave the Collège de Montaigu; three years later he treated him again for the same malady.

Erasmus intended to revise the *Adagia* completely, but was occupied during the winter preparing Valla's *Annotations* for the press. From the preface which he wrote to the book it is obvious that he was well-aware of its importance as the basis of a new science, Biblical philology, and of the impact it was likely to have as such.

Inquiry into the text of the New Testament was a necessity fostered by the new theological and historical interests of the age. Some time around 1440 Valla had undertaken his examination of the *Vulgate*. He had worked from three Latin and three Greek manuscripts. With his penetrating mind and excellent command of Greek he had had no difficulty in pointing out some hundreds of errors in the official version. After seeing Valla's manuscript, the humanist pope Nicholas V, whose secretary Valla had been, encouraged the scholar Gianozzo Manetti to make a completely new translation of the Bible from Greek and Hebrew texts, but this was never done.

From the point of view of the Church there was nothing wrong in publishing a list of errors in the *Vulgate*, which had not in any case been declared *ex cathedra* to be the official version. But Erasmus knew his scholastics well. Valla was no favourite of the doctors, who called him 'the Epicurean pig' and 'that grammarian of intolerable temerity who, having harassed all the disciplines, did not scruple to assail the Holy City with his petulant pen'. It was easy to foresee what the more conservative doctors would say about Erasmus's bringing out the work of the man who had attacked the wealth and secular power of the papacy and thereafter dared to exert textual criticism upon the Holy Scriptures.

Erasmus was prepared for the arguments which would inevitably come, and he provided the *Annotations* with a preface addressed to the papal protonotary, Christopher Fisher, who was himself eager to see the book published. Maintaining the esteem he had had for Valla ever since defending him against the attacks of Cornelius fifteen years earlier at Steyn, Erasmus opened the book with an all-out attack against the enemies of humanism and modern theology, who, he insisted, were in each case one and the same. 'If one ponders the extent to which the Goths have succeeded in confusing the disciplines, and how they teach sham learning, one will see Valla's indignation as having been moderate and will judge his wrath pious and necessary. . . .' He cited the decision of the Council of Vienne in 1311 to revise the *Vulgate* according to original texts, the decree which had never been put into effect. Various editions of the *Vulgate*, he continued, were in fact different readings; it could do no harm to correct them according to the originals. Thus, he concluded, one should pay thanks to Valla, who laboured towards this end, and who gave us the method which we must follow in the critical examination of sacred texts.

The book was published by Erasmus's new printer, Josse Bade (Badius), in March 1505. It was well received and enhanced his already sizable reputation as a humanist and theologian. The conservatives were of course scandalized, and they prepared a multitude of arguments against it. One of these was that Valla had been a person of such depravity that everything he had said should be considered null and void. Another was that all the decrees of all the councils during a millennium had been based on the text of the *Vulgate* (which was not, strictly speaking, true) and thus any changes in its text would invalidate the doctrines of the Church. Finally it was put forward that it was the Latin Church which had the honour of being Christ's favourite daughter, and, consequently, the Latin text of the *Vulgate* must of necessity have been inspired by the Holy Ghost to the extent that the Greek originals had been. For the time being, however, no printed attack was made against Erasmus.

We have little information concerning the next eight months of Erasmus's life, and thus do not know how he reacted to his new fame during the spring and summer of 1505. The *Adagia* was reprinted during this time, and for the first time the name Desiderius appeared on the title page before Erasmus Rotero-damus. Sometime around his thirty-fifth birthday he had presented himself with this additional name.

It is well known that humanists, like scholastics, never tired of playing with the meanings of names, attributing great sig-nificance to them. Desiderius means 'the desired one', and we may conclude that Erasmus, in spite of his continuing financial difficulties, was perhaps not unduly pessimistic now about his future. For many years he had felt quite the opposite of a *desiderius*: he had had to leave his father's house at an early age; his guardians had tried to rid themselves of him; his favourite in the monastery had turned a cold shoulder to his protestations of devotion; and he must have felt unwanted almost always during the ten years which followed his arrival in Paris, not least of all during the two years' voluntary exile in Louvain. Now success had finally arrived with the *Adagia*, and perhaps for the first time in his life he could see himself as a man to whom such a name as Desiderius was not inappropriate.

During either the summer or autumn of 1505 he made a second journey to England. In one letter he informs us that he wanted to get 'important advice from sensible people', and in another he asserts that he was in need of money and had been invited by Mountjoy. The visit lasted until June 1506, and was no less pleasant for him than the first had been. In a way it seems to have been a continuation of the first, except that now relations were assumed on a higher level.

When Erasmus first visited England both Colet and More had divined a distinguished humanist in the unknown Dutch monk. Now they were already foreseeing in the distinguished scholar the future leader of European humanism. In 1499 Colet had been teaching in Oxford and dreaming of ways to introduce human-ism into the lower schools. Now he joined his friends More and Erasmus in London, where he had become dean of St Paul's School. More, who in 1499 had still been searching for his path in life and wondering whether to become a monk, was now the very embodiment of the 'humanist man'. He had meanwhile married, immersed himself in Greek studies and, a year before, had sat in parliament. Erasmus pronounced him 'the most delightful character in the world' and 'a man born and made for friendship'.

It had been six years since they had last discussed their problems together and explained to one another their views, without however attempting to synthesize them. Now each knew what he was after. More and Colet hoped, roughly speaking, to blend learning with Christian life and civic duty, much like the Italians Bruni, Poggio and Salutati. Colet tended to emphasize the role of learning at the expense of politics, while More concerned himself largely with the latter, including every sort of social problem. Erasmus was somewhere between the two, his chief aim having by now become the propagation of 'real theology', the 'philosophy of Christ', and of antique culture, all on the widest possible level. He considered this, as well as vigilant mistrust of rulers and politicians, to be his civic duty; yet he expected his ideas to be victorious through the collaboration of learned men and enlightened rulers, much like Voltaire after him.

At this time the dreams of a humanist victory and of religious reform, i.e. the elevation of the layman and of all human values through an infusion of humanism into the Church and the schools, seemed about to be fulfilled. The powerful patrons of humanism, such as the mother of Henry VII, the archbishop of Canterbury, the bishops of Winchester and Rochester, did much to encourage this belief. The bishop of Rochester, John Fisher, was chancellor of Cambridge and had been president of Queens' College for some months. Colet, More and Erasmus hoped that the movement for religious reform would emanate from Queens.' The statutes of the college drawn up at that time show the influence of Erasmus quite clearly. It was probably only in the following year that Fisher took him from London to Cambridge and offered him a professorship there, which he accepted. He was expected to lecture on St Paul's Epistle to the Romans from the autumn of 1506 onwards.

In the meantime he had joined forces with More to translate

selections from the works of the Greek satirist Lucian. Often called the Voltaire of antiquity, Lucian was the darling of the Renaissance, as he was to be of the Enlightenment. Poggio, Filelfo, Agricola, Melanchthon, Rabelais, and later Diderot, Voltaire, Goethe and Wieland were among his greatest admirers, and many of them attempted to translate him. Lucian's merciless satire, imbued with a gleeful maliciousness, his superior, ethically impeccable and triumphantly intellectual attitude – probably the only such attitude of the ancients to survive intact adoption by the modern era – were an enormous help to them in the struggle against prejudice, superstition, decadence, inertia and officially-entrenched stupidity.

The literate classes were longing for satire and they found it in Pulci's *Morgante*, Brant's *Ship of Fools*, the Italian novellas, Rabelais's *Gargantua*, the satires of Benir, Aretino and Ariosto and in Erasmus's *The Praise of Folly*. At the same time, however, it was the translation, publication and especially the dedication of editions of ancient authors which was necessary to snare patrons. In a way, publishing Lucian meant to Erasmus a surrendering of part of his moderate and conciliatory attitude, in that he was translating that very author whose satire was most bitingly effective in its direct application to Erasmus's own age. It meant recognition of the fact that the struggle against the common enemy was not going to be won easily – that enemy to whom a knowledge of Greek was tantamount to heresy and an understanding of Hebrew the mark of a Jew in disguise (Savonarola, Pico and Reuchlin, amongst others, had actually been accused of being Jews). Thus in turning from Platonistic dialogues to the strongest satire available, Erasmus was tacitly admitting, as had so many before him, that the battle would be fought with every available weapon.

It was during this period that King Henry VII promised Erasmus an ecclesiastical benefice. Of all the possibilities before him, this one worried him perhaps most of all. His fears were compounded by a letter received from Steyn some time in 1505. After Prior Werner's death Servatius, Erasmus's closest friend in the monastery, had become his successor. In his letter

Servatius matter-of-factly demanded an account of Erasmus's departure from Paris. He accused him bluntly of having squandered ten years there without any visible result, and finished by declaring that he had no confidence either in Erasmus or in his writings. Over-sensitive as always, Erasmus was stunned by the blow, though he had long been expecting something similar from Steyn. It hurt him that his influence over Servatius had dwindled to this extent and that his former friend had, presumably in the name of duty, become a rigid and impartial superior with no special place in his heart for the renegade monk. Though extremely humiliating, the letter was somewhat less alarming than it would have been a year before.

Aside from Andrelini, Erasmus had no real friends at the French court. But at the English court his allies were both numerous and powerful. He applied for a dispensation from his vows to Pope Julius II, and there is little doubt that his English friends helped him to procure it. The dispensation, granted in Rome on 4 January 1506, included the assumption, based on information supplied by Erasmus himself, that he had been born the illegitimate son 'of a bachelor and a widow'. The document spoke at length about 'Our beloved son's zeal for religion, honesty of life and character, and other laudable merits . . . for which you have been commended to Us by faithful testimony, and which have induced Us to show you special grace and favour'. It absolved Erasmus of 'all defects concomitant with illegitimate birth'. It also gave him permission to hold certain benefices in England, which implied that he would not be required to return to Steyn. Yet it did not completely remove this threat, which continued to hang over his career.

Erasmus replied to Servatius's letter on 1 April 1506, explaining how highly he was esteemed by the most eminent men in England, and how Henry VII had promised him a sinecure. Then he went on to say that he felt his life to be 'dwindling': his health had always been far from robust, and study and misfortune had used up his slender store of strength. For a long time now, he wrote, he had been concluding that all endeavour and wisdom were in vain. Thus, he continued, he had resolved to utilize the little time left him in meditating upon death and in preparing his soul for it. It was a restrained letter, beginning with the extent of his success among the English and concluding, rather incongruously, with his contempt for the world and the futility of it all. We must conclude that he was still afraid of Servatius, though by now such fears were largely unwarranted. In any case, the next day he wrote a letter fairly bursting with ambitious plans to another friend.

As it happened, Erasmus did not receive the promised benefice from the king. It was probably while he was preparing his Cambridge lectures that he learned that Giovanni Battista Boerio, physician to Henry VII, was seeking a tutor to accompany his sons on a journey to Italy. It was an opportunity to fulfil his life-long dream, and Erasmus joyfully accepted the post. It was in fact something of a sinecure, for the boys already had tutors of their own, and Erasmus was merely to supervise their studies. They departed in June 1506, but dallied two months in Paris where Erasmus was enthusiastically welcomed by his friends. A rumour that he had died in London had been circulating in Paris, and Fausto Andrelini met him with tears of joy. He and Josse Bade celebrated the reunion with their friend with a great feast. Bade had more than this to celebrate, as it happened: in less than a year he had sold out the entire reprint of the *Adagia*. He asked Erasmus to enlarge the book for a third edition, but by now Erasmus had no time.

Nevertheless he did revise for publication his translation of Euripides' *Hecuba* and *Iphigenia*, as well as the selections from Lucian. The latter were published in one volume divided into two parts, the first containing Erasmus's translations and the second those of More. Erasmus wrote a preface to his section in which he urged a resolute and methodical fight to 'unmask and reduce to silence' all the impostors who deceived the people with false legends, superstitions and the empty formalism of religion which corrupted the teachings of Christ. The tenor of More's preface to his own section was similar.

The company left Paris for Orleans, where Erasmus had spent many depressing months six years before, then rode up the

valley of the Loire, crossed the Bourbonnaise to Lyon and from
there followed the ancient road of the Roman legions and of the
pilgrims across the Alps into Italy. Somewhat bored by his
travelling companions, Erasmus rode ahead of the party and
amused himself with the composition of a poem entitled *Carmen
alpestre vel potius equestre* (which, being a pun, is better left un-
translated). In it he described his situation and spoke of the
infirmities of old age. Not inappropriately, he dedicated the
poem to his Swiss physician, Wilhelm Cop.

One may well wonder at the fact that Erasmus, some few
weeks before his thirty-seventh birthday, felt old. It must be
remembered first of all that at this time to be thirty-seven was
to be well advanced into middle age, and that Erasmus, neurasthenic and weak compared with such hearty contemporaries
of his as Aretino, Columbus, Michelangelo and Luther, as well
as hypersensitive and somewhat vain, looked upon old age as a
refuge in which his knowledge, wisdom and moderation would
at last appear appropriate in the eyes of the world. How quickly
age was descending upon him! he exclaimed in the poem.
Looking back on his life, he conjured up the young Erasmus,
always eager to study, write poems, learn Greek and embark
upon the road to fame; and in the middle of all this he had
suddenly become old, he lamented with ill-concealed pleasure.
And what had all these labours and studies profited his soul?
Nothing. From now on he would renounce the world, bid
farewell to jests, trifles, philosophy, learning and poetry. All
he desired was a heart full of the love of Christ.

One cannot attribute too much significance to a farewell to
poetry which is written in verse, and which bids goodbye to
learning at the very moment the author is en route to Italy to
continue his studies. The poem tells us little about the present
course of Erasmus's life, but it does afford certain insights into
his mind. It may be that these fits of melancholy, so noticeable
in his letters of appeasement to the priors of Steyn, were something more than mere sentimentalism or deceit. In fact the lack
of any such motive in the poem would seem to prove that this
melancholy did play at least a minor role in his character. It is

possible that, for the sake of his vanity, he whose outward guise and manner were anything but prepossessing had created for himself the consoling delusion that he was sacrificing himself for others instead of tending to the salvation of his own soul as he longed to do – or had convinced himself that he longed to do.

At this juncture in Erasmus's life biographers have usually paused to sum up the first thirty-seven years of his life, and to pass judgement on the highly controversial matter of his relationship with the so-called northern Renaissance and that of Italy. About his first thirty-seven years there is general agreement, but about the second matter none whatsoever.

Had an avalanche buried the little party as it descended towards Turin, the name Erasmus would be found only in Dutch histories, like that of Agricola. He had taken thirty-seven years to achieve a measure of fame, but he would need three more to write *The Praise of Folly* and earn immortality. And he would need still fifteen more to achieve that which is even more important: the shaping of humanism, and the adding to it, besides his ideas on pedagogy and philology, the concepts of tolerance and pacifism. Had Erasmus died at this point his name would not be bound with humanism as it is nor, in all probability, would humanism itself have its present meaning for us.

The disagreement concerning Erasmus's role in the Renaissance begins with the assumption that there were in fact two Renaissances, a northern and an Italian one, each of which can be separated from the other in time and space. This argument has more than once enshrouded Erasmus in various national colours. Johan Huizinga, the Dutch scholar, tried in his generally authoritative work on Erasmus to demonstrate that in all his disparate qualities of seriousness, sincerity, mendaciousness, vanity and pettiness he was in every way a Dutchman. The noted historian Michelet asserted that Erasmus, by virtue of the extreme clarity of his thought, had been an *esprit italien* and by no means typical of Holland. Imbart de la Tour blamed him for possessing an intellect but no soul, and concluded from his enduring influence in France, where he was probably best understood and where his work bore most fruit, that his spirit had been basically French. Renaudet, a noted scholar and author of five books on Erasmus, maintained the following:

> He remained a child of the Low Countries, a dweller beside the great rivers and grey seas of the North. . . . He knew and loved Flemish and Gothic art. . . . His religion remained faithful to the images of medieval piety. In the course of a controversy with Lefèvre d'Étaples . . . it came to light that the Christ of Erasmus still remained the *Ecce Homo* crowned with bloody thorns, the compassionate God of the ateliers of Flanders . . . whereas the Christ of Lefèvre remained the metaphysical God of Marsilio Ficino.

In spite of Renaudet's statements we have no proof that Erasmus loved Flemish art, or for that matter any other art. He displayed a consistent lack of interest in the matter. Nor is there any reason to believe that he had any special attachment to 'the great rivers and grey seas of the North'. His usual references to his homeland were to the effect that the climate was detrimental to his health, the winds pestilential, the customs barbarous, and so on. The matter of the Northern Christ as opposed to the Southern one is as well impossible to substantiate. The metaphysical Logos of the neo-Platonists cannot be considered the exclusive property of Origen, Pico, Ficino or Lefèvre d'Étaples – the last of whom was in any case a Norman. It belonged equally to such northerners as John Colet, Matthias Grunewald, Johannes Reuchlin and many others. Similarly, the *Ecce Homo* concept, with its thorns and drops of blood, is not in any way restricted to the north: St Ambrose, Pope Gregory the Great, St Francis of Assisi, Thomasius a Celano, Giacopone da Todi, Cimabue, Giotto, Dante, Petrarch, St Bernardino of Siena, Fra Angelico da Fiesole, Savonarola and Michelangelo are not to be deprived of it so casually as this. One imagines Erasmus smiling ironically at such arguments, and dismissing the folly of dissecting the person of Christ as an example of the scholastics' mania for setting up categories which are both invalid and inane.

There is no doubt of course that Erasmus was born a Dutchman, and certain things can perhaps be accounted for by this
fact. There is, though, something charming, if naïve, in the
rivalry among those scholars who seek to claim him for one
nation or another: Imbart de la Tour for the French; Michelet,
magnanimously presenting him to the Italians; and a few
English writers who have sought to include him among the
ranks of the Oxford Reformers. In the midst of all this it is
necessary to remember that Erasmus insisted that he was a
citizen of the world. He called Holland his *patria*; but Latin, the
universal language, was his mother tongue. It was Christian
civilization, built on the foundation of Graeco-Roman culture,
which he regarded as his paternal domain. In fact, his usual
disregard of national differences was responsible for a number of
serious errors of judgement he was to make regarding national
divisions and aspirations. Humanism was by its nature a supra-
national movement, and the neo-Platonists' 'unity of the human
spirit' was not only the aim of Erasmus's actions but also their
very basis. In the light of his own views on the matter such
categorizations as 'French mind', *'esprit italien'* or 'Oxford
Reformer' are, at best, beside the point.

It has also been the fashion to claim that Italian humanism
was in a lamentable state at this time, and that Erasmus had
nothing to learn in Italy. Similarly, some have maintained that
around the turn of the century the northern Renaissance had not
only found its own feet but had cut itself off from its Italian
roots, and, once separated, had blossomed into something
incomparably superior to its humble Italian origins.

What Erasmus himself thought he had to learn in Italy will
be discussed in the following chapter. It should be mentioned
here, however, that he later intended to settle in Venice, and still
later in Rome; and he was to state quite plainly that he regretted
ever afterwards the fact that he eventually decided to live elsewhere. It is of course true that the humanists of Italy, like their
counterparts in many other places, had by now lapsed largely
into rhetoric for rhetoric's sake. As early as 1485 Pico had
attacked them on this score, comparing their empty eloquence

with 'the worst kind of Oxonian Nominalism'. At the end of his life Erasmus too was to fling harsh accusations at them.

Yet it would by no means be true to say that the death knell of Italian humanism had begun to toll. Pietro Pomponazzi (1462–1525), head of the Academy in Rome, was one of the most original and provocative thinkers of the day, as was Gianfrancesco Pico (1470–1533), nephew of the prince of Mirandola. Pietro Cardinal Bembo (1470–1547), a writer of first-rate prose and author of the famous love poems to Lucrezia Borgia, was to become one of Erasmus's most valued friends; and Jacopo Cardinal Sadoleto (1477–1562) remained throughout his life a staunch propagator of Erasmianism in Italy.

Nor is it right to assume that the appearance of these and others like them signalled a last, brilliant flowering of Italian humanism: for ninety years later, during the period between the Massacre of St Bartholomew and the Thirty Years War, Italy was still fertile enough ground to produce humanists of the calibre of Tommaso Campanella (1568–1639) and Giordano Bruno (1548–1600), while from beyond the Alps little was heard except the raging of zealots and the clash of arms.

For the sake of perspective, of course, one might place Erasmus behind the fence of the northern Renaissance; but any effort to separate him from his Italian predecessors has little chance of success. In his textual criticism of the New Testament and in his views on latinity he followed in the footsteps of Lorenzo di Valla. In his philological methods he was highly indebted to Angelo Poliziano, whose essays he was to use as models in his new edition of the *Adagia*. The *Dialoghi* of the Neapolitan humanist Pontano exerted great influence on the dialogues of his famous *Colloquia*. In his polemical writings against monasticism he often borrowed even his train of thought from Poggio. In his pedagogical theory he was highly indebted to Vittorino da Feltre and Leonardo Bruni d'Arezzo; his maxim that 'Men are not born, but made by education' was in fact theirs. Marsilio Ficino's neo-Platonism and his 'pious philosophy', which reached Erasmus through Pico, were largely included by Erasmus in his 'philosophy of Christ'. The ideas of pacifism, tolerance and the essential unity of human thought also came to him from the Florentines, and blended with his own commitment to peace, harmony and human perfectibility.

Beyond the Alps humanism was enriched by something it had lacked in Italy: the movement towards religious and social reform. This cannot be said to have been of humanist origin, for it had been expressed in various ways before the advent of the movement. But it is obvious that humanist influence, from the *devotio moderna* to the circle of Erasmus and his English friends, was of inestimable importance in its development. Any effort to alienate Erasmus from either movement inevitably destroys his claim to greatness, for the very heart of his historical role lies in the fact that he united in his person the best of Italian humanist thinking and the new directions it took in the north.

If by some miracle one could separate Erasmus from his achievements as a reformer, he would still be known to us as the author of *The Praise of Folly*; but if one could, as scholars on occasion have tried to do, separate him, or the northern Renaissance, from Petrarch, Bruni, Poggio, Valla, Ficino, Pico and Poliziano, then it is clear that there would be precious little left of either. Indeed, had there been any such separation we should have neither the sonnets of Shakespeare nor many of his plays.

IV

'Citizen of the World'

Erasmus, his two pupils and their entourage descended from the pass of Mont Cenis during the last days of August 1506 and headed for Turin, capital of Savoy. At this time the dukedom of Savoy was a poor and backward area, and the contributions of the Piedmontese to the Renaissance had been negligible. There was not a single professor of European standing in the university at Turin. It is likely that Erasmus knew in advance that he could easily manipulate the doctors of that institution. In any case, on 4 September he took advantage of the favourable situation and appeared before the theologians of the University of Turin to receive the degree of master and doctor of divinity. After eleven years of intermittent study he had finally acquired the document for which Bishop Henri had dispatched him to Paris in the first place. Like so many other things of the kind, it seemed a matter of importance until it was acquired; after that it was immediately forgotten.

They followed the Po down to Pavia, and along the way Erasmus had an opportunity to see the famous Certosa, one of the greatest monuments of Gothic and Renaissance architecture. It seems to have been the only such edifice which ever made any impression on him. Seventeen years later, in the *Colloquia*, he was to recall the Certosa with its magnificent tombs of white marble – but only to criticize the rich who had built such lavish sepulchres for themselves, and to recall how the monks had chanted the Office while jostled by swarms of sightseers.

1. Petrarch (?) by Bellini (Mansell Collection)

HIC AENEAS AFOELICE A ANTIFAR IE AD FE EDE

2. Aeneas Sylvius (Pope Pius II) crowned Poet Laureate by Frederick III, painting by Pinturiccio in Sienna Cathedral (Mansell Collection)

3a. Pico della Mirandola (far left) from Botticelli's fresco 'LucretiaTornabuoni and the Seven Liberal Arts', now in the Louvre (Archives Photographiques, Paris)

3b. Marsilio Ficino (right), Angelo Poliziano, Cristoforo Landino and Gentile de Becchi (left) from Ghirlandaio's fresco 'The Sacrifice of Zacharias' (Mansell Collection)

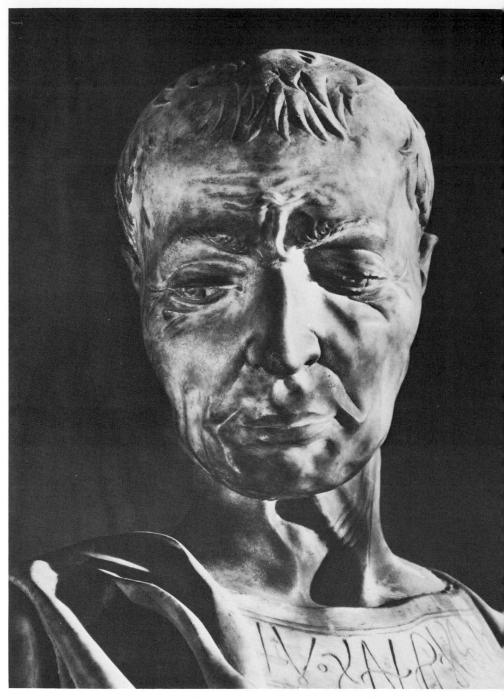

4. Poggio Bracciolini (?) head from the statue of Donatello in the
Cathedral, Florence (Mansell Collection)

5a (*right*). Erasmus's 'Terminus' device. Drawing by Holbein (Öffentliche Kunstsammlung, Basle)

5b (*left*). Title page of the Aldine edition of the *Adagia* printed in 1508 (British Museum)

Tho: Moor Lᵈ Chancelour

6. Sir Thomas More by Holbein in the Royal Collection, Windsor
(By Gracious permission of Her Majesty the Queen)

7a. (*right*). A drawing of John Colet (?) by Holbein in the Royal Collection, Windsor (By Gracious permission of Her Majesty the Queen)

7b. (*left*). Bishop John Fisher by Holbein in the Royal Collection, Windsor (By Gracious permission of Her Majesty the Queen)

8a. (*left*). Etching after Hans Holbein from *In Praise of Folly* from the 1703 Leiden edition of the *Opera Omnia* (British Museum)

8b. (*right*). Melanchthon *c.* 1543 by Lucas Cranach, now in the Uffizi, Florence (Mansell Collection)

9. Erasmus at about 55 by Holbein, now in the Louvre (Archives Photographiques, Paris)

10a. (right) 'Martin Luther in Pathmo' etching after Heinrich Goding (Staadtliche Kulturinstitut, Worms)

10b. (left). Luther in about 1527, portrait after Dürer (?) (Mansell Collection)

11a. *(right)*. Title page of the Leiden edition of the *Opera Omnia* (British Museum)

DESIDERII ERASMI
ROTERODAMI
OPERA OMNIA
EMENDATIORA ET AVCTIORA,
AD OPTIMAS EDITIONES PRAECIPVE QVAS IPSE ERASMVS
POSTREMO CVRAVIT SVMMA FIDE EXACTA,
DOCTORVMQVE VIRORVM NOTIS ILLVSTRATA.
TOMVS PRIMVS,
QVI CONTINET
QVAE AD INSTITVTIONEM LITERARVM SPECTANT,
VT VERSA PAGINA DOCEBIT.

BONA CAVSA TRIVMPHAT.

LVGDVNI BATAVORVM,
Curâ & impensis PETRI VANDER AA, M DCC III.
Cum speciali Privilegio Illustr. ac Praepotent. Ordd. Holl. & West-Frisiae.

11b. *(left)*. Erasmus's Statue in Rotterdam, from the Leiden edition of the *Opera Omnia* (British Museum)

12.   Erasmus in about 1532 by Holbein (Öffentliche Kunstsammlung, Basle)

Passing through Milan, which had been occupied by the French since 1500, they arrived in Bologna, where the Boerio boys, Giovanni and Bernardo, had hoped to enter the university. But they found it closed. The warrior pope, Julius II, had set out to reconquer all the territories which the Papal States had lost during the period of the papal captivity at Avignon. Having occupied Perugia, Urbino and a number of smaller places (including the castle of the princes of Mirandola, which had the distinction of being bombarded personally by His Holiness), Julius was now advancing on Bologna to drive out the ruling family, the Bentivoglio. The city was preparing to undergo a siege, and Erasmus, together with the Boerio boys and their tutors, took refuge in Florence.

At this time Florence was a republic again, though only temporarily. It remained neutral between the ravagings of the conquistador pope and the marauding of the French armies, and, if only for a short time, it was enjoying a great measure of civil liberty thanks to its *gonfaloniere*, Piero Soderini, and its foreign secretary, Niccolò Machiavelli. The centre of the town, in which Erasmus took rooms, looked much as it does today. The Renaissance, as far as Florence was concerned, was still in full bloom: during that autumn of 1506 Michelangelo, Andrea del Sarto, Botticelli, Raphael and Leonardo da Vinci were all living and working in the city. On any given day it was possible to see Leonardo strolling along the Arno with his retinue of handsome *apprendisti*. Michelangelo's *David*, still sparkling white, had been standing only four years before the Palazzo della Signoria. The cupola of the Duomo was still the largest in existence and was called the eighth wonder of the world. The *Mona Lisa* was on public display, perpetually surrounded by such crowds that it was difficult to get a glimpse of it.

It is a pity that Erasmus had no eye for all this, that he never mentioned the Duomo, the Campanile, Michelangelo's *David* or any of the other things which made Florence uniquely beautiful among the cities of Europe. One fears that he scarcely noticed any of it. It is sadly ironical that the man who combined in himself the most progressive trends of the era, who literally showered the benefits of his learning upon his contemporaries, and whose grasp of all the issues was clearer than anyone else's – with the possible exception of the foreign secretary of the town he was now living in – was blind to artistic beauty.

His *amor Dei intellectualis* did not include metaphysics, art or poetry (if we mean by poetry not skilful versification but transfiguration, i.e. true poetry). The paradox lies in the fact that Erasmus, who worked so long in the world for that which we call the divine, was blind to those manifestations of the divine in man which are the essence of our culture. As far as Italy is concerned, however, it must in fairness be added that neither Colet nor Rabelais, among others, ever wrote a word about the monumental artistic achievements of that country which they knew so well. And even in the works of many Italian humanists, Ficino, Pico and Poliziano for example, we find nearly nothing about art or artists. Humanism, that is to say the *bonae literae* of Erasmus (which may be translated either as *polite literature* or *true learning*) simply did not include the other arts, and many of its greatest representatives considered them unworthy of their attention.

Erasmus was now living only a few minutes from the San Marco, where both Poliziano and Pico were buried side by side, as they had wished. But nowhere does he mention ever having visited the church. The only thing he does tell us about Florence, in fact, is that he saw the humanist Bernardo Rucellai.

Rucellai was an old man by now, and he had known Pico, Poliziano and Lorenzo de' Medici intimately. After Lorenzo's death in 1492 it had been in Rucellai's garden that the meetings of the Platonic Academy were held. There is little doubt that, lonely and melancholy as he was, he would happily have talked about his former friends to the Dutch humanist, and told him of the glories he had witnessed. Erasmus for his part had not only highly praised the work of Valla, Poggio, Pico and Poliziano, but was continuing it. In the light of this, and the fact that he was perfectly aware of the new standing of the venacular in the land of Dante and Petrarch, it is nearly incredible that the visit ended in the disaster it did. His host addressed Erasmus in Italian, whereupon Erasmus exclaimed: 'By the grace of God, excellent sir, do not serve yourself with this language; I cannot comprehend it any better than the language of the Indians.' One sees why the conversation progressed little further, and was never to be repeated.

The sporadic warfare going on in the area soon ended, and Erasmus left Florence with the boys and their tutor, arriving in Bologna on 11 November. On a sunny autumn day with the roses still in bloom they watched the triumphal entry of Pope Julius into the city. In accordance with the etiquette of war the city gate had been demolished and a triumphal arch erected, bearing the inscription 'To Julius, our liberator and most beneficent father'. The procession was led by cavalry, which was followed by infantry and regimental bands playing martial music. After them came the cardinals, on foot, and the pope, borne aloft in his *sedia gestatoria*, dressed in a purple robe shot with gold and fastened with gems. An immense crowd lined the way to cheer the pope, the splendid spectacle and the end of their independence. Erasmus was deeply scandalized by the 'pagan triumph' celebrated by the Vicar of Christ after 'bloody victories to the detriment of the Church of Christ', and later was to air his disgust in the most pointed manner.

After they had settled themselves in Bologna he wrote a letter to Servatius, maintaining that he had come to Italy to continue his studies in divinity and in the Greek language, the only guide in theology. Having written this, he spent more than a year in the city occupying himself with nothing but study of the classics and the preparation of a new edition of the *Adagia*. Although he had thumbed his nose at Rucellai, he now made friendship with the humanist Paolo Bombasio, professor of rhetoric and poetry in the university. Bombasio was considered one of the greatest Greek scholars of the day, although unfortunately he left behind no books to corroborate this opinion. Erasmus praised him highly in many letters, and their friendship was to endure a long time. Bombasio eventually became secretary to Pope Clement VII, and died during the sack of Rome in a manner

eminently befitting a humanist: a stray arrow pierced his forehead as he was bent over his lectern.

In October 1507, on his thirty-eighth birthday, Erasmus wrote
a long letter to the printer Aldo Manuzio (Aldus Manutius) in
Venice. At this time every literate person in Europe was familiar
with the name Aldus. Aldine editions had bewitched the public
somewhat in the way the works of Michelangelo had, and it was
obvious that if there was one greatest printer in the world it
was 'Aldus the Roman'. The beauty of the books he printed, the
perfection of his settings, the overall harmony of line-length
and spacing, the almost mystical coordination of colours and
paper with the spirit of the text, all combined to make him the
envy of printers then and – in spite of the infinitely superior
equipment of the present day – ever since. By no means the least
of his attractions was the incomparable accuracy of his type-
setters.

Aldus was not only a great printer but an outstanding publisher. He had more than once risked his entire business by turning out an array of Greek and scientific texts, which were never
very popular. Between 1494 and his death in 1515 he printed
twenty-eight first editions of Greek and Latin classics, including
Aristotle (1495), Homer (1504), Plato (1513), the works of Pico
and Poliziano and such writers of the vernacular as Dante and
Bembo.

Erasmus was therefore neither exaggerating nor attempting to
flatter when he wrote a letter to Aldus expressing his wish to be
printed by him that he might 'ensure his immortality' (referring
to himself as usual in the third person). He requested that Aldus
publish Plato, whose works were eagerly awaited by all humanists, as well as a first edition of the Greek New Testament with
its Latin translation – which he, Erasmus, would happily prepare
for the press. He added that for this work he would like to use
the small type known as 'cursive', those letters in which Petrarch
had penned his manuscripts. Could not the printer, he asked,
create type to imitate this elegant script? Together with this

letter he sent Aldus the Paris edition of his Euripides translations, an ugly book full of misprints. What, he asked in conclusion, would Aldus say to the idea of an accurate and beautiful reprinting of this book?

Unfortunately Aldus's reply has been lost, but we know that it contained an invitation to come to Venice. Thus, late in 1507 or at the beginning of 1508 Erasmus left Bologna for Venice. Beatus Rhenanus tells us (in one of his favourite stories about Erasmus), that, arriving in the city by boat, he immediately hastened to Aldus's shop near the Rialto. Out of modesty – he was famous enough by now – he merely mumbled his name to an employee, and was kept waiting a very long time. Before him sat Aldus, correcting proofs, believing Erasmus to be one of the stream of visitors who constantly pestered him. It may be that Aldus, knowing everything about Erasmus, had expected to see him in a long black gown with a black mantle and white hood, a rare sight in Venice. (It happened, however, to be the same as the dress of the physicians of Bologna, who treated plague victims: and Erasmus had already narrowly escaped the fury of a Bolognese mob who thought he brought the contagion among them. On that occasion, speaking scarcely a word of Italian, he had been rescued by an intelligent woman who realized he was a cleric. After that he had exchanged this garment for those of a secular priest and, with papal dispensation, was to remain thus garbed for the rest of his life.) At long last it occurred to Aldus that the visitor who was waiting so tolerantly and patiently could be none other than Erasmus of Rotterdam, and he jumped up to welcome him warmly. He found lodgings for him in the nearby house of his father-in-law, Andrea Asolani.

The intellectual life of Venice was not very lively, except for a learned society formed around Aldus and known as the Neacademia. Their discussions were held exclusively in Greek, and they welcomed Erasmus with enthusiasm. Some of the members were humanists of distinction, as for example the cleric Pietro Bembo, author of the love sonnets to Lucrezia Borgia (whom

he had wooed in vain). He was later to become secretary to
Pope Leo X, after which he was made bishop of Bergamo and
a cardinal.

Another cleric, no less talented, was Girolamo Aleandro, a
young man of twenty-eight. Handsome and fond of good living,
Aleandro had lived in penury like Erasmus, and he too had
tutored the sons of the rich to earn his bread. Now he shared
his room in Asolani's house with the Dutch monk for the length
of the latter's stay. They became close friends, and Aleandro
was frank enough to admit to Erasmus his total indifference to
religion. They were to meet again in 1520, when Aleandro came
to Louvain as papal legate to the empire, and as the staunch
defender of Roman orthodoxy against the criticism of the
humanists and the onslaught of Lutheranism. It was in fact
Aleandro who was to be responsible for the burning of the first
Lutheran heretics in the Low Countries, and who became the
leader of the most arch-conservative elements within the
Church.

Other scholars whom Erasmus met in the Neacademia were
Ioannes Lascaris, the same humanist Charles VIII had taken to
Paris as a prize of his Italian campaign, and who was now
French ambassador to the republic of Venice; Battista Egnazio,
a patrician who was a disciple of Poliziano; Frater Urbano, a
Franciscan, author of a Greek grammar in Italian; and the
Cretan Marcus Musurus, professor of Greek literature in the
University of Padua.

Erasmus never ceased to praise 'the selfless friendship of those
humanists, and the generous help which they placed, in accordance with the noble spirit of the Aldine Academy, at the disposal
of a foreigner whom they did not know, for the benefit of a
work which was intended for the general education of the
human mind'. Lascaris, who had once been sent to the Greek
Islands by Lorenzo de' Medici to collect manuscripts (and who
then kept the larger part of what he found for himself), used to
come to Aldus's shop in the evening when the employees had
left and Erasmus would be working alone. He would bring with
him one of his Greek manuscripts so that Erasmus might search

for new material for the *Adagia*. Aleandro did the same: in the morning he would sometimes surprise Erasmus with a manuscript found in the depths of some library.

Erasmus had spent much of his year in Bologna working on the *Adagia*, but he still found it unfit for printing. 'With great temerity on my part, we began working at the same time, I writing, Aldus printing.' In the noisy printer's shop Erasmus sat and worked, usually from memory, so occupied with his task that he had, as he put it, 'no time to scratch his ears' during the eight months of work. A special proof reader was assigned to him, and finally the last corrections were made. Aldus was also going over the proofs, and Erasmus asked him why. 'Because I too want to learn', he replied. Later, when the *Adagia* had been printed, Erasmus continued to work with Aldus, probably in the preparation of his edition of Horace.

The collaboration was fruitful in every way. For a time Erasmus considered stopping in Venice until all the classical authors should have been issued by Aldus, which is to say, for the rest of his life. In the meantime he had acquired all the tricks of the trade in the printing shop and had adapted himself to its speed. In the coming years he would more than once have to write and publish simultaneously, using the new invention for its primary purpose: the dissemination of learning and the guiding of public opinion. As we have said before, Erasmus was the first to adopt this attitude, and, for a time, the most successful in it. Neither his name nor his achievement can be separated from the triumph of book printing, so closely are they bound. His admiration for Aldus was based, apart from the excellence of his craftsmanship, on the fact that he printed those things which were most useful in raising the intellectual level of Europe. He had a profound distaste for those printers who pandered to the common taste and threatened to turn the restoration of classical values 'into a tragic and senseless mess'. He was in fact to live long enough to see this tragedy enacted.

There were significant differences of opinion between the two men, however. As Huizinga aptly remarked: 'Erasmus was one of those true book-lovers who pledge their heart to a type or

size of book not because of any artistic preference, but because
of readableness and handiness.' He wanted his books to be small
and inexpensive, whenever possible. Moreover, Aldus and his
friends were interested in little except classical antiquity,
especially Platonism. Erasmus both agreed and disagreed with
them in this, somewhat as Machiavelli did when stating that, in
a narrow sense, 'Renaissance means the resurrection of dead
things'.

To the new edition of the *Adagia* Erasmus added a commentary criticizing the institutions of the present society and recom-
mending the restoration of ethics, both Christian and antique, in
reforming it. Certainly, however, he never advocated the
resurrection of a dead society. This may account for the fact
that Bembo and Aleandro, searching as they were for the ghost
of the past, and having no firmer pedestal beneath them (their
paganism being in the last analysis nothing more than an affecta-
tion), surrendered cynically before the Counter Reformation;
while Erasmus, unyielding, stood alone in a hostile world.

It is possible that these differences were instrumental in per-
suading Erasmus to leave Venice, especially in that his friends
there had so little interest in the reforms he advocated. There
were, however, other reasons. Erasmus 'shuddered', as he says,
in the face of his landlord Asolani's parsimony. The meals were
ludicrously frugal: there was no breakfast, the first food being
served at one o'clock in the afternoon; bread was baked once in
a fortnight and was therefore stone-hard; seven leaves of lettuce
were served to be divided among nine people; and, most disagreeable of all, the wine was concocted by adding water to
dregs 'which had stood ten years'. When Erasmus complained
of all this, Asolani appealed to his feelings, and said that he
should take into consideration the southern climate, which
lessened the body's need for food. To this Aldus himself added
a few tales concerning foreigners who had come to Venice and,
unable to curb their northern appetites, either died before their
time or went home with dreadful diseases.

This is one side of the story, comically exaggerated by
Erasmus himself. By his enemies it was exaggerated at his ex-

pense, however. Julius Caesar Scaliger depicted him as a full-blooded man of the Renaissance who, a parasite at Aldus's table, devoured all the food thereon and did the work of half a man while drinking enough for three under the pretext that he needed stimulation. Scaliger also charged that Erasmus was inconsolable over the fact that the Venetians, jealous of their wives, kept them from him, and therefore he abandoned the city after emptying Aldus's larder, cellar and purse. Be all that as it may, it was in Venice that Erasmus suffered his first attack of stones, probably brought on by drinking. He put it down to the food at Asolani's, however, and was to take revenge on the man in the *Colloquia*. He believed that wine was the best treatment for his malady, this being the prevailing medical opinion at that time. In any case, health seems once again to have become uppermost in his mind, and he left Venice.

Before we trace Erasmus to Padua, the next stage in his journey, we must make a few remarks concerning the new edition of the *Adagia*. The first Paris editions had contained 818 adages; the Aldine edition 3,260. In subsequent editions Erasmus was to increase this number slowly until in that of 1536, the year of his death, they numbered 4,151. The change, however, did not lie in the number of aphorisms, representing by now nearly the whole range of classical literature, but in the accompanying commentaries. These were, in part, miniature essays in which the author followed the pattern set by Poliziano in his *Miscellanae*, much as Montaigne was to pattern his own *Essays* on Erasmus. In some of them we find Erasmus's opinion of various friends, in others there are attacks against the abuses of government and against those who acquire wealth by brutal exploitation. They were still somewhat reticent in tone and overburdened with commonplaces, but the refreshing breeze of political and religious liberalism could already be felt.

It was in this revised form that the *Adagia* became the favourite manual of many generations. It provided the intelligent reader with those quotations from the classics which would permit him to mingle in educated society – at least as long as classical allusions were still in fashion. Some of Erasmus's biographers, notably Huizinga and the American Preserved Smith, have tended to belittle the importance of all this. It seems likely that they are not quite fair, in so far as they underestimate the importance which a general knowledge of the classics held for our ancestors. In truth we are no longer in a position to assess the need which was felt for a book such as the *Adagia* in Erasmus's day. The philosophers of antiquity stood alone in their unchallenged superiority, for the world was just beginning to reach the far side of that gulf which had opened up after Plotinus and was not to end until Spinoza; and the literature of the ancients was as well infinitely superior to nearly every product of national literature which had been created since. It is not surprising then that there was passionate and general interest in the classics – and not surprising that this is difficult to understand in our own century, which has witnessed a lessening of interest in those things which constitute the basis of our civilization.

The *Adagia* was reprinted some fifteen times during Erasmus's life, not counting abridgements and pirate editions, and some fifty times more in the following hundred and sixty years. It was translated into many languages during the sixteenth century, including such as Lithuanian and Hungarian. It was still widely read during the Enlightenment. It was highly praised by Herder; Lessing admitted its influence on his work, and Goethe drew heavily on it in his *Xenia* and *Wilhelm Meister*. In a letter from Goethe to Schiller dated 16 December 1797 we find the latter being advised to obtain a copy of the book, for in it he would find the real treasures of the ancients, 'the real stuff'.

In either October or November 1508 Erasmus moved to Padua. Having left his two former charges at the University of Bologna, he now took another pupil to finance his travels around the country. This was a youth of eighteen, Alexander Stuart, archbishop of St Andrews and natural son of James IV of Scotland. Erasmus seems to have been very fond of him, and later described his beautiful appearance, his love of learning and of music and his eloquent conversation.

Every morning at seven o'clock Erasmus and his pupil attended the Greek lectures of the humanist Marcus Musurus between the somewhat forbidding walls of Padua's anti-humanist university, the last and most intransigent stronghold of Latin Averroism. It was so cold that winter that most of the students remained in bed until a much later hour. Once, Erasmus tells us, there were only three gathered to hear Musurus, the third being the humanist Raphael Regio, professor emeritus of Latin, now a toothless old man of over seventy. When Erasmus inquired about his presence, Regio replied: 'I should not like to die without having tasted lectures in Greek.'

Early in December it became known that Pope Julius, not content with his previous victories, was planning to attack Venice with the help of his allies, the League of Cambray. The university soon closed its gates. Before Christmas Erasmus, his new pupil and the latter's entourage moved to Ferrara, seat of Duke Alfonso d'Este and his wife, Lucrezia Borgia. Ferrara was famous for the numerous poets living there, patronized (and occasionally murdered) by Duke Alfonso. Erasmus was to meet neither the duke nor any of his poets, but he was welcomed with an oration by the famous humanist Celio Calcagnini, a friend of Copernicus, who wrote a work of which only the memorable title has survived: *That the Sky Stands Still and That the Earth Moves*.

From Ferrara they went to Sienna, where Alexander Stuart continued his studies. Erasmus stayed on to tutor his pupil for some months, instructing him not only in Latin and Greek, but 'trying his best to transform . . . the youth into the visible image of God', as he later put it in his *On the Education of Boys*. Then, probably in April 1509, he left Stuart in Sienna and made his way to Rome.

Two years later another Augustinian monk, Martin Luther, was to visit Rome and be deeply scandalized by the worldly, im-moral and altogether corrupt life of Pope Julius II and his court.

The criticism voiced by the reformer was essentially the same as that of the humanist before him – except that 'Erasmus said it better', as Luther was later to concede in a fit of generosity. A few weeks after his four months in Rome Erasmus would write *The Praise of Folly*, which may be considered an outcome of the visit.

> If wisdom would come to the popes, what comforts it would deprive them of! [Folly exclaimed] It would deprive them of all wealth, honour and possessions; all the triumphal progress, offices, dispensation, tributes and indulgences; the many horses, mules and retainers; in short, it would deprive them of all their pleasures. . . . The Christian Church was founded on blood, made strong by blood and enlarged by blood; and nowadays they use the sword to continue the good work, just as if Christ, who keeps watch over what is His in His own way, had perished. . . . Here you can see a tired old man [a reference to the pope] act with youthful energy and disregard all labour and expense simply in order to overturn laws, religion, peace and humane institutions. Nor is it difficult to find learned sycophants who will give to this obvious madness the name of zeal, piety and fortitude. They can show how a man can draw his sword and run it through his brother's gut and at the same time live in that perfect charity which Christ tells us a Christian owes his neighbour.

The last remark was an allusion to Caesare Borgia, who had murdered his brother, the duke of Gandia, and was made General of the Church by his father, Pope Alexander VI.

In spite of the fact that they both condemned what they saw in Rome, Luther and Erasmus were even at this early date far apart in attitude. Luther was to emphasize repeatedly in his writings that it was his visit to Rome which opened his eyes to the true nature of the papacy. Erasmus was less naïve, and knew before he got to Rome what he would see there (which, in any case, was no secret). But Erasmus's interests, unlike Luther's, were broader than those of a pious but rebellious provincial. He did not visit Rome as a pilgrim, to begin with, and unlike Luther he had never believed in pilgrimages. He came to Rome to gather impressions, and it must be said that he was one of the first modern authors to do so. In Luther this sort of curiosity extended only to those matters connected with his own reformatory aims.

Erasmus was repelled by Rome, and at the same time enjoyed it hugely. 'One is always pleased there by the sweet liberty,' he wrote, 'rich libraries, the charming friendship of writers and scholars and the sight of antique monuments.' He attended a bullfight, and was horrified by the 'cruel game, a remnant of old paganism'. On Good Friday he heard a sermon delivered by the prelate Tommaso Inghirami, known as 'the Cicero of his time', who larded his message with mythological allegories and flattery of Pope Julius, but neglected to mention the death of Christ. Inghirami, who was also the pope's librarian, later conducted Erasmus through the workshops of Raphael. Carrying his native philistinism to absurd lengths, Erasmus tells us nothing of what he saw there or of what was said. When going from the library to the workshops, they had to pass the Sistine Chapel, where Michelangelo was at work high up on his scaffoldings. The doors were closed, however (an unnecessary precaution in Erasmus's case, one is tempted to add), and not even the pope was permitted to disturb the painter at his work.

Erasmus was at once amused and scandalized by it all. He saw the murderous verses, the pasquinades posted in the Piazza Navona, and we may assume that by now he had, in spite of himself, absorbed enough Italian to understand them. Typical of those of the period was one which lampooned the feuding of two cardinals in love with the same prostitute. Another concerned a papal servant who took bribes from foreign applicants and had, in this case, sold a customer an Irish bishopric which, when the man went to assume it, he found occupied by adolescent twins of unpromisingly robust health. Others concerned the warrior pope, sanctimoniously praised for having outdone his predecessor, whose violence had been restricted to cutting off Malthus's ear; and one showed how Julius was rejuvenating himself by watching from his balcony while horses coupled in the courtyard below.

Erasmus, who had evidently been bored by the Florentines,

was interested in, if appalled by the Romans. He not only spoke with scribes, notaries, advocates, pimps, bankers, secretaries, courtesans and lackeys, those whom he described in *The Praise of Folly*, but interested himself in every aspect of the life of the city. Years later, in Basle, he concluded that the phrase *civis Romanus* had become empty. 'It is more,' he wrote, 'to be a citizen of the free city of Basle.'

Thanks to the Venetian edition of the *Adagia*, his name had become as well known in Rome as those of his great Italian predecessors, the humanists of the previous century. Domenico Cardinal Grimani, patriarch of Aquileja, a man of exceptional erudition (for which he was rewarded with 18,000 ducats per annum), received him in his palace as an equal. Grimani agreed wholeheartedly with Erasmus's aims, not only the pedagogical ones but also those ecclesiastical reforms outlined in the *Enchiridion*.

He met another influential prelate, Giovanni Cardinal de' Medici, son of Lorenzo, disciple and friend of Ficino, Poliziano and Pico. He had acquired his red hat at sixteen, and his father had sent him to Rome with the warning: 'Take care, my son, you are going into the den of all the vices of the world.' But by now the cardinal had adapted himself to the circumstances of Rome, and he loved humanism and the arts. He was the focus of the opposition gathering against Julius II, who disliked him violently. Four years later, when he acceded to the papal throne, Giovanni de' Medici told his cousin Giulio (later Pope Clement VII): 'God has given Us the papacy, now let us enjoy it.' They proceeded to do so, and quite soon a lampoon was posted on the Pasquino of the Piazza Navona to the effect that Giovanni might make a good pope – if only he believed in God.

Having met Hadrian of Utrecht while still at Louvain, Erasmus had by now met all the men who were to be pope during his lifetime, with the probable exception of Paul III. For the time being, however, it was widely believed in Rome that the next pope would be Raffaello Cardinal Riario, archbishop of St Giorgio. This prelate doted upon Erasmus even more than

SCOTLAND

NORTH
SEA

KINGDOM
OF
DENMARK

ENGLAND

London

Amsterdam
Rotterdam

HOLSTEIN
Hamburg
Bremen
MECKLENBURG
MÜNSTER
UTRECHT
BRUNSWICK
BRANDENBURG
Berlin
POLAND

Ghent
Antwerp
Brussels
Cologne
Liège
HESSE
SILESIA

THE

Caen
Rouen
Reims
LUXEMBURG
WETTIN
LANDS
K. OF
BOHEMIA
Prague
MORAVIA

Paris
Orléans
Tours
Troyes
Mayence
Worms
Nuremberg

Nantes

LORRAINE

Rhine

BAVARIA

EMPIRE

DUCHY
Dijon
FREE
COUNTY
OF Besançon
Basel
SWISS
CONFEDERATION
Munich
AUSTRIA
Vienna
Salzburg

Poitiers

BURGUNDY
TYROL
TRENT
Trent

Bordeaux

Lyons
SAVOY
MILAN
VENETIAN
Venice
FERRARA
HUNGARY

Toulouse

Avignon
GENOA
MODENA
BOLOGNA

K. OF
NAVARRE

Marseilles
FLORENCE
PAPAL
STATES

REPUBLIC

SPAIN
SIENA
UMBRIA

Rome

Naples

KINGDOM
OF THE
TWO
SICILIES

EDGAR HOLLOWAY

0   100   200   300 MILES
0   100   200   300 K.M.

Western Europe, c. 1475

the others. One day he surprised him with the request of Pope Julius (although the idea probably originated with Riario himself) that Erasmus should write a treatise for the pontiff justifying the creation of the League of Cambrai and the war against Venice.

Erasmus of course liked Venice almost as much as he detested war. Although he was not very familiar with political machinations, he undoubtedly realized that a coalition of the pope, the emperor and the kings of France and Hungary stood every chance of dismembering Venice, the only naval power left in Europe which was strong enough to resist the Turks. Unfortunately the treatise which he produced has been lost, but we know that instead of accusing Venice of occupying territories rightfully belonging to the Holy See he discussed the problem of war in general and advocated Christian moderation. The pope was not pleased.

Meanwhile he visited Naples and the Cave of the Sybilla, and was considering taking up permanent residence in Rome. He probably would have done so had he not received a letter from Mountjoy. In April 1509 Henry VII had died, and his successor was the young prince to whom Erasmus had been presented in 1499, and who, two years before, had written a letter to Erasmus in Bologna boasting of his proficiency in Latin. 'Now all bitterness must instantly leave your soul', wrote Mountjoy, well aware that it was not like Erasmus to have forgotten the eighteen pounds taken from him at Dover. That he was correct in this is attested by the fact that Erasmus had employed 'English' as a synonym for 'greedy' ever since.

Mountjoy urged him to hasten to England, where, he wrote, the cause of literature was flourishing, the sky was laughing and tears of joy were flowing from all eyes. The floweriness of the style indicates that the lines were written by Mountjoy's secretary, the humanist Andrea Ammonio, rather than by Mountjoy himself. The letter ended by saying that the archbishop of Canterbury was devouring the *Adagia* page by page and was praising its author to the high heavens. 'He promises you a benefice upon your return,' continued the letter, 'and sends you five pounds for travelling expenses.' To this sum Mountjoy added five pounds of his own. Erasmus pondered the matter, hesitating. Cardinal Grimani did his best to keep him in Italy, but the temptation proved too great. He left Rome in July 1509, never to return.

Renaudet has maintained that this was the greatest mistake in Erasmus's career, and one which was to have disastrous consequences not only for his own work but for the future of Europe. In a few years, he argues, Erasmus would almost certainly have been made a cardinal by Leo X, and his influence in the Lateran Council would have resulted in the most far-reaching reforms. Renaudet also points out that with Erasmus in Rome the most powerful members of the Sacred College, such as Riario, Grimani, Giulio de' Medici, Egidio of Viterbo, Este of Eger, Bakócz of Esztergom, Ximénes of Toledo and Albert of Mainz, all on the side of reform, would have won the day. He believes as well that Erasmus, a born mediator, would have prevented the excommunication of Luther and brought about an early compromise with the reformer. This, he points out, would have spared Europe the Massacre of St Bartholomew, the Thirty Years War and the hatred and misery which ensued during the 125 years following the Reformation.

We shall not presume here to pass such definitive judgement on what is, after all, a matter of speculation – albeit enticingly plausible speculation. That Erasmus's decision was a mistake, however, one is inclined to accept. This much at least we have on the authority of Erasmus himself, for he regretted the decision for the rest of his life.

As he hurried northward he called on Bombasius in Bologna, giving him a vivid account of expectations in England. Just before this, in Siena, he had bidden farewell to his former pupil Alexander Stuart, who was to die at the side of his father four years later at Flodden. Before they parted company the young man presented Erasmus with two beautiful gifts. One was a gilded goblet, the other a ring set with a carnelian engraved with Erasmus's device, Terminus, god of boundary lines, the only god to stand up to Jupiter. With this was the inscription CONCEDO

NVLLI, I concede to none. It was this defiant motto which was printed on the title pages of his books.

He crossed Switzerland to Constance, sailed down the Rhine and, after stopping briefly in Louvain, arrived in England in the autumn. From this whole period, his arrival in England until he went to Paris nearly two years later to publish *The Praise of Folly*, not a single letter survives, and Erasmus's life is shrouded in mist. We know that after arriving in London he stayed at More's house, and while awaiting the arrival of his books he suffered an attack of stones. It was while undergoing the terrible pain which accompanies this affliction that he wrote *The Praise of Folly* in several days. Later he lived with Mountjoy at his country estate, but there is no information concerning this period. We do know, however, that he wrote nothing else during the following year and a half.

The dearth of correspondence from the years 1503–4, when Erasmus was in voluntary exile in Louvain, indicate that he had felt lost and unhappy. There is some reason to believe that the same explanation holds good for this visit to England. Arriving in the country with the remainder of the ten pounds that Mountjoy and King Henry had given him and the promise of a benefice, he may well have begun to question the wisdom of returning to a place which, on the last occasion, had deprived him of a larger sum and had reneged on a similar promise. After the luxury of his life in Italy he may also have felt dismay at having abandoned the prospect of wealth to live in a country in which, as he had learned, it was not so easily obtained.

The benefice which Mountjoy had promised him in May 1509 was at last granted in March 1512, by the archbishop of Canterbury: a pension accruing from a rectory in Kent. It is likely that during the thirty-four months of waiting for the promise to be fulfilled Erasmus lost some of his well-known patience.

As it turned out, however, Henry VIII on whom he had pinned his hopes did not much care for him. Three years earlier Erasmus had dreamed together with Colet and More of a movement for social and religious reform, spreading across the land from Queens' College and embracing the learned class of the entire realm. Now, however, there was nothing but silence at Cambridge.

The Praise of Folly is perhaps too well known to need more than the briefest of summaries here. In the form of an oration held by Folly herself, it is constructed with great dramatic skill. Folly reviews all the stupidities of her earthly realm, maintaining that folly is a remedy against the suffering in the world and a necessary attribute of all persons. As examples she conjures up the quackery of the physicians, the pettifoggery of the lawyers, the revelling of kings, popes, bishops, cardinals, knights and merchants, all of whom live happily – as opposed to the doctrinaire who, shrinking from folly, leads a life of deadly tedium. Customs and institutions are as well subjected to the same charming treatment: the adoration of saints does not differ much from polytheism; people delude themselves with indulgences and are encouraged in this by greedy clerics; the expostulation of dogmas leads us to absurdities; real happiness is found in self-forgetfulness, the self-transcendent tenderness of lovers, those whom Plato called the happiest of all.

Folly continues in this manner until the reader is prepared to conclude that Erasmus, with his words carefully chosen to avoid blasphemy or even profanation, is going to make sport of the whole spectrum of human nature. But he does not. Slowly and almost imperceptibly Folly increases the violence of her abuse, and the reader, previously inclined to agree with her, finds himself repelled by her arrogance. Wise men, says Folly, prefer prudence and clear understanding – but where does this lead? The wise may either retreat, taking nothing seriously and laughing at the human comedy, into the conceited foolishness of believing that they understand it all and are above it; or they may do their best to strip men of the various guises they wear in life. This is folly as well, since destroying the masks of illusion automatically destroys a comedy which cannot be played without them.

Folly asserts that life must be lived by her rules, and that all men, whether her followers or her enemies, are by their very nature fools. The kind of Socratic wisdom which can be pitted against her, she insists, is also impracticable, for true prudence lies in desiring only that degree of wisdom which is proper to mortals. It is at this point that the reader is finally brought to the point of open revolt, and he will have noticed that in explaining that life was folly she inadvertently indicated the remedy for the situation. Putting the book down, the reader inevitably retains two paramount impressions: first, that there is an inordinate amount of stupidity, hypocrisy and corruption in the world and in each man; second, that a radical programme based on the teachings of Christ (and Socrates) is the only possible solution to the evil inherent in human nature. The second idea is in effect the underlying motive of the book, the message embodying the whole of Erasmus's goal. It is a plea to resist indifference and satanical cynicism, and a warning that there can be no easy and immediate transformation of man. It is also an optimistic reaffirmation that the aims of humanism will, slowly but surely, prevail.

The immediate and enormous success of the book marked the rise of Erasmus's new fame not only as a humanist but also as a writer and as the intellectual leader of the Continent, a reputation unequalled until Voltaire. After the first edition of 1511 the book was reprinted thirty-nine times before 1536. German, French and English translations soon appeared, followed by Italian and Dutch versions. In 1515 Hans Holbein, then eighteen years old, drew thirty-seven illustrations for the work. In 1730 *The Praise of Folly* was translated into Icelandic, and soon afterwards into Swedish and Danish. The Enlightenment favoured it even more than the previous two centuries, and even today the book is reappearing with ever-increasing frequency in Europe and America: in English alone there were three editions in the sixteenth century, nine in the eighteenth, and eleven so far in the twentieth. It must be added, however, that in the

English-speaking world the book is largely the preserve of scholars and students of history or literature, while in France, and especially in central Europe, it is still considered obligatory reading on the part of every educated person.

Opinions of *The Praise of Folly* have always varied. Martin van Dorp, a conservative professor at Louvain, though not inimical to Erasmus, nevertheless wrote to him in 1514: 'Your *Folly* has caused great disturbances even among those who were formerly your most devoted admirers. . . . It is not for me to give you advice, but I humbly believe that you could make everything good by publishing a counterpart to *The Praise of Folly – The Praise of Wisdom.*' Erasmus commented to More: 'I cannot imagine what was going on in Dorp's head. Well, that is what theology does to people.'

He went rather further than necessary, however, when he reassured the good Dorp that the book was not be taken seriously, that he had composed it to pass the time while he was in More's house, too ill to do any serious work. Consequently, the opinion that the book was written by an otherwise serious author for his own distraction was voiced not only by some of Erasmus's contemporaries but more recently by such a fine scholar as Huizinga. J. A. Froude, a noted English scholar of the last century, was even convinced that Erasmus was 'a sarcastic sceptic' and 'an Epicurian', and asserted that the book contained all the 'spiritual dynamite' the Renaissance needed. Some thirty years ago another Englishman added: 'Instead of speaking of "spiritual dynamite" it would be simpler, perhaps, though it would not sound so well, to call the *Folly* a theological squib. It is a squib which today, perhaps, dances and crackles a little disappointingly.'

Among the myriad divergent views of the book it is interesting to note such unexpected stands as that taken by the authors of the *Great Soviet Encyclopaedia*, who rebuff Huizinga and other western writers for 'playing down the social and political context of Erasmus's immortal work'; and that of the Hungarian ideologist, Imre Waldapfel, who praises Erasmus for having 'laid bare the structure and injustice of feudal society, the rot of its ruling clique and clergy who kept the people in darkness and ignorance, the conceit of its ideologists and the buffooneries of its lackeys and beneficiaries'.

One might easily select better balanced judgements of the *Folly*, but these are most likely, perhaps, to propitiate the spirit of Erasmus, who would surely have been amused that the doctrinaires of the present day are still intent upon avoiding any painful application of the message of his book to themselves, and that his purpose in writing it is still the subject of more or less scholarly contention. He would, presumably, have agreed with Anatole France, one of his more recent disciples, who remarked that people search in the great books of the past not so much for what they contain as for what it is hoped they contain, and that posthumous fame evidently owes much more to a misunderstanding of any given author than to any real comprehension of his intentions.

The success of *The Praise of Folly* during the past 450 years must be attributed to the fact that it is a literary masterpiece, and a splendidly anomalous one at that. In this connection at least it may be said that its message, whatever it ultimately is, is not of primary importance. In spite of the efforts of Hegel, and more recently of certain of his disciples, to present us with an absolute aesthetic, we are still reduced to conjecture as to why the *Folly* must be considered a masterpiece.

First of all, it is a very special kind of satire. It has been shown that Erasmus borrowed his method of irony from Lucian – or at least there are strong natural affinities between them. Allowing this, it must still be said that while Lucian looks down from his Stoic belvedere and shrugs in the face of human stupidity, Erasmus is not loath to accept his share of the general responsibility and, reserved and dispassionate on other occasions, musters a spirited and peculiarly humanistic and Christian sense of irony in the *Folly*. It was this new brand of gentle irony, deeply concerned but sharply effective, which lent charm to the book and which has lost little of its effectiveness today.

Another reason for the book's success is that it is at once a revolt against the Middle Ages and, outwardly at least, a typically medieval book in its form. It is closely related to Sebastian Brant's *Ship of Fools* of 1494, which was translated into Latin as *Navis stultifera* and published by Josse Bade in 1505. Erasmus read the book and later became a friend of its author. In *Ship of Fools* Brant described various types of foolishness and ridiculed them in his defence of conventional behaviour. Erasmus, on the other hand, attacked foolishness as the essence of conventional behaviour. The *Folly*, typically medieval in construction and utterly classical in its implications, was thus a satire on medieval thinking. Holbein's thirty-seven illustrations for the book depict medieval types, the same vision the book must have evoked in most of Erasmus's contemporaries. All this too accounts for the fact that the *Folly*, like its author, defies any attempt at rigid categorization. Its only valid classification is in fact inclusion among such satires as those of Petronius, Lucian, Rabelais, Cervantes, Swift and Voltaire.

In August 1511, a few days after he had recovered from an attack of 'sweating sickness' – a mysterious disease which seems to have been epidemic and often fatal – Erasmus travelled from London to Cambridge, where he was to lecture in Greek. Fisher had had the post created for him. Until then Greek had never been taught in Cambridge.

Like so many of Erasmus's journeys, this one was fraught with mishaps and tribulations. Although often on the road, he disliked travelling and was a poor rider. During this journey his servant's horse went lame. On the first day they had nothing to eat since, unlike France and Italy, inns and hostels were rare along the English highways. On the second day there were incessant thunderstorms, and Erasmus's horse 'fell three times on its nose' in the mire. He arrived in Cambridge exhausted and soaked to the bone, and after taking over his quarters in Queens' he hastened to the physician, a Dutchman, and alchemist of some fame. He assured Erasmus that he could rejuvenate him.

The letter in which Erasmus described his hazardous trip to Cambridge to Colet also contains a passage concerning his desperate financial situation: 'I see before me the path of

Christian poverty. I have so little hope of any profit that I realize that I shall have to leave here whatever I am able to tear from my patrons.' This theme, though usually treated lightly or even jestingly, is often repeated in his letters from Cambridge: 'Oh, this begging! You laugh at me, I know, but I hate myself for it. I am fully determined either to obtain some fortune which will relieve me of cringing, or to imitate Diogenes altogether.'

In spite of his respect for Erasmus, Colet sent him ironical and sometimes irritated replies to these letters. Erasmus's financial situation seems to have been confused throughout his stay in England. When appointed lecturer in Cambridge he was promised a salary much higher than the usual ten pounds a year. Later on, we do not know exactly when, he accepted a second post. According to local tradition, this was the Lady Margaret chair of divinity, which brought with it some thirteen pounds a year. Besides these two salaries, he received a yearly stipend of twenty pounds from Mountjoy and something like twenty-five pounds from Warham, whom he called his most generous bene-factor. If he did in fact receive all these amounts, which is far from certain, he had nearly seventy pounds a year altogether.

If we compare this with the ten pounds which the master of newly-founded Christ's College received, we must assume that Erasmus was living on a truly lavish scale, that he was spending an inordinate amount on manuscripts or else that his patrons were breaking their promises. After March 1512 he received the pension accruing from the rectory of Aldington, Kent. The rectory was worth thirty-two pounds a year. Rather than reside there, Erasmus merely drew the pension of about twelve pounds (which was later increased), while the priest who actually occupied the post had to content himself with the remainder. Erasmus himself was to denounce this unfair practice in his books.

For the first time in his life he had a fixed occupation and adequate lodgings. The famous tower study, overlooking both town and river, was his. These assets, however, were offset by the disadvantages. His lectures excited little interest, and his classes remained small. Cambridge was a typically provincial town, and its university was inferior to Oxford's both in size and reputation. Unlike such places even as Deventer, Oporto, Modena and Palermo, it did not have a printing press until 1520. And Queens' was a clerical community, only slightly better in this respect than the Collège de Montaigu. Erasmus's colleagues were Scotists, and utterly undistinguished Scotists at that. For them, as Renaudet has remarked, Erasmus was and remained 'un étranger d'esprit aventureux'. A few young men, such as Henry Bullock and Thomas Lupset, helped him in his work and spent evenings with him 'in perfect and delightful talk', but they were poor substitutes for Colet, More, Ammonio, Linacre, Grocyn and the others who were in London. 'There is absolutely no reason,' Erasmus wrote to Ammonio in November 1511, 'for you to congratulate me on my Cambridge retreat. Shame alone curbs my complaining.'

His complaining, however, continued; and it was probably justified. The climate of Cambridge was clearly detrimental to his health. Wood and coal, which were transported up the Cam, were evidently scarce in all seasons. It rained throughout November 1511, and Erasmus became so hoarse that he sometimes could not speak at all. During the next months he had an attack of stones and suffered agonies. His Dutch physician prescribed the usual remedies: barley water, syrup of vinegar and cherry preserves. Erasmus wrote a letter to Ammonio, who had left Mountjoy's service to become secretary to Henry VIII, and asked for several casks of Greek wine, which he considered the best medicine for his affliction.

Tormented by his longing to return to Rome, he comforted himself with continuous work and a lively correspondence with Ammonio, who was also dreaming of leaving England to return to Italy. Andrea Ammonio resembled Fausto Andrelini, Erasmus's friend of his Paris days. He was a humanist of no small reputation, albeit a writer of nothing but amateurish poetry. He had been born in Lucca and had come to England in 1504 in the service of the pope. Like Andrelini, he always secured the most desirable positions for himself with skill and ruthless intriguing, yet he too displayed more sincere affection and selfless friendship for Erasmus than one might have expected. He kept his friend well-informed of political matters and the affairs of London society, and took trouble to obtain patrons and money for him. The charm of the correspondence between them, however, lies in the gossip which the two émigrés exchanged about their English hosts – whom they understood far better than they ever allowed outside that correspondence.

The inclement winter of 1511–12 was followed by a 'dusty and pestilential' summer. In 1513 plague struck Cambridge and raged unchecked throughout the summer and autumn. Erasmus fled to the country, staying with friends there. Discovering that the wine which Ammonio was sending him from London would not reach him in the countryside, he returned to Cambridge, preferring to risk the plague rather than do without the Malvasian he believed the only cure for his kidney or bladder ailment. In January 1514, shortly before he left Cambridge for good, he suffered a really severe attack of stones. He was dismayed at this turn of events, having believed himself cured by the white wine. From then on he experimented with red Burgundy.

Perhaps because of the view prevailing among continental humanists that England was a remote, unhealthy and fairly barbarous place, Erasmus's friends worried about him during his thirty months at Cambridge. As early as November a letter arrived at Queens' from Paolo Bombasio in Bologna, inquiring after his friend, whose death had been rumoured all over Italy. We do not know what reply Erasmus gave to this, although one can imagine his insisting with grim humour that the rumours were essentially true. During the summer of 1513 when plague broke out at Cambridge, it was officially stated in Basle that he had died during the epidemic. This was still believed in Vienna as late as 1514.

One wonders why he did not leave Cambridge since he quite evidently felt himself to be submerging in insular backwaters. Besides the fact that he evidently did not realize how famous he had become on the Continent by now, there are two likely explanations. First, he may yet have kept his belief that the king would fulfil the high hopes which the humanists had placed in him, i.e. 'to make learning and literature flourish in his realm, instead of pursuing the vainglories of war'. Second, it is possible that he preferred the security he was enjoying to placing himself at the mercies of his French publisher, who paid notoriously small fees.

Illness, depression and loneliness served to make him industrious, however. In September 1511 he had sent Colet the manuscript of a booklet, *A Method of Study*. A month later he completed a Latin transcription of St Basil's commentary on the book of Isaiah, dedicating it to Bishop Fisher. In December he presented Ammonio with his translation of Lucian's *Icaromenippus*, a charming satire on the senselessness of philosophical disputes.

Early in 1512 he wrote *De copia*, usually known in English as *On Fluency*. For the next two centuries this book was to be Europe's standard textbook of literary style, being reprinted more than one hundred and fifty times. Together with *A Method of Study*, it will be examined later in connection with Erasmus's pedagogical works, written for the most part towards the end of his life. It must be mentioned though that *De copia* is far from an ordinary textbook. It went a long way towards adapting Latin to the needs of the time, ignoring the custom of 'imitating the worm-eaten Roman usage of yore'. With a Rabelaisian fullness and playfulness, towards which he was always inclined but seldom permitted himself, Erasmus proved in this book a true son of the Renaissance. In a display of formidable linguistic virtuosity, he provided an imposing list of paraphrases for the young Latinist, including such things as two hundred variations on the theme *As long as I live I shall remember*. None of the two hundred was laboured, and all were examples of a rather unwieldy language being moulded into forms of almost Greek naturalness. In reading this list, and others, one is rewarded by such touches of special and unexpected charm as *Tum demum Mori sui oblivisci poterit Erasmus cum ipse sui desinet memor esse.* (As long as he is master of his memory Erasmus will remember More.)

During the year 1512 he compared texts for the projected edition of the Greek New Testament and that of St Jerome. He also prepared a new and slightly enlarged edition of the *Adagia* and translated two works of Plutarch, whom he regarded as one of the earliest ancestors of humanism. In the meantime the fourth edition of *The Praise of Folly* and editions of both *A Method of Study* and *On Fluency* were being brought out simultaneously by Bade in Paris. A few weeks later Bade sent him fifteen guilder in payment for *On Fluency*, and a letter in which he explained:

Ah, I know well what you will say: What a small sum! But it is too obvious that no remuneration whatsoever could be adequate to your genius, your knowledge, your industry. I am sure God will repay you and that your own virtue will be, as it already is, your finest reward ... and you will help your little Badius, too, who has a numerous family and no earnings whatsoever besides his daily trade.

Erasmus's reaction to this is not difficult to imagine, but the reply he sent to Bade was friendly, and he promised him and his large family every sacrifice on his part. After he finished the revision of the *Adagia* he visited London and gave the manuscript to an agent, Francis Berckman, to deliver to the publisher. That Berckman gave it to Froben in Basle rather than to Bade in Paris is owed, so far as we know, to a mysterious misunderstanding. Froben, having just printed a pirate edition of the same work, was understandably enchanted. Erasmus pretended to be indignant with Berckman's 'perfidity', though he does not seem to have hesitated to enter into a business relationship with Froben, one which was in fact to endure for the rest of his life. Bade was thus amply repaid for his years of cheating, and Erasmus was spared the necessity of quarrelling with him. From then on he discovered that it was quite possible to have several publishers at once, and he continued to give work, the Lucian translations and *On Fluency*, to Bade, presumably for the sake of his great family. 'If it is agreeable to your interest and honour,' wrote the chastened Bade, 'I will suffer, and that with equanimity.'

During the thirty months Erasmus spent at Cambridge it became clear that the optimism which the humanists, like the populace in general, had felt at the beginning of the reign of Henry VIII was misplaced. Already in 1511 Pope Julius II had made peace with his arch-enemies, the Venetians, and had allied himself with Ferdinand of Spain and with Henry VIII in order to drive 'the barbarians', meaning his former allies the French, out of Italy.

Erasmus detested nationalism as the major obstacle to the further development of European civilization, unity and peace. It must be said however, that, while not usually having an appreciative eye for national characteristics, he did entertain a sort of admiration for the French, praising them for their wit and humour, the natural intelligence of their women, the excellence of their cuisine and the civilized manners of their society. Adding all this to his momentary displeasure with England, it is not surprising that his sympathies were now with the French. He excused the English king, however, assuming that he had been enticed into the war by the wily pope.

As King Henry campaigned against the French in the Low Countries, the armies of the French king were also rapidly losing ground in Italy. In June 1512 Julius II won a major victory over Louis XII, and was planning to occupy Paris when, early in 1513, he died. During the upheavals on the Continent Erasmus kept himself busy in England writing an essay on the art of letter-writing, exerting textual criticism on Seneca and composing an extremely dull commentary on the so-called *Disticha Catonis*, a collection of equally dull moral precepts wrongly attributed to Cato the Censor, and used, thanks to the authority of both Cato's name and Erasmus's, as a textbook in grammar schools throughout the sixteenth century.

He made up for this insipid exercise, however, by composing a venomous satire entitled *Julius Shut Out*, presumably just after the death of the pope. In it he tells the story of the martial pope's attempt to enter the gates of paradise, and how, after heated argument, he is turned away. The booklet was published anonymously since it was much more dangerous to single out a pope, even a dead one, than to attack popes, cardinals, kings and other potentates impersonally, as he had done in the *Folly*. His authorship was obvious to everyone, however, and when asked about it he skilfully avoided owning to it, although his pride never permitted him to deny it outright. The booklet became very popular and was often reprinted, though never by any of Erasmus's regular publishers.

During the summer of 1513, sitting in plague-stricken Cambridge, Erasmus was 'ready to fly away' at any moment. The country was preparing for full-scale war against the French. English raids across the Channel multiplied during the summer, and the Scots, allied with Louis XII, attacked the English. They were defeated in September at Flodden, where their king, James IV, was killed together with his son, Alexander Stuart, Erasmus's former pupil.

Peace was restored soon afterwards, but by now Erasmus had lost all interest in remaining in England. 'I have been living a snail's life here,' he wrote in a letter to Ammonio in November 1513, 'most people having gone away out of fear of the plague; though even when all are present it is a lonely place for me.' Two months later he left Cambridge for London, and in June he embarked for the Continent. During the following years he made three short visits to England, but never again displayed any inclination to remain there. His disappointment in Henry VIII was never forgotten. In the remaining twenty-two years of his life he was to be invited by such figures as Emperor Charles V, Francis I, Ferdinand of Austria and several popes to take up permanent residence at their courts. He would always excuse himself with a polite letter, sometimes explaining that authors are like certain Flemish tapestries: they must be viewed from a distance if they are to retain their attractiveness.

Arriving in Antwerp, he went to visit Mountjoy, now lieutenant of the castle of Hammes, some twenty miles away, which was attached to 'His Majesty's town of Calais and the marches under his obeisance'. There he found a letter from Servatius awaiting him. This message was considerably milder in tone than the one Erasmus had received ten years before.

Servatius very politely asked his subordinate to return to Steyn. We may assume that his concern for the state of Erasmus's soul was now augmented by the desire to have 'the light of Christianity' beneath his roof once again.

Erasmus replied at length, rejecting Servatius's invitation in no uncertain terms:

> Whenever I have thought of rejoining your society I have been reminded of the jealousy of many, the contempt of all, the coldness and silliness of the conversation, utterly lacking any savour of Christ . . . in fact of a whole way of life in which, if the ceremonies were removed, I know not what would be left to choose. And, finally, I have thought of the weakness of my constitution, increased by age, infirmity and work, which would prevent my satisfying you while at the same time I should destroy myself.

He enumerated his plans: the translation of the New Testament, the commentary on the Epistles of St Paul and the edition of St Jerome; and he concluded by saying that he wanted to live in liberty and to complete his earthly task. Only in the final passage, after many Greek quotations which Servatius could not be expected to understand, did he mellow somewhat and express his hope that they might speak together during the coming year after he returned from Basle, that they might discuss 'all the secrets which cannot be dealt with in letters'. And he bade farewell to his 'once-sweetest companion'.

The meeting was never arranged, however. Servatius was to survive his former friend by several years, and no doubt he was aware of it later when a wooden statue was erected in front of Erasmus's alleged birthplace (probably the house of his grandparents) in Rotterdam; for the erecting of a statue to a commoner, and a contemporary at that, was unheard-of in the sixteenth century. Fortunately he did not live long enough to witness the victory of Protestantism in the Netherlands and the disbanding of the monasteries. At that time the surviving monks, mostly old men, would be moved into the almshouse of Gouda, and the beautiful library of Steyn, including all the works of Erasmus, would be auctioned off.

V

The Leader of Humanism

Erasmus's voyage up the Rhine in the summer of 1514 was really a triumphal procession. In each city delegations awaited him, dinners were given in his honour and he was showered with gifts. It was not only the community of German humanists who were responsible for this, but the middle classes of the towns as well, those who had become aware of their real power and needs during the years of the intellectual revolution kindled by humanism. Nor was Erasmus honoured merely as the author of famous books: they were celebrating the cause he stood for. They paid homage to him for his *philosophia Christi*, so far as they understood it, his perception of religion as an inner commitment, his appeal for ecclesiastical reform and the simplification of the faith down to its essential doctrines. He was celebrated for his endeavours to restore human values to a society which had finally begun to realize its own sorry state and to long for change, for his indefatigable efforts to spread learning and for his hope that human reason would prevail and that men would be persuaded that changing their world for the better depended on the growth of knowledge.

Certainly the majority of his admirers and disciples, possessing minds far less subtle and complex than his, did not fully apprehend many of his ideas, though these were expressed with the utmost clarity and directness. They were, however, ready to follow him, and were themselves aware that this was the most important thing.

Having so recently left sombre England, Erasmus regretted as he travelled up the Rhine that he was coming to know Germany so late in life. In his euphoria, as he later confessed, he began to dream of earthly paradise as being within the reach of mankind – much as Pico had dreamed some twenty-five years before that world-government, the unification of the three great religions and eternal peace would all be achieved by the early sixteenth century. This happy period, when every conceivable issue was raised and discussed in an atmosphere of unparalleled freedom, was not to last very long. After the rise of Luther the boil of sectarianism slowly but irresistibly infected and destroyed those ways of thinking which were not pertinent to it. In 1514 Erasmus felt he was witnessing the advent of eternal spring; twenty years later he was to look back on this time as the Indian summer before a seemingly endless winter.

Although he does not say so, he may well have been preoccupied with the thought that in his present success he had at last attained the unattainable, that he had risen from an unknown and impoverished scribe to a world-famous author sustained by nothing but his own intellectual power, utterly above competition, surrounded by friends and followers, at once sociable and splendidly alone. Listening to the solemn and pompous eulogies in which he was called 'the phoenix of learning', 'the light of mankind', the 'eighth wonder of the world' and 'the most enigmatic and incomparable character', he must have smiled to himself at the sweet irony of it all. The author of *The Praise of Folly* was indeed a vain man, but one whose good taste consisted largely in an exquisite sense of proportion.

At Mainz, then the centre of German learning, he met Ulrich von Hutten, courtier in the service of Archbishop Albert von Hohenzollern. Hutten was a peculiar sort of humanist, at once talented, insolent, truculent, romantic, noble in his goals and unscrupulous in attaining them. Twenty-six years old, he was the leading poet of Germany, and desired nothing more than to play Alcibiades to someone's Socrates, sword in one hand and pen in the other. Thus there is nothing surprising in the fact that he became fond of Erasmus. It is somewhat surprising, however, that Erasmus was well-disposed towards him. This may be ascribed, perhaps, to the effervescent mood in which his German reception had put him.

In Frankfort he met Johannes Reuchlin, the great Hebraist, hero of the most famous trial of the time. Hochstraten, chief inquisitor of Germany, had been provided with false charges by his hireling, a converted Jew by the name of Pfefferkorn. The charges were used to justify the burning of all Hebrew manu-scripts with the exception of the Old Testament. Reuchlin led and won the battle against this atrocity, and was consequently accused of heresy. At this time the fight had been going on for five years, with all the humanists of Germany backing Reuchlin and all its fifty thousand monks against him.

Erasmus had already corresponded with Reuchlin from England; and later, from Basle, he was to intervene on his behalf with Cardinal Grimani in Rome. He also wrote a bold letter to Hochstraten, lecturing him on moderation, and stating sarcastically that if being a good Christian meant hating the Jews, then assuredly the population consisted of very good Christians indeed.

He proceeded to Strasburg, the first free imperial town he had ever been in, and was much taken with it. 'There I have seen,' he wrote, 'old men who were not morose, nobles without arrogance, magistrates without hubris . . . a democracy without turbulence, wealth without wantonness, prosperity without insolence.' The humanists of Strasburg received him with open arms. He met, among others, Jacob Wimpfeling and Sebastian Brant, author of *Ship of Fools*.

Arriving at last in Basle, he entered the printing shop of Johannes Froben in a manner reminiscent of his first day at Aldus's in Venice. This time he varied the joke by delivering a letter from himself to Froben, introducing himself as an intimate friend of the humanist, and explaining that Erasmus had entrusted him with the business of publishing his books, so that whatever he did Froben could take as being done on the authority of Erasmus himself. Then, to Froben's horror, he set to work as if he were taking over the shop. Finally, however,

Froben realized the joke and took it in good part. They became good friends, in spite of some irritating faults which the printer later revealed. He was a naïve man, and, as the episode with Erasmus's servant[1] indicates, something of a boor at times. Nevertheless, he was essentially well-meaning, an excellent printer and a man of unshakable honesty. Erasmus remarked of him that 'he was a man on whom you could count to play cards fairly even in the dark'.

This first visit to Basle was to last two years, and in many ways it resembled Erasmus's visit to Venice, where his love affair with book printing had begun. The work he turned out in Basle, however, was superior in nearly every way. It was of wider scope, better planned and better executed than almost anything he had done before. For the first time he was defining in clear-cut terms that movement which, from 1516 onwards, was to be known as Erasmianism and which was to take him to the peak of his career.

In April 1515 he interrupted the visit to make a short trip to London, probably to get manuscripts he needed for the new edition of either the New Testament or St Jerome. During the same year he was appointed councillor to Archduke Charles (later Emperor Charles V) by Jean le Sauvage, chancellor of the Low Countries. It was a purely honorary title, but it brought 200 florins a year. Shortly after this the king of France, Francis I, presented him with a canonry at Tournay. These benefices together with the much-increased income from the sale of his books, had finally placed him 'beyond the reach of envy'.

Between 1514 and 1517 he published a dozen new works. His continuing interest in the classics was demonstrated by two of Plutarch's treatises which were printed now by Froben to celebrate Erasmus's arrival in Basle. A few weeks earlier, Bade had published the second series of his Lucian translations in Paris, a continuation of the work he had begun with More. In the following year Froben published his edition of Seneca. He also brought out a less important work, the *Parabolae*, in 1514.

Much greater than either of these in its effect was the 1515

[1] See Chapter I, p. 5.

edition of the *Adagia*. The four-thousandth adage of this edition was a new one: *War is sweet to the inexperienced*. This quotation from Pindar was followed by an essay against war. Lifted *in toto* from the work, it was later published separately and ran through twelve editions. Two years later Froben published the *Querela Pacis*, which in spite of its title, is not so much a 'lament of peace' as an attack against war.

A new motif in Erasmus's writings, through a direct development of his *philosophia Christi*, pacifism remained from this time a central feature of his thoughts. He was proud of pioneering it, and considered it his greatest title to fame. The pacifist ethic was not, of course, Erasmus's invention. It had first appeared in force in the western world among the early Christians, who drew the same conclusion from the teachings of Christ as Erasmus. According to the testimony of Tatian, Justian and Tertullian, the early Christians held the profession of soldiering to be incompatible with their beliefs. Legionaries were, in fact, neither baptised nor admitted to religious services until the Synod of Antioch (in 274 or 276). It was St Clement of Alexandria who took note of the fact that most of the legionaries adhered to the cult of Mithras simply because they were not permitted to become Christians, and under his influence the decision of the Synod of Antioch was taken and quickly seen to bear fruit: thirty years later it was the Christian veterans who revolted against Diocletian, and twenty years after that the Roman Empire was officially Christian.

This new attitude toward the bearing of arms was reinforced by St Augustine, who developed the theory that a war to resist aggression or to enforce justice was not only permissible but a Christian duty. The matter of 'enforcing justice' was sufficiently vague, from the Church's point of view, to support any number of wars thereafter. Aquinas restated Augustine's stand in his *Summa Theologiae*, laying down the guide-lines to follow in establishing what was just or unjust. His view was taken almost as law by the Church from that time on. One result of this was that pacifism was thought of as cowardice, at best, and punished as heresy at worst. The concept nearly disappeared during the

Middle Ages. Remnants of early pacifistic thinking could, however, be detected in the beliefs of the Waldenses, the Lollards and a few other heretical sects.

It was revived in Dante's *De monarchia*, with which Erasmus was familiar. Yet Dante's peace was the Ghibelline, eschatological and transcendental concept of peace: the anticipation of the establishment of a universal Christian monarchy in which the whole world would be ruled justly, and the existence of inimical camps rendered impossible. Two hundred years after Dante this dream already appeared hopelessly antiquated.

Erasmus hoped to guide his contemporaries along a more realistic path, but his fervour matched Dante's: his own memories of war were no less disquieting than the poet's had been. The Holland of Erasmus's childhood suffered under the legacy of Charles the Bold: poverty, piracy, famine and anarchy. As a boy of eight Erasmus had seen 200 prisoners of war broken on the rack outside the gates of Utrecht on the orders of the town's bishop. He had witnessed Julius II entering Bologna at the beginning of a seven-year period during which he was to treat Europe as his private field of honour. And then Henry VIII had joined in the general mêlée, thwarting any chance of success of the reformatory programme of More, Colet and Erasmus.

A few years earlier in London, More had drawn Erasmus's attention to a tract by Cardinal Cusanus, the only one of his works in print at that time, which concerned the Turkish wars. Cusanus was pleading for arbitration and peaceful settlement to Pope Nicholas V, and disparaging the idea of yet another crusade against the Infidel. Pico della Mirandola, it will be remembered, had considered a secure peace to be a *sine qua non* of human dignity. Vitrier, abbot of St Bertain, had condemned war in outspoken terms to Erasmus. And Colet in 1513 had delivered a sermon at Greenwich in the presence of Henry VIII in which he courageously denounced war as barbarous and unchristian. But Colet and Vitrier were not writing books on the subject, and the ideas of Cusanus, Ficino and Pico were known in detail to relatively few people. Erasmus's *Dulce bellum inexpertis* (War is sweet to the inexperienced) was the first book in European history devoted entirely to the cause of pacifism. It was written for the public at large, imbued with obviously real concern and buttressed by irrefutable arguments. In Erasmus's words its appearance marked 'the beginning of another war, that between the better part of human nature and the other, destructive part'.

The pamphlet *Dulce bellum inexpertis* begins with the statement that war is so unquestionably accepted by men that they marvel at anyone who is not pleased by it. Erasmus portrays man as the only creature nature has brought forth naked and helpless, with soft flesh, innocent eyes, arms meant to embrace, and the ability to kiss, laugh and weep, 'a token of meekness and mercy'. Nature, he continues, has endowed him with a hatred of solitude, a love of company and a fervent desire for knowledge. Contrasting the heroic concept of man as his own means and end, to the unheroic idea of the warrior whose aim is destruction and, ultimately, self-destruction, he paints a portrait of Alexander the Great – whom he considers insane. He movingly describes the growth of civilization in a manner reminiscent of the fifth book of Lucretius' *De rerum natura*, and follows this with Christian arguments against war.

Then he turns on St Bernard de Clairvaux, who praised soldiers, and St Thomas Aquinas, who sanctioned the 'just' war. Why, he asks, should we be more moved by the teachings of St Bernard or the disputations of St Thomas than the word of Christ? How can there be a just war? Was there ever a war which lacked a pretext? Would the Romans be justified in reoccupying Spain because it was once their province? How would it benefit us to subdue the Turks when, even should we succeed in baptizing them, we should become pagans in the bestial process? The best defence against the Turks, he continues, is the unity and solidarity of Christians and their rulers. He tells how he wrote the book *Antipolemos* for 'Julius, Despot of Rome, the second of that name' during the time he was committed to making war against the Venetians. Now, he adds, he is happy that he can commend the same ideas to Leo X, the son of that Lorenzo de' Medici who had taught us that by supporting the causes of learning and peace a man heaps more glory upon himself than he could ever hope to do with any number of wars.

In the *Querela pacis*, published two years later (1517), Erasmus went still further. In this book he stated the idea that 'man alone in all nature possesses self-destructive tendencies', and went on to propose Christian remedies for this. Examining the causes of war, he began with the disputes concerning hereditary rights to thrones, and continued with nationalism, boundary disputes and conflicts of economic interest (citing the frequency of wars against France owing to its wealth, yet condemning Charles VIII's invasion of Italy as open robbery).

He concluded by analysing tyranny, which, in order to maintain its hold over the people, must avail itself of every opportunity to wage war. His enumeration of the causes of war seems fairly complete, even in this age of vaster experience. It covers a good deal of ground the Marxists were later to tread, but does not limit itself to the social causes which Rousseau held to be predominant, nor the idea, which so obsesses the followers of Marx, that the roots of all conflicts are economic.

The *Querela* concludes with several concrete proposals for lessening the danger of armed conflict between nations: education against nationalism, the establishment and recognition of unalterable frontiers between states, international laws for the regulation of royal succession, the restriction of the ruler's power to declare war, the establishment of an international body of savants to arbitrate impending conflicts, and, finally, the mobilization of the intellectual forces of the Church, the universities and the schools for a concentrated attack against the romantic glorification of war and for the purpose of imbuing society at all levels with a disgust of it. The book ends with a passionate plea, not to the rulers of Europe but to their subjects: 'I appeal to you all, who are considered to be Christians: conspire together in this same manner of thought. Here you should show how much the unity of the masses can do against the tyranny of the mighty.'

Although there is a certain amount of naïveté in all this, as in all humanist proposals for restraint, moderation and reason, it should be emphasized that Erasmus's explanation of the causes of war is, *mutatis mutandis*, extraordinarily close to the view of present-day political theorists. He was the first man in modern times to point out the connection between war and the duality of human nature, i.e. the conflict between man's destructive and aggressive instincts and his 'higher nature'. It is significant that Erasmus, abandoning moderation for once, faced this problem with courageous honesty at a time when war was thought to be as inevitable as any other aspect of human life.

Both tracts which analysed the causes of war and recommended specific remedies for them were written during a propitious lull, the few peaceful and optimistic years before the calamitous third decade of the sixteenth century. The *Querela pacis* enjoyed the same measure of success that *Dulce bellum inexpertis* had. In the next hundred and fifty years it was published in thirty-two Latin editions, translated into seven languages and often reprinted at the height of the religious wars. Both pamphlets were read by the rulers of Europe, and caused at least mild uneasiness in some of them. Later, when rigid intolerance slowly gained the upper hand throughout Europe in the wake of Reformation and Counter Reformation, no other book of Erasmus's was to suffer so much reviling as the *Querela*. In spite of the admiration that Francis I felt for its author, it was condemned by the Sorbonne in 1525 and publicly burnt. The Spanish translation was banned by the chief inquisitor Juan Valdes, in 1559, and burned in the Spanish Netherlands. Nothing of this sort took place in the Protestant countries, though this by no means implies that Luther or Calvin had any use for pacifism.

In the meantime, however, both books added greatly to Erasmus's reputation and won him valuable friends. One of these was Johannes Faber, later minister to Ferdinand of Austria and then bishop of Vienna, who, together with his sovereign, showed a thoroughly Erasmian attitude in foreign affairs and in matters of religion. Another friend won by his 'evangelical pacifism' was the humanist Juan Luis Vives, who became one of

Erasmus's staunchest supporters in Spain. The Swiss reformer
Ulrich Zwingli, whom Erasmus had already influenced with his
translation of the New Testament, published a year earlier in
1516, welcomed the *Querela* as 'the Psalm of Christian Concord'.
Thanks to Zwingli, Erasmus's pacifism was to enjoy at least one
immediate success: it was with arguments drawn from it that
Zwingli persuaded his fellow citizens to remain neutral in the
war between the Swiss Confederation and France. Thus no one
from the canton of Zürich was slain in the bloody fiasco at
Bicocca in 1521.

It has been mentioned that Erasmus was appointed councillor to
young Prince Charles, archduke of Austria, in 1515. Being a
conscientious man, he felt obliged to repay the honour (and
earn the stipend) by writing a book entitled *On the Education
of a Christian Prince*, which was published in 1516. In the first
chapter of this book, called in Latin *Institutio principis christiani*,
he states that the chief aim of education is virtue, and the second,
wisdom. Apart from the Bible, he recommends the reading of
Plutarch, Seneca, Cicero and, above all, Plato. The prince
should be moulded to Christian specifications, however, and
not made to conform to the shadows of Achilles or Alexander
the Great, and certainly not to those of Lancelot or King Arthur.
Developing his theme, he set down the whole pattern that
education should follow. After the basic character of the prince
has been formed the study of history and geography should be
pursued, and technical training should complement these. The
prince must acquire a thorough knowledge of the laws, customs
and institutions of his country in order to understand and win
the hearts of all his subjects.

Erasmus, More, Machiavelli and Voltaire held strikingly
similar views on the advantages of education. Yet Erasmus, for
all his being the strongest advocate of these views, was not so
naïve as to think them likely to succeed. Perfect princes are
rare, as he remarked, and for this reason he advocated the curtailment of princely power. In the *Institutio*, in which he

expressed himself with great moderation, he preferred 'a limited monarchy, checked and decreased by an aristocracy and by democracy'.

In his commentary on one of the entries of the 1515 edition of the *Adagia* he expressed himself more forcefully: 'The eagle is the image of the king, for he is neither beautiful, nor musical, nor fit for food; but he is carnivorous, rapacious, a brigand, a destroyer, solitary, hated by all, a pest to all, who, though he can do more harm than anyone, wishes to do more even than he is capable of.' And in the same edition the comments after the entry *Aut regem* sound amazingly like something which might have been heard at the French National Convention of 1791:

> Do we not see that noble cities are erected by the people and destroyed by the princes? That a state grows rich by the industry of its citizens only to be plundered by the rapacity of its rulers? That good laws are enacted by the representatives of the people and violated by kings? That the commonalty loves peace and the monarchs foment war? The guardians of a prince aim never to permit him to become a man. The nobility, feeding on public corruption, endeavour to make him as effeminate as possible through pleasures, lest he learn what a prince ought to know. Villages are burnt, fields are devastated, temples pillaged, innocent citizens slaughtered, all things spiritual and temporal destroyed while the king plays at dice or dances, or amuses himself with fools or in hunting and carousing.

Both sections of the *Adagia* were printed separately and widely circulated. During the War of Religions the French anti-monarchists (called Monarchomachs), who anticipated the French Revolution by two centuries, echoed these views, without precedent in the sixteenth century. It should be added, however, that Erasmus, realizing the decadence of the monarchies, knew with Machiavelli that the virtues of the Roman Republic, such as they were, could not be resurrected.[2] On the other hand, Erasmus had no high opinion of the uneducated masses, and

---

[2] It was to take many years for republican ideas to ripen even to such a limited extent as they did in Erasmus's homeland, the United Provinces, after the Dutch liberated themselves from Spanish rule.

believed anarchy to be an even greater evil than tyranny – though it should be added that he was never inclined to choose the lesser of two evils, preferring to repudiate both.

Many of Erasmus's other political opinions sound equally modern. Two decades after the discovery of America and the Portuguese landing in Goa, he stated that 'Colonization is nothing but robbery masquerading as the propagation of Christianity'. In his advice to the Christian prince he recommended a liberal economic policy combined with a certain amount of state control; he had little confidence in unrestrained free enterprise. He advocated the supervision of markets, weights and measures, the disbanding of mercantile coalitions and the punishment of speculators and any others who might cause prices to rise. He advised the suppression of money-lending and brokerage, an increase in the taxation of luxury articles and a decrease in taxes on bread, wine, clothing and all other necessities.

He asked for measures against the accumulation of private capital, and presented convincing arguments against the private ownership of the means of national wealth, the buying and selling of public office, the system of punishment which did little to prevent crime, and the whole feudal system of taxation which did nothing to ensure that public funds were spent for the public good. He advocated the limitation of the number of monasteries and a system of public care for the aged and infirm. As the Italian humanists had done before him, he advised the rich and powerful to place their sons in useful professions and to disinherit them if they refused to learn and work.

In the last chapter of the *Institutio* Erasmus turned again to the pacifist cause, and explained for the benefit of the young prince that war, condemned by Christ, should never be undertaken by a ruler either against a Christian state ('cross against cross, Christ against Christ') or even against the Infidel. It should remain the last resort, self-defence, since no such thing as a just war exists. Several years after this he was to maintain that the pope should be forbidden to enter into any political alliances in order that he might remain free to arbitrate in international disputes; and, similarly, that no ruler should be permitted to declare war or to enter into any alliance without the consent of his councillors.

Erasmus's political ideas were often compared with those of Machiavelli, whom he never read. *Il Principe* was not published until 1536, and then only in Italian. There can be little doubt that Machiavelli's insights into politics and psychology were superior to Erasmus's, and in many ways their views were in fact opposed. Machiavelli saw national states and warfare as facts to be reckoned with, while Erasmus wanted simply to abolish both. Machiavelli saw man as intrinsically evil, while Erasmus saw him as essentially good, believing that the desire for learning is innate and that man is born predisposed to the Christian ethic – the neo-Platonist view of Ficino and Pico. Beyond this, however, the differences virtually cease, and many a conclusion reached by Machiavelli in his *Discorsi* corresponds exactly with that of Erasmus on the same subject. They were agreed that man can be changed: in the case of Machiavelli, that innate evil can be surmounted, and in the case of Erasmus that innate goodness can be made to flourish. And they were agreed that education is the means to achieve this, since it is education which leads to virtue and virtue which is the key to their common goal: the well-being of the human community.

Social questions were largely ignored prior to the middle of the eighteenth century. The poor were looked upon with commiseration at best, and charity was the universally recommended palliative for their affliction. It occurred to no one to consider a comprehensive programme to solve the problem, and such proposals of Erasmus's as public care of the aged and infirm were by way of being pioneering efforts, as were his recommendations for the abolition of feudal taxation, state control of capital and the revision of the penal system. Most of these ideas were not heard again until the Enlightenment, when they were voiced by Voltaire, Montesquieu, Diderot and d'Alembert. Others were not to find expression until the nineteenth century, or even later.

In February 1516 the *Novum instrumentum* left the press of Froben in Basle. It was the first edition of Erasmus's Latin translation of the Greek New Testament, accompanied by the Greek original and annotations. About half the volume of 679 pages was devoted to annotations to the text and elucidation of the errors in the *Vulgate*. Sandwiched among the commentaries were strong attacks against ecclesiastical abuse.

The three original prefaces to the *Novum instrumentum* were revised by Erasmus from time to time. In the first of these he recommended the diligent study of the New Testament, and asserted, in contrast to the teachings of the Church, that no layman should be denied the opportunity to study the Bible any more than he should be denied the sacrament of baptism. The Bible, he continued, is more instructive of religion than all the writings of all the theologians past, present and future. Mindful that the vast majority of people did not read Latin, he recommended that the New Testament be translated into the various vernaculars.

In the second preface he explained something of the philological methods he had followed, while in the third, entitled *Apologia*, he gave an account of his desire to improve on the *Vulgate* with a translation strictly following the Greek originals. The work was dedicated to Pope Leo X, and appeared by privilege of Emperor Maximilian. The text of the *privilegium*, in keeping with the strongly anti-papal leanings of the emperor, also advocated the reading of the New Testament, and added that this might 'persuade the pope to enlarge further Christian piety' and prompt him 'to make Christians once more acquainted with their Holy Scriptures, even with the teachings of their Master'. Lest the sarcasm be missed, the title-page carried an allegorical drawing of *Envy Defeated*.

In the fifteen years since Erasmus had first conceived the idea of translating and annotating the Greek New Testament he had gradually come to think of it as the chief aim of his life, his first duty as a Christian and his personal means of earning heavenly reward. It was a direct and logical consequence of the *philosophia Christi*, which aimed at the restoration of the authority of the Gospels over that of theology and tradition. Such men as Wycliffe, Hus and the leaders of the *devotio*, all of whom attributed a central role to the Bible but had little or nothing to do with humanism, shared with the rest of the age an ardent interest in Holy Scripture. Between the appearance of the Gutenberg Bible and the end of the fifteenth century a hundred and twenty-four editions of the *Vulgate* had been printed, though none of them authorized by the Church. Rabbis had edited the books of the Old Testament repeatedly, and it was considered the shame of Christianity that the Greek New Testament had never been printed except in Latin translation. The plan of Erasmus was thus met half-way by the wishes of the population, and the allusions of Emperor Maximilian to the failures of the popes were widely recognized as not being without foundation.

Erasmus was of course aware of the dangers involved in publishing such a work. In the spring of 1515 he visited England to procure manuscripts of the New Testament before beginning his task, and while there he wrote a letter to Pope Leo X. The letter was couched in the most flattering language, and English scholars from Dr Johnson down to the present day have seldom failed to be shocked by it. Erasmus asked the pope's permission to dedicate to him the edition of St Jerome and 'everything else I shall ever write'. It was a skilful ruse, for at the same time he wrote another letter to Cardinal Grimani announcing his intention of publishing the *Novum instrumentum*, obviously hoping that the cardinal would announce the news to the pope, who would then be persuaded to accept the dedication. Such a dedication would have provided Erasmus with no small measure of protection. Unfortunately, however, no reply came from Rome for the time being.

Back in Basle, he immediately began the translation. The enormity of the task should not be underestimated. Erasmus was armed with phenomenal powers of concentration and the ability to work fourteen to sixteen hours a day with great speed. On the other hand, the philological methods at his disposal comprised the bare skeleton of modern methods, if that. For his textual criticism he had only one authority to rely on, Valla, and no real reference works, not even encyclopedias.

Aside from occasional outside help, he had two assistants in the work. One was a certain Nikolaus Gerber, who proved an unfortunate choice. The other, the cleric Ioannes Œcolampadius, who later became the aide of the Swiss reformer Zwingli, was said by Erasmus to have 'a golden stream in his head, a radiant library and a manuscript of Jerome'. Since Erasmus did not know Hebrew, Œcolampadius took on the task of looking up all references in the Old Testament, and he did a splendid, if less than perfect job. Œcolampadius was a man of 'infinite and bottomless piety', and he looked upon his temporary master as a saint. When asked what payment he required for his help, he replied, 'The remuneration of anonymity', and meant it. The only present he accepted was one of Erasmus's manuscripts, the introduction to the Gospel According to St John. He was in the habit of kissing this as if it were a relic, and kept it hanging on a crucifix before him as he prayed – until one day another, presumably still more fervent, admirer of Erasmus stole it.

Of the ten Greek manuscripts Erasmus had to work from, four were brought from England, five he found at Basle and one was lent by Johannes Reuchlin. Reuchlin's codex (which is still extant, as are the others) was the oldest and by far the best of Erasmus's sources. Unfortunately, however, he used this copy only for the Apocalypse, which was missing in the others. He used the second best of the codici, number two of the Basle manuscripts, only occasionally, believing that its Greek text had been tampered with to make it conform to the *Vulgate* – which was not the case. Thus the best of the texts were slighted in favour of the eight which Erasmus believed to be 'very ancient', though they were mediocre copies from the fourteenth and fifteenth centuries.

The last six verses of the New Testament were missing altogether in the ten Greek manuscripts, and Erasmus was unable to find them elsewhere. Thus he retranslated Apocalypse, xxii: 16–19 and 21, from the *Vulgate* back into Greek, having found the original Greek text of only the twentieth verse in Valla.

Though he added a remark, confessing the stunt and stating why he had felt obliged to perform it, it has never failed to make modern scholars shudder with horror, as perhaps it should.

After completing 'the work of six years in eight months . . . to the detriment of our health', Erasmus handed his manuscript over to Froben in February 1516. Still no answer arrived from the pope, but Professor Dorp of Louvain, who had previously urged Erasmus to undo the damage wrought by the *Folly* by writing a *Praise of Wisdom*, sent him an anxious letter imploring him not to alter the *Vulgate*. What would happen, asked Dorp, if he should happen to come up with a text at variance with the old one? And why for that matter suppose that the Greek Church, that cause of so much mischief, had kept a better text of the Holy Scriptures than the Latin Church, infinitely nearer to Christ? He begged Erasmus not to challenge the authority of the *Vulgate* even should he discover it to have been corrupted.

If Erasmus was timid to the point of cowardice in everyday affairs, he was heroically resolute where his work was concerned. Nevertheless it was true that, as it stood, the book was a potential source of danger. Besides the anti-papal jibes in the imperial *privilegium*, there were still more serious attacks in the commentaries, not against the person of the pope but against the papacy itself. For example, Erasmus commented upon the passage 'Thou art Peter and upon this rock I will found my Church' to the effect that the words were addressed to St Peter alone; there is no reason, he said, to assume that they were meant to refer to the bishops of Rome, or that they were to apply in perpetuity. People had been burnt at the stake in Paris, Naples, Toledo and elsewhere for less.

In the light of this it is not difficult to see why Erasmus decided to dedicate the book to Leo X, with or without permission. The dedication, he hoped, would still be enough to protect him. As it turned out, it was a risk well taken. A few months after the publication of the book, while Erasmus was visiting England for the fifth time, he received a letter which the pontiff had written a year before. The pope had learned about the book, as Erasmus intended that he should, from

Cardinal Grimani. He expressed enthusiasm and pronounced it a magnificent undertaking. This letter was immediately published by Froben, and it gave Erasmus some much-needed reassurance. It was followed later by a formal brief in which the pope expressed his delight 'not only because you have dedicated [the work] to Us, but because it contains a new kind of science . . . and therefore We give you all credit due to a true Christian'.

The *Novum instrumentum*, the first Latin translation of the New Testament in nearly a thousand years, was intended to be closer to the reader of the sixteenth century, and more vivid to him, than the *Vulgate*. Its language is fluent and elegant, in spite of Erasmus's statement that 'it is not so much elegant as lucid and exact'. A noted liberal theologian of the present century, A. Bludau, who wrote an exhaustive study of the *Novum instrumentum*, has gone so far as to speak of the 'humanist dawn' evoked by Erasmus's translation, as opposed to the 'medieval dusk' of the *Vulgate*.

Erasmus employed a fresh, distinctive and vibrant language to replace the worn-out Graeco-Hebraic Latin of the *Vulgate*, often too rigid to match the complex and fluid phrasing of the Greek and the sometimes exotic sense of the Hebrew; all too often the *Vulgate* lacks that supreme clarity which, since the work is in Latin, is at its disposal. One would not like to be unfair to the *Vulgate*, however. It abounds in passages which are superior to Erasmus's reading; and it has, moreover, an overall uniformity and cohesion, luxuries Erasmus did not permit his own text. But it also has a monotonous quality which all but destroys the authors' more impassioned passages, and its very uniformity of tone prepares an easy path for orthodox interpretation. It may be said that the *Vulgate*, most probably the product of a committee of pious and learned men who edited the translation of St Jerome, is a fairly reliable but somewhat colourless text; while Erasmus's *Novum instrumentum* is, for all its inaccuracies, the noble and eminently readable effort of a single man searching for the unadorned word of God.

The *Novum instrumentum* is at variance with the *Vulgate* in some four hundred instances, each of which is elucidated in the annotations. Erasmus could scarcely have suspected that his exegesis would shake the very foundations of the Christianity he hoped to strengthen. That he was so daring in his performance of textual criticism on the Bible owed to his belief as a Catholic that it was in a real sense proof against false attack. But he also believed in the existence of a Greek text, a faultless original which, once found, could be deciphered properly with the aid of reason. What he failed to realize was that the text of the *Vulgate*, though corrupt in many instances, was by no means as corrupted as he, Luther, Zwingli and Calvin assumed.

Four and a half centuries after the appearance of the *Novum instrumentum* Erasmus's translation is still a subject of scholarly contention. Some of the points at issue are negligible, while others must remain unresolved; for all the evidence is not yet gathered, and, in the case of the Church, the *Vulgate* continues to be regarded as an incontestable authority, sacred and not to be tampered with by unauthorized scholars, however well-meaning.

No attempt will be made here to pass judgement on the 400 passages in which Erasmus's translation differs from the *Vulgate*; to do so would mean becoming involved in theology at the expense of philology. The Council of Trent established the *Vulgate* (during the session of 1546) as the official text of the Church, and condemned Erasmus's translation. Thus the Church shares the views of Professor Dorp and rejects the 400 changes as incorrect. The Protestant translations of the New Testament, however, beginning with Luther's translation of 1519, were based on Erasmus's version, not on the *Vulgate*. According to Bludau, the German Protestant theologian of this century, at least 330 of Erasmus's changes are justified, although some scholars have mentioned a rather lower figure. In any case, there are at least seventy instances in which Erasmus, it must be admitted, was indisputably wrong.

Along with his textual criticism Erasmus included a great deal of explanation. Many of his thousands of remarks on the language, meaning, style and historical background of the New Testament are still valid, and some of his more general conclusions are echoed by later theologians. Thus, for example, his opinion that St Luke could not have witnessed the events he described, a view which has gained wide acceptance, as have his doubts about the authenticity of the Apocalypse, which he did not find in the canon of the Greek Church. Similarly, he doubted the authenticity of St Paul's Epistle to the Jews, finding in it 'his spirit, perhaps, but surely not his style'. He discussed these and other problems freely, and whenever he entertained doubts either about the text or his ability to understand it he invariably admitted them. After some of the more sensitive, hence dangerous arguments, he concluded ironically that, if forced to, he would bow to the authority of the Church.

The annotations provided Erasmus with ample opportunity to digress in the form of essays against ecclesiastical abuse, ceremonial and superstition. Most of his contemporaries welcomed these passages as extensions of what he had begun in the *Enchiridion*. Some, however, including even a few of the more progressive spirits, were scandalized and felt such essays to be out of place in a commentary upon Scripture. These passages thus became at once the most popular parts of the book and a chief cause of the attacks against it.

The annotation to the verse, 'Some have made themselves eunuchs for the Kingdom of Heaven's sake', reads as follows:

> In this class we include those who by fraud or intimidation have been thrust into a life of celibacy in which they are allowed to fornicate, but not to marry, so that if they openly keep a concubine they are Christian priests, but if they take a wife they are burned.

On Matthew, xi: 30, 'My yoke is easy and my burden is light', he remarked that Christ's light burden has been made heavy by the Church. Scholastic theologians have loaded man down with doctrines turned out from their own syllogisms and from Biblical quotations which they have misinterpreted. It is not possible, he continued, for a man to acquaint himself with all these even in a lifetime, and, since theologians earn their bread in this manner, the number is still increasing. Christ did not put riddles to us that we should solve them or else be damned. His teachings are easy to understand.

The commentary on Matthew, xxiii: 5, is similar in tone. By the Jewish Pharisees Erasmus is put in mind of these clerics who are as well Pharisees, and even worse ones. For a price, he says, these men will show us the milk of the Blessed Virgin, the pieces of Christ's cross (which are so numerous by now that a ship could not hold them all), the comb of St Ann, the sandals of St Thomas Becket or the foreskin of Jesus. By these Pharisees, he continues, we are given to understand that we must tolerate the stupidity of the common people – though it is Pharisaic rapacity that keeps the people ignorant.

Commenting on other passages, he attacks hypocrisy, intolerance, indulgences, pilgrimages and everything else which is incompatible with the teachings of Christ. Thus the *Novum instrumentum* included the whole of his 'philosophy of Christ': the restoration of the role of the New Testament and the programme of reform, restated here in terms less moderate and more likely to have strong and far-reaching effects.

Any recapitulation of the *Novum instrumentum* would be incomplete without mention of the Greek text which formed a part of it. This first edition, as it were, of the Greek New Testament was probably the least successful part of the book. It is a slipshod work, abounding in faulty passages, typographical errors and misreadings, for most of which his assistant Gerber was to blame. Erasmus was horrified at the profusion of errors and immediately set about revising the text for a new edition. He was to continue amending the book until the fifth edition, in 1535, a year before his death. He had to face much criticism for the *Novum instrumentum*, and where this dealt with the text of the book (as opposed to its purpose) it was, admittedly, often justified.

Nonetheless, the book was a triumph for Erasmus in the meantime. As soon as it appeared lavish praise began pouring in from all sides, if not from all quarters. Colet wrote that 'the name of Erasmus shall never perish'. The archbishop of Mainz declared himself happy to have been born a contemporary of him 'who has restored the ancient glory of theology'. Thomas More wrote an epigram in honour of the work, and defended it publicly against its detractors. Bishop Fisher, far from being shocked by the liberties Erasmus had taken with the *Vulgate*, was inclined to think that the translation ought to have been still freer. Philipp Melanchthon proclaimed its author 'the rising sun of truth which hath dispelled the darkness'. Ulrich Zwingli memorized portions of the Latin text and the commentaries. Luther, who was at the University of Wittenberg at this time, lecturing on the Epistles of St Paul, took Erasmus as his chief authority in exegesis from the day he first laid hands on the book, quoting him directly in every important question, immediately abandoning his former scholastic methods and, ironically, explaining the Bible in accordance with the humanistic and rationalistic guide lines of Erasmus's commentaries.

There was also opposition to the book from the beginning, not so much for its errors as for Erasmus's commentaries and, especially, the threat it posed to the *Vulgate*. In Cambridge, where Erasmus had lectured just two years before, the book was banned as soon as it arrived – a fact seldom mentioned by most of Erasmus's English biographers. One early critic, Bishop Henry Standish, preached a sermon in London charging Erasmus with the falsification of the New Testament; and he urged the lord mayor, the nobility and the populace to prevent the complete ruin of Christianity by destroying all copies of the book at once. On one occasion the bishop threw himself on his knees before Henry VIII and, raising his arms heavenward, implored the monarch to defend his crown and realms against Erasmian heresy; whereupon he was told to shut up.

Revised editions of the *Novum instrumentum* were printed in 1519, 1522, 1527 and 1535. The 1519 edition bore a text still further from the *Vulgate*, one which Erasmus had allegedly written in 1506; and in 1522 he was forced by conservative pressure to restore the text of the first edition and to print it side-by-side with that of the *Vulgate*. The book was reprinted at least sixty-nine times between 1516 and 1536, not including four editions of the Latin text by itself, and two of the Greek text printed by Aldus's successor, Asolani.

Thus the New Testament was printed the equivalent of once

every 90 days for a period of twenty years. According to the most conservative estimates more than three hundred thousand copies were in circulation. Clearly every scholar and most literate people from Spain to Poland and from Scotland to Italy were familiar with it.

Still more important is the fact that Erasmus's *Novum instrumentum* served as a basis of, and inspiration for, the vernacular translations which followed it. It is generally accepted that the preface to the 1519 edition suggested to Luther the idea of his German translation. Luther used both the Greek and Latin texts of Erasmus in his work. The first English New Testament, also based on Erasmus, was translated by William Tyndale and printed at Cologne in 1525. It was followed by the Hungarian versions of Benedek Komjáti (1533) and János Sylvester (1540), the Spanish of Francisco de Enzinas (1543) and many more, based on Erasmus. It is beyond the scope of this book to examine how far the spirit of Erasmus and his bold enterprise survived in these other translations, the sole reading of millions of people in centuries to come. We shall content ourselves with adding that in the preface to the *Novum instrumentum* Erasmus expressed the hope that such translations would be the result of his labours; and in this his wishes were fulfilled.

In the spring of 1516 Erasmus left Basle for Antwerp, where he stayed in the home of his young friend Pierre Gilles, the town clerk. Gilles was also a friend of Thomas More, and he served as the model for the character in More's *Utopia* in whose garden the sailor tells his story. At this time he was busy correcting the manuscript of *Utopia*, which was to be printed a few weeks later by Maertensz, More's printer, who also worked for Erasmus from time to time.

It was during this period that Quentin Matsys painted his diptych of Erasmus and Gilles, who sent it as a token of their friendship to More. Pierre Gilles, so far as we can judge, was a charming young man, a typical Renaissance intellectual. Beside him in the painting, Erasmus looks pale and harassed. Several more drawings and paintings of Erasmus, especially by Dürer and Holbein, are no less interesting for the fact that each seems to have been painting a different subject. The Erasmus of Matsys looks like a listless dreamer with a decidedly mystical bent. Neurasthenic he certainly was, but mysticism was the furthest thing from his nature. It may be that Matsys, impressed by Erasmus's reputation as an 'enigmatic character', remained more faithful to the legend than to the evidence before his eyes. Dürer's Erasmus is a South German burgher, a typically Baroque and Lutheran bulwark of anti-Renaissance sentiment. One is inclined to accept Holbein's hare-lipped version, with its clear if almost maniacal blue eyes fixed upon desk and ink-pot, as the truer; but there are no proofs at hand.

During the summer of 1516 Erasmus made the first of two short return visits to England, where he saw More, Colet, Warham and Fisher. His main object now was to obtain the dispensation which he had already been seeking with Ammonio's help. The bishop of Worcester, Silvestro Gigli, who happened to be going to Rome for the Lateran Council, undertook to deliver the necessary documents and to plead Erasmus's case. After a delay of more than six months Erasmus finally received the dispensation he had so long desired. The delay was caused not by the pope, always well-disposed towards Erasmus, but by his Cancellaria, who, knowing Erasmus to be wealthy, were determined to squeeze a sizable sum out of him, which they did.

In April 1517 he re-visited England, staying this time in Ammonio's house. In a ceremony at Westminster Abbey he received absolution from his friend, and at one stroke the nightmare of 30 years was ended: he was released from his vows as an Augustinian canon (though not of course as a priest) and freed from the sin of having taken holy orders without first receiving dispensation for his illegitimate birth. This was to be the last service Ammonio performed for his friend, for a few months later he died of the sweating sickness, a mere eight hours after taking to his bed.

During both visits Erasmus's friends, as well as Warham and Wolsey, did their best to keep him in England by promising him high ecclesiastical honours. He declined, however, and returned to the Low Countries where he remained for the rest of 1516 and the first half of 1517 in the house of Pierre Gilles in Antwerp. Recognized now everywhere he went, he was applauded by the people in the street. When he stayed at a hostel admirers would flock to watch him, looking on silently as he ate. Some tried to bribe his servant to let them peep through the keyhole as he slept, or snatched as souvenirs the stubs of the candles he burned through the night. Amused by this, Erasmus remarked that they would do better to use his ideas as candles.

His reputation was enhanced by the steady flow of books from his pen. In 1516 alone, the *Novum instrumentum*, the first volume of St Jerome, the *Education of the Christian Prince*, and a translation of Gaza's *Greek Grammar* were all published. These were followed the next year by the *Querela pacis*, *Scarabaeus* and a volume of correspondence which, following custom, was edited by someone other than the author, Pierre Gilles in this case, who explained in the preface that the author was too modest to publish his private letters, and thus the task must fall to his friends.

His correspondence had grown enormous over the years, so large, in fact, that the postillion stopped at his house before proceeding to Antwerp's city hall. He was harassed now by visitors, most of whom bored him to tears, especially the Spanish, it seems, who stood about 'like statues' and, once seated, displayed 'verbose solemnity'.

The lords of Europe were competing vociferously to lure him to their own countries. The bishop of Paris, Ponchet, let him know that Francis I was prepared to honour him with a generous prebend if only he would come to France. Cardinal Ximénes, primate of Spain, invited him to Toledo, and Archduke Charles, having in the meantime become king of Spain, asked him to accompany his entourage to his new court in the same city. The duke of Saxony offered him a chair in the University of Leipzig, hoping to have the benefit of his advice at all times. The humanist Willibald Pirckheimer, a wealthy patrician and a patron of Albrecht Dürer, invited him to the free imperial city of Nuremberg where he could 'find freedom above all'.

Not surprisingly, Erasmus plotted his next move with care. Spain held no attractions for him. He had many enemies in the Sorbonne against whose powers neither King Francis nor Pope Leo could protect him completely. He saw Germany as a land in upheaval with rulers who were against the pope, bishops who were altogether subservient to the pope and a peasantry and landed aristocracy who were jealous of the wealth of the burghers. Most of all, perhaps, he was disturbed by the nationalism of the Germans, that disease he was so quick to sniff out wherever he went. From the Low Countries he wrote: 'Here I am barked at as nowhere else, and there is no remuneration for me. I cannot stay here.' The 'barking' refers to the hatred which the theologians of Louvain expressed for his edition of the New Testament and for his erudition in general.

At last he made his choice, and in July 1517 he moved to Louvain, where he had already spent two unhappy years and was now to spend four more. It would be hard to find a satisfactory explanation for the move. Perhaps by this time Erasmus no longer attached so much importance to where he lived, or at least felt secure enough to take up residence in a stronghold of his enemies. Louvain was still the bastion of scholasticism it had been 15 years before. Yet both Jean Briard, the vice-chancellor of the university and a man of exemplary honesty, and Jean Paludan, the rector, proved good friends to him in spite of their conservatism. They often came to his house in Louvain, confessing their doubts; but they always heard him out, and were usually won over in the end. In order not to provoke the theologians further Erasmus declined the professorship offered him, and lived the life of a private citizen as far as possible.

His optimism about his cause now seemed justified. The magic blend of his 'philosophy of Christ', that which he advocated as the sole remedy for the ills of the Church and society, at last began to show signs of being generally accepted. His supporters were to be found not only in the ranks of the humanists, bishops and princes, but in the vast majority of the learned classes throughout Europe. His main points had already been largely accepted: the central role of the New Testament in matters of faith, the simplification of the creed to essential doctrines, the creation of a well-informed and humanistic laity which would slowly take over power from the hierarchy of the Church, and the condemnation of scholasticism and all the abuses of the medieval Church. It now looked as if this programme, though still faced by a stubborn if dwindling opposition, had no real obstacles left in its path, and that it would soon become a reality.

By Erasmianism we generally mean the whole programme of religious reform advocated in the *Enchiridion*, combined with a humanistic attitude towards society and learning. During the Reformation the emphasis of the movement was to shift decidedly towards humanism, learning and tolerance. Its adherents tended to think of their cause as European civilization's last bulwark against the disintegration taking place before their eyes. Because of this attitude Erasmianism meant something quite different in 1526 or 1536 from what it had in 1516, and varied still more from place to place.

In Spain, for example, Francisco Cardinal Ximénes, archbishop of Toledo, was Erasmus's first follower, although with his rigid orthodoxy and highly authoritarian views he was a most peculiar sort of follower. Yet it was Ximénes who reformed the monastic orders in Spain, founded the University of Alcalà de Henares and commissioned its professors to prepare a trilingual edition of the Bible; and all of these acts were inspired to one degree or another by Erasmus's 'philosophy of Christ'. Ximénes died in 1517, and after an interim of seven years it was another Erasmian, the humanist Alonso de Fonseca, who became archbishop of Toledo and the most influential man in Spain. Encouraged by Emperor Charles V, the movement gradually became as much the leading spiritual trend in Spain as the *devotio moderna* had once been in the Low Countries. It was supported by most of the clergy, both higher and lower, the civil service and devoted circles of Erasmians in every major town. For nearly a decade it seemed assured of ultimate victory.

In Poland Erasmianism remained a movement of the *élite*. Its influence was greatest in the highest circles of Church and state, especially in such men as Andreas Cricius, bishop of Przemysl; Justus Decius, a royal councillor; and Christopher Szydlowieczki, chancellor of Poland. In the 1520s these men and others like them succeeded in winning over King Sigismund II, an extraordinary piece of good fortune.

There is something particularly moving in the affection the Polish humanists felt for Erasmus. When they married, for example, it was their custom to send their 'father', as they called him, a gift. We know that when the humanist physician Antoninus Cassoviensis married the daughter of the famous Cracow goldsmith, Terctander, the young bride sent a box of embroidery-work to Erasmus. This same Cassoviensis had visited Erasmus in Basle in 1524 and treated him successfully for his bladder stones. At that time he invited him to Cracow where, as he said, Erasmus could work in peace, utterly undisturbed by wars, civil or religious. Erasmus declined, however, saying simply that a captain cannot desert his post so long as the battle goes on.

More important than all this were King Sigismund's activities, both inside Poland and beyond her frontiers. With papal consent the king introduced Erasmian reforms in the Polish Church. He also maintained strict neutrality in all European conflicts, and did his best to mediate in them. The most successful enterprise of this kind was his intervention in Hungary in 1527, when both the *voivode* of Transylvania and Ferdinand of Austria claimed the country's throne and were preparing to go to war over it. Sigismund sent his chancellor, Szydlowieczki, to both parties with the typically Erasmian message that it behoved them to try other means before resorting to war, 'for war between Christian princes is fratricide, to the detriment of the unity of the Christian Republic in the face of the Turkish threat'. The attempt succeeded, and the pretenders concluded an agreement which they kept for a time.

The effects of Erasmianism lasted longer in Poland, perhaps, than anywhere else after Erasmus's death, especially as far as tolerance was concerned. When the Zwinglian refugees from Northern Italy were expelled from Geneva by Calvin and found no Lutheran country which would permit them to enter its borders, it was Catholic Poland which offered them hospitality.

The history of Erasmianism within the court of Francis I and among the French humanists is complex; and the matter of Erasmianism and the Vatican lends itself even less to brief treatment. Leo X, mindful of his father Lorenzo's successes with his 'Florentine Peace' and the teachings of his tutor, Pico della Mirandola, followed a policy which encouraged European unity, and applied it vigorously. He favoured Erasmus, in whom he saw an incarnation of his late tutor, the 'Prince of Concord', in every possible way, and he seems to have understood him perfectly even in those matters in which they did not see eye to eye. In the early 1520s, however, Leo's policy of peace and unity faded in the face of Luther's growing strength, and as pressure was applied on him from various quarters he gradually abandoned Erasmianism for the simpler expedient of pitting Erasmus against Luther – which turned out not to be so simple after all. Some ten years later, when Alessandro Cardinal Farnese acceded to the papal throne as Paul III, there was hope that Erasmianism might be revived in the Vatican.[3]

The religious and social tensions which had long been building up in Europe seemed to increase rapidly about the time Erasmus moved to Louvain. Aleandro, who had a careerist's keen eye in political matters, had, as papal legate to Germany, warned Pope Leo that the country was on the point of secession. 'I fear a great revolution is about to take place in this part of the world', Erasmus wrote in September 1517. News of the traffic in indulgences in Germany, one of the most scandalous instances of this sort of abuse, could only add to his fears. Albert Cardinal von

[3] See page 249, *infra*.

Hohenzollern had sought to gain papal dispensation to hold, besides his own archbishopric of Mainz, those of Magdeburg and Halberstadt as well. Pope Leo asked an enormous sum for the favour, but gave the cardinal permission to sell extraordinary plenary indulgences in order to raise the money. The banker Fugger lent half the amount Albert had to pay, and took charge himself of the traffic in indulgences.

In the midst of all this Erasmus learned of the 95 theses which Luther had written at Wittenberg. We do not know his immediate reaction, but we may surmise that he largely approved. There was in fact little in the theses that he himself had not said previously, in some instances repeatedly. Having acquired the text of the theses, he sent them to More and Colet, writing in a letter to the latter that 'the Roman Curia has simply cast aside all shame'. A few months later, as he passed through Strasbourg on his way to Basle, Erasmus met the humanist Capito and expressed to him his admiration for the theses of Luther, knowing that Capito was in correspondence with the young monk and would surely send this piece of information on to Wittenberg.

Later, during the summer of 1518 when he learned that Luther's enemies were about to move against the reformer, he added the following lines, typical in their conciliatory tone, to the preface to the new edition of the *Enchiridion*: 'So if anyone admonishes us that the deeds of charity are better than papal indulgences, he does not altogether condemn indulgences, but prefers to them what is more surely taught by Christ.' In a letter dated 17 October 1518 to the humanist Lang, he was considerably more outspoken:

> I hear that Luther is approved of by all good men, but it is said that his writings are uneven. I think his theses will please everyone, except a few, concerning Purgatory, which those who make their living therefrom do not want taken from them . . . I see that the monarchy of the Roman high priest (as that See now is) is the plague of Christendom, though it is praised through thick and thin by shameless preachers. Still, I hardly know if it is expedient to touch this open sore. . . .

Besides revealing his appreciation of Luther, this letter shows some of his earliest reservations. By Luther's 'uneven' writings Erasmus referred to the *Sermons*, published by Froben, some of which he disliked because of their demagogic and inflammatory character. Luther's first letter to Erasmus, dated 18 March 1519, was respectful, even affectionate. He called Erasmus 'our glory and our hope', and asked: 'Who is there whose innermost self Erasmus has not penetrated, whom Erasmus does not teach, in whom Erasmus does not reign?' The letter was clever in its diplomacy and was written for the sole purpose of winning Erasmus over to Luther's cause. It was, however, anything but sincere.

By this time Luther had already developed his own doctrine of justification by faith alone, and he had certainly not failed to notice that in Erasmus's translation of the New Testament there was nothing which would support this singular view. Moreover, Luther had already complained to a friend some two years before that his respect for Erasmus was decreasing day by day, for he did not 'sufficiently reveal the grace of God', was 'much more ignorant than Lefèvre d'Étaples', and because 'human conditions prevail in him much more than divine'. For the time being, however, nothing was more vital to Luther than the support of Erasmus, the most celebrated and influential mind in Europe, even if only in the form of a secret alliance. As far as the prevalence of human conditions over the divine was concerned, this letter was not the first and far from the last example on Luther's part of just that.

Luther's letter to Erasmus was not immediately answered. Instead Erasmus wrote to Frederick the Wise, duke of Saxony, asking him (this was still before Luther's public debate with Eck at Leipzig) not to hand the reformer over to his blood thirsty enemies. Finally, at the end of May, he sent the reformer an amiable but restrained reply. Luther must have been displeased, however happy he was for the help Erasmus had been giving him behind the scenes.

Dearest Brother in Christ [wrote Erasmus], your letter, showing the keenness of your mind and breathing a Christian spirit, was most pleasing to me. I cannot tell you what a commotion your books are raising here.[4] These men cannot by any means disabuse themselves of the suspicion that your works are written with my help and that I am the standard-bearer, as they call it, of your party . . . I have testified to them that you are entirely unknown to me, that I have not read your books and neither approve nor disapprove anything . . . I try to stay neutral in order to help the revival of learning as best I can. And it seems to me that more is accomplished by a civil modesty than by impetuosity.

In the years that followed Erasmus did his best to protect Luther from persecution, maintaining that his voice was a new, courageous and valuable one which should be heard and not suppressed. Voicing his fears that 'Martin will perish for his uprightness', as Hus had, he tried to convince him to practise moderation. He gave the same advice to Luther's enemies as well. At the same time, however, each continued to voice doubts about his comrade-in-arms. Erasmus was aware that Luther would stir up German nationalism and might very well excite revolt and religious strife in which learning could only suffer, if not perish.

Thus quietly aiding Luther with the protective mantle of his influence, he carefully dissociated his name from that of the reformer. As a result Luther profited from Erasmus's help just as he had from his writings, from humanism itself and from the atmosphere which humanism engendered. But, unlike Melanchthon, his aide-de-camp, Luther was devoid of humanistic idealism. He never thanked Erasmus for his help, nor does he seem to have appreciated the nobility of Erasmus's attitude. Since it was not accompanied by submission to his doctrines it probably did not even occur to him to think of it as nobility.

In 1517, and for several years thereafter, Erasmus and Luther seemed to represent much the same spirit of reform. In Germany

---

[4] The phrase *tragoedias excitare* has the double meaning of *to raise a commotion* and *to wreak tragedy*. The *double entendre* is worthy of Erasmus, and we may assume that it was intentional. He was later to refer to the 'Lutheran tragedy', which enraged Luther, though Erasmus merely meant by it that he considered the schism of the Church a tragedy.

it was said that the renegade Augustinian canons were working together, the older and more famous of the two simply prompting the other. That this was not the case became obvious only when Erasmus, having unintentionally helped prepare the path for the Reformation, slowly turned from moderate support to equally moderate opposition. He did this not from any change in his own views, which remained as remarkably consistent as always, but because from his vantage point Luther appeared to have changed.

However radically stated, Luther had included some of the principles of Erasmus's more comprehensive programme in his theses; but as he went on to develop his theology he took a stand that was irreconcilable with Erasmianism. Erasmus, feeling himself to be something like the master of a hotheaded pupil, was cautious enough to support Luther longer than the latter had expected; for Luther had noticed their essential differences much earlier, of course. His political instincts were sharper than Erasmus's, and it must be admitted that his thinking was in many ways more realistic.

After a few years it became clear that their mutual suspicions were well-founded; that the questions on which they were agreed, e.g. 'the papacy, indulgences and similar trifles', as Luther said, were indeed just that. It became equally clear that in all other matters their point of departure was as different as their goal, that there was hardly any aspect of character in which they were not antithetical, and that they already embodied in themselves, as they were to symbolize after their deaths, the whole conflict between humanism and Reformation.

During their lifetimes it was said that if they were locked up together in a cell Luther would murder Erasmus or else Erasmus would commit suicide. Be that as it may, the French scholar Georges Duhamel was more to the point when he wrote in his book, *Erasme, ou le spectateur pur*, that one could live quite easily in a world inhabited by millions of Erasmuses (in spite of having to put up with so much lecturing), but to live in a world inhabited by millions of Luthers would drive anyone to suicide.

Erasmus the humanist and cosmopolitan had chosen the

middle way. Beside him Luther seemed still more radical, rustic, violent and intransigently German, even to the point of being, in Erasmus's words, 'the tree which bore the poisonous fruit of nationalism'. In religion Erasmus advocated above all the right kind of life; Luther, the right kind of faith. Erasmus's *philosophia Christi*, however critical of the Church, was no threat to Catholic orthodoxy, nor indeed to Christian unity. Erasmus wanted less theology; Luther, whatever he may have wanted, brought with him more theology than had appeared at any one time since the Council of Nicaea (325). Erasmus hoped for an end to religious discord and for the ultimate harmony which Pico had dreamed of; Luther brought in his wake more religious strife than anyone had imagined possible – although it must be added that Erasmus rightly blamed the Church for this as much as he did Luther or the other reformers.

Luther maintained that man is condemned to a state of wretchedness, and he considered Erasmus's ideas on free will and human dignity profanations of the glory of God. Though well read, he displayed little interest in the aims of humanism or in learning itself, with the exception of theology. The two men were agreed in their condemnation of scholastic theology, but Erasmus saw in Luther a man of the past, a man with the Roman mania for doctrines, a mystic who despised human reason but who nevertheless tried to use it to explain the unexplainable down to the last mystery. In short, he saw him as a new type of scholastic, 'a Goth'.

For Luther, on the other hand, Erasmus's reason was the abuse of reason, the 'haughty scepticism' of a man he called 'the incubus of the Devil'. Erasmus's world was the serene realm of the neo-Platonists, devoid of devils, witches or demons. Luther was convinced that he had met the devil in person, at Wartburg. He believed that every earthly matter is subjected incessantly to divine interference; and like St Augustine, with his credulity and his belief in predestination, he believed not only in Satan and his minions but in burning those whom they possessed.

Before the advent of Luther the *philosophia Christi* had seemed well on the way to enjoying ultimate victory over the worst legacies of medieval Church and society. It had arrived at a fortuitous moment. It was feasible, a characteristically Erasmian blend of natural evolution and moderate reform. The appearance of a new theology, however, forced the Church to strengthen its own already over-elaborate structure. In the swiftness of the opposition's victory, and in the Church's over-reaction to it, there was a revival of religious life on both sides, but not a revival which had any room for the *philosophia Christi*, let alone for humanism itself. In the ensuing battle of the faiths, the fears which Erasmus had voiced as early as 1518, that both Catholics and Protestants would turn against learning, proved justified.

To see this one need only remember the fates of Servetus, Campanella, Giordano Bruno and Galileo; to compare the first edition of Giorgio Vasari's *Lives of the Painters* with the second edition, published in 1568 during the Counter Reformation;[5] or to witness the state of the University of Heidelberg in the 1520s when, thanks to the effects of the Reformation, there were fewer students left than professors. In comparing the books published in France and Germany in 1510 with those published 25 and 50 years later, one finds that religious pamphlets of the most odious sort had almost entirely supplanted the classics and the works of serious contemporaries.

The tragedy of the *philosophia Christi*, Erasmus's personal tragedy, was that at the very moment it seemed assured of success it met with a stronger, more passionate, less rational and yet more realistic movement, and thus found itself in the impossible position of having to compete with two warring orthodoxies. Against such enemies the noble synthesis of a rationalized and demythicized Christianity seemed fragile, as did humanism and neo-Platonism themselves. Until the arrival of Luther Erasmus had been the uncontested prophet of the age, much as Voltaire was to be two and a half centuries later. But, like Voltaire, he was neither a leader of men nor a practical politician, and Luther was both. Voltaire was lucky enough not to have to face

[5] In the first edition of his work, for instance, published eighteen years earlier, Vasari stated in a sympathetic tone that Leonardo had been an atheist; in the second edition, after the re-establishment of the Roman Inquisition by Pope Paul IV (1555–59) he omitted all reference to this fact.

Robespierre or Bonaparte, for whom he helped prepare a path, and who, in a way, even continued his work. It was Erasmus's misfortune that he had to face Luther, Zwingli and Calvin as contemporaries; he helped prepare their paths, but the continuation of his work was the last thing any of them had in mind.

Erasmus has sometimes been accused of cowardice for not having sided with Luther; or, conversely, of heresy for not having sided wholeheartedly with Luther's opponents. If these charges were justified Erasmus would certainly have written a book against Luther, as he was urged to do, when the reformer was in greatest danger. But he refused. And had he in truth really sided with Luther in his heart there is no reason to doubt that he would have gone over to him, which, however convenient it might have been at first for Luther, would inevitably have been a source of great embarrassment to him later on.

The only criticism one can make of Erasmus in all this is that he remained rigidly uncompromising in the face of the inevitable, that he was unable to adapt himself to change even when it was upon him. But, whatever one's view of this, it must be allowed that his attitude itself was utterly new to history. Erasmus refused to choose between what he thought to be two evils, to acquiesce to the still flourishing medieval compulsion to choose between Thomas and Scotus, Ghibelline and Guelf, pope and emperor, Protestantism and Catholicism; and this at a time when social pressure still forced one and all to take up that violent partisanship which was considered a natural and unavoidable state of affairs. In the book entitled *The Letters of Obscure Men*, the anonymous author (probably Ulrich von Hutten) described how he had tried to ascertain which party Erasmus belonged to. At the end he concluded with awe, '*Erasmus est homo per se*', 'Erasmus is his own man'.

This attitude was to become the hallmark of humanism thereafter, and is especially in evidence in the modern world, in which it is at last being generally realized that neither of two opposing forces must necessarily be altogether in the right, and in politics seldom is. Erasmus, the first man to take the difficult stand of refusing to choose where there is in fact no choice, quickly found himself in an almost untenable position. As accusations flew at him from both sides he comforted himself with an ever-increasing amount of work, with attempts at mediation between the two camps, and with the continuation of his endless, but already hopeless fight for the spiritual unity of Europe.

The years at Louvain were probably the most trying of Erasmus's life. The local theologians relentlessly harassed him. Shortly after his arrival he attended a mass at which he heard himself attacked from the pulpit. The preacher, one Nicolaus Egmondanus, professor of theology, accused him of having falsified the text of the Gospels and of being deaf in his pride to the 'trumpets of truth'. This same White Friar, when lecturing at the university on St Paul, remarked that just as Saul of Tarsus had needed to be converted, so Drs Luther and Erasmus should also be converted immediately that they might become the servants of Christ rather than His persecutors. When Erasmus took the Carmelite to task in the rooms of a mutual acquaintance and demanded to know exactly which passages he thought he had falsified, he replied that he had never seen Erasmus's translation of the New Testament. This does not mean that Egmondanus put an end to his abuse. On the contrary, he was to continue slandering Erasmus for another ten years. Pushed beyond endurance by this inane vituperation, Erasmus was more than once to ask Popes Hadrian VI and Clement VII to 'gag the Carmelite's diarrhoeic mouth'.

Besides wasting a good deal of time fending off such attacks, Erasmus felt compelled to reply to the pamphlets of the critics of his *Novum instrumentum*, to refute refutations, as it were. Reading nowadays those unbound pamphlets, one feels pity for Erasmus, who felt he must answer such adversaries as these. It would be surprising that he bothered at all if it were not for the fact that the charges usually mentioned heresy; when this happened the violence of his rebuttal more than once surprised even Erasmus himself.

The worthiest of the critics was Lopez Zuñiga, professor of theology in the University of Alcalà de Henares and a member of the committee which had prepared the *Complutensian Polyglot Bible* (*Complutum* being the Latin name of Alcalà de Henares), an undertaking of which Erasmus had no knowledge. The work consisted of the Hebrew Old Testament, the Greek New Testament and the *Vulgate*. It was a scholarly effort, but one which, unlike Erasmus's, attempted no new translation. Its commentaries were few, moreover, and so devoid of original thought that they were of little use to anyone. In certain passages, where the *Vulgate* differed glaringly from the Greek text, the professors simply altered the Greek original to make it conform to the Latin. The committee had set out to produce a conservative and traditional text, one which would offend no one and would cause trouble neither for the Church nor for themselves, and that is what they did.

The trilingual work was printed in 1514, but the sheets were stored away, probably to await the final approbation of Rome. The Greek New Testament and the *Vulgate* were published together in 1522, each in 600 copies, but failed to attract much attention. Philologically speaking, the entire effort was masterly (forgeries included) but uninspired. From the historical point of view the results were by any standard negligible.

Zuñiga, who had seen Erasmus's New Testament in 1516, noted down a number of critical remarks. He showed these to Ximénes, who was well disposed towards Erasmus. The cardinal advised Zuñiga to send his objections to Erasmus himself, and forbade him to publish them unless the humanist failed to reply. Zuñiga did not send his criticisms to Erasmus, but published them after the cardinal's death in 1517. Some, but by no means all, were well-founded. However, the whole tone of the professor's attack was vulgar and offensive in the extreme. He condemned Erasmus for his classical culture, charged him with heresy and finished by asserting that Erasmus's manipulations of the New Testament were as unkempt as one might expect from a filthy Dutchman who stank of beer and rancid butter.

Erasmus replied with an apologia written in two days. In it

he admitted none of Zuñiga's corrections, yet in the next edition
of the *Novum instrumentum* he incorporated nearly forty of
them! With this he hoped the affair would end; but Zuñiga,
having in the meantime moved to Rome, soon published another pamphlet, *The Impieties and Blasphemies of Erasmus of
Rotterdam*, in which he called his adversary the standard-bearer
of Lutheranism. This was followed by another pamphlet in
which he charged him with heresy on 60,000 counts, all listed.
Zuñiga was unable to publish this until the death of Leo X
(1521), the latter having prohibited his printing anything at all
against Erasmus. When Leo's successor, Hadrian VI (1522–23),
upheld this ruling the Spanish professor had to restrain himself
until yet another vacancy should occur on the papal throne and
he could at last give the world the *Suspect and Scandalous
Assertions of Erasmus*.

When this appeared Erasmus again wrote an apologia. In the
meantime the new pope, Clement VII (1523–34), was following
the example of his predecessors, and threatened Zuñiga with
imprisonment if he dared to print anything against Erasmus.
Since the new pope was comparatively young and healthy and
Zuñiga was an old man by now, he decided to publish the
pamphlets anyway, but anonymously. He managed to complete
two more before he died, having spent the last fourteen years of
his life searching for error and heresy in the writings of Erasmus.
One might conclude that he had lived and died in unrelenting
hatred of the Dutchman, but this seems not to have been the
case. Shortly before his death Zuñiga ordered that all his manuscripts should be sent to Erasmus when the end came. He
expressed the hope that the Dutch humanist would remember
him with affection.

The details of Erasmus's protracted controversy with Edward
Lee, later archbishop of York, are too numerous for anything
but the briefest treatment here. Colet, Fisher, Pace, Lupset,
More and nearly all the English humanists tried to restrain Lee
and the same pressure was applied on Erasmus. Unfortunately
Lee was all too correct in some of his criticisms of the *Novum
instrumentum*; and Erasmus's vanity was piqued, not least because

his opponent was a much younger man. He went so far as to enlist the aid of his German friends in the quarrel. Thus, besides a series of pamphlets by Erasmus against Lee, a whole book, a veritable anthology of abuse, was turned out by various humanists and professors in 1520. It contained letters and poems against Lee and an epitaph in which the authors made clear their hope that Lee would hang himself after reading the book. Some of the contributors compared him with Caligula and Judas. Ulrich von Hutten raged, 'You filth, if you do not beg forgiveness of Erasmus I shall throw your name, like a piece of excrement, across the picket-fence of posterity that people may remember your stench forever!'

Erasmus spent the summer of 1518 in Basle working on the revised edition of the *Novum instrumentum* and a new edition of the *Enchiridion*. In the preface to the latter he defined his *philosophia Christi* more clearly than ever before. He reaffirmed that the theologians had hopelessly obscured the teachings of the Gospels. Since Christ had been dead for centuries, as far as the ignorant were concerned, a body of learned men should be commissioned to make a compendium of the faith:

> ... in which simplicity would not detract from erudition, nor brevity from precision; all that is of faith should be condensed into a very few articles, and the same should be done for all that concerns the Christian way of life. Those who receive such instruction would understand that the yoke of Christ is not heavy, but light, and ... that they have found fathers, not tyrants, and shepherds, not robbers; that they have been called unto salvation, not dragged into slavery.

In September he returned to Louvain, exhausted by his sojourn in Basle and much in need of the relaxing trip down the Rhine. In a letter to Beatus Rhenanus he described an incident on the journey:

> After we arrived at Boppard, someone recognized and betrayed me to the customs officer. His name is Christoforus Cinicampus, in common speech Christopher Eschenfelder, customs officer at

Boppard-am-Rhein. He fairly leapt for joy and dragged me into his house. The books of Erasmus were lying everywhere amidst customs agreements. He exclaimed at his good fortune and called in his wife, children and friends. Meanwhile he sent out two tankards of wine to the sailors who were calling for me, and yet another two when they began calling out again, promising them that when they returned he would remit the toll to the man who brought him a visitor such as myself.

Continuing his journey down the river, and then in an open coach, 'with strong and pestilential winds blowing from the South', and finally through a rain-storm, he reached Aachen after a few days. He was at the end of his strength after the exhausting last stages of the journey, but an insistent canon took him out of the hostel to stay in his own home, where he was served cold carp for supper. Erasmus had loathed fish all his life, as we have learned, especially after his days in the Collège de Montaigu. He had been known to feel nausea just passing a fishmarket. The first morning at the canon's he was served eel for breakfast, and after this he was definitely unwell. Discovering that mackerel was being served for lunch, he said a hasty farewell and continued his journey. Riding on horse-back now, he noticed that a boil-like swelling had appeared on his left hip, and another on his groin. He refused to summon a physician during the journey, although his servant and his secretary begged him to do so. He did not want to be blamed for having brought the black death with him; for he was certain that this was what he had.

He avoided his own house once they reached Louvain, fearing that his friends would visit him and contract the disease. Instead he accepted the invitation of the printer Dirck Maertensz, who displayed an admirable indifference to the danger. Erasmus applied rose oil to his abdomen to alleviate the pain when the biggest of the boils (by now there were three) began to suppurate. The first physician to arrive assured him that he had no reason to fear that it was plague; he promised to return at once with medicine. In the meantime a second physician was summoned, a Jew; he examined the patient's urine, and sighed 'If only I were as healthy as you!' Erasmus expressed doubts about this judgement, but the physician replied that if he really needed proof then he was willing to lie down beside him to show that there was no danger of contagion.

Erasmus was reassured by this, but when the first physician failed to return with the medicine he called in yet another one. Then he questioned his secretary and his servant, who hesitated but finally admitted that the first physician had said that Erasmus did in fact have the plague, 'the real, unadulterated and genuine German plague'. 'I didn't believe it', he wrote to Rhenanus. But when the third physician examined him from the distance of the doorway and then had medicine sent in with a servant, Erasmus writes that he commended himself 'to our Physician Jesus Christ'.

Three days later, however, his condition began to improve, and after two weeks of living on nothing but chicken and red wine he was well again. Those medical men of the present day who have given their attention to the matter are as much at a loss to diagnose Erasmus's illness as were his own physicians. Professor Wertheman, who supervised the examination of Erasmus's remains when they were exhumed at Basle in 1930, had two theories. One was that it may have been a mild case of bubonic plague after all; the other, which he considered more probable, was that the illness was a manifestation of a venereal disease which Erasmus had contracted but was not aware of as such. That he had in fact had syphilis was proved beyond doubt by the microscopic examination of his bones.

No one has ever attempted to set Erasmus up as some sort of plaster saint, and it is therefore simply as a matter of passing interest that we mention Professor Wertheman's view that the disease was acquired, not inherited. This supposition, however, was based on the opinion prevalent in the 1930s that syphilis had been introduced to Europe from the Americas, brought back by Columbus's crew in 1494. According to this theory, Erasmus could hardly have been born with hereditary syphilis in 1469. The American origin of the disease is widely doubted nowadays, however. In any case, Professor Wertheman's findings appear conclusive, so far as concerns Erasmus having had the disease, and it must be considered a matter of luck that he lived as long as he did in an age when it often killed in a few weeks or months.

In October 1519 Erasmus sent a letter to Albert of Mainz, in whose diocese Luther was living. Albert was the prelate whose shameless trafficking in indulgences finally provoked Luther to write his theses. Curiously enough, the bishop was not so inimical to the idea of reformation as one might expect. Later on, both Melanchthon and Luther attempted to win him over. In his letter to Albert, Erasmus explained first that he had nothing to do with either Luther or Reuchlin; yet, he insisted, when the former had spoken out, perhaps immoderately, against indulgences and the power of the pope his opponents had surpassed him in rashness. In fact, Erasmus continued, Luther was merely impulsive, not impious. He had little reverence for Aquinas and for the mendicant orders; he wanted to diminish the profits resulting from the sale of forgiveness and to place the Gospels above the writings of the scholastics. Intolerable heresy indeed!

The letter was entrusted to Ulrich von Hutten, a member of Albert's court, who first showed it to a highly pleased Luther. Then, before delivering the letter, Hutten published it. Erasmus was incensed at this unscrupulous provocation, believing that the public disclosure of his relations with Luther would endanger his position as a mediator. In his letters, however, he continued to defend Luther to such an extent that more than once Luther's friends succumbed to the temptation to repeat Hutten's indiscretion. When pressure was applied on Luther to recant, some months later, Erasmus produced still more new arguments in his defence, views on tolerance which he was to uphold and expound until his death: 'Force is not the anchor of salvation,' he wrote to the duke of Albertine Saxony. 'To exert pressure is the act of a tyrant, to yield to it is the act of an idiot.'

The theologians of Louvain did not leave him in peace for a single moment during all this. The 'champions of bad literature', as he called them, solemnly ratified the condemnation of Luther's books at a university ceremony in the presence of Jacob Hochstraten, Grand Inquisitor of Germany. Egmondanus, leader of the theologians, declared that as long as Erasmus refused to come out against Luther in his writings he too must be considered a heretic.

It was about this time that Erasmus learned that Colet, perhaps his best friend, and the one man who understood all the issues at stake, had died.

> The death of John Colet has been as bitter to me as the death of any man in the past thirty years [he wrote to Fisher]. I know that it is well with him that he is free of the calamities of this wicked world. . . . All that is left for me is to discharge the offices due to the beloved dead; if my writing has power I shall not suffer his memory to die to posterity.

During the same month he wrote to Lupset and to other friends, asking them for material, which he then used to write a moving account of Colet's life.

In June 1520 Pope Leo signed the bull *Exsurge Domine*, threatening Luther with excommunication if he failed to recant within sixty days. The bull had not been promulgated, but all knew of it. Erasmus resolved to do everything he could to prevent this extreme measure from being taken. During July Henry VIII came to Calais to negotiate with Francis I and Charles V. On this occasion More went to Bruges, where Erasmus saw him for the last time. Then Erasmus went to Calais and was granted an audience by King Henry. They discussed the matter of Luther. Unfortunately their conversation was not recorded, and Erasmus nowhere tells us what was said. We know only that he met with a cool reception, and that he soon wrote to a friend saying that he now feared the worst for the reformer.

Three weeks later the papal legate Hieronymo Aleandro arrived in the Low Countries. He published the papal bull in Antwerp and secured from Charles V a decree which ordered the burning of Lutherans in the country. After visiting Bruges and Antwerp Aleandro proceeded to Louvain, where he oversaw the burning of Luther's books (which, incidentally, he brought with him for that purpose, no copies being available in Louvain) and accompanied this with a diatribe against Erasmus. A pamphlet concerning all this appeared almost immediately; it was published anonymously, but Erasmus's style is easily discernible in it. It contains a devastating satire on Aleandro, and the reader is assured that the inquisitor might be able to burn Luther's books but he would never be able to refute a single page of any of them.

A few days after the book-burning Erasmus wrote to Pope Leo, politely expressing his disapproval of the bull and asking him not to move against Luther with undue haste. In November 1520 after attending the coronation of Charles V, he went to Cologne where the emperor was meeting with Duke Frederick, elector of Saxony, Luther's protector. Aleandro was also in the city. Frederick insisted to the emperor that he would permit none of his subjects to be outlawed without a hearing. He also told Aleandro that his conscience would not permit him to hand an innocent man over to anyone, 'not even to a papal legate'. The next day the elector sent for Erasmus. Their conversation was recorded almost word for word by Georg Spalatin, the duke's chaplain and an admirer and translator of Erasmus.

Standing before a large open fireplace, hands clasped behind his back, Erasmus was questioned by Frederick. Had Luther fallen into error, he asked, or had he not? Erasmus remained silent for some time as the benignant old man watched him. At last he declared: 'Luther has erred on two points: attacking the crown of the pope and the bellies of the monks.' It was one of the several occasions in Erasmus's life when a pronouncement of his immediately became a popular saying.

On this occasion the duke invited him to draw up the twenty-two propositions on how the Lutheran affair ought to be handled. Erasmus immediately complied with a manuscript entitled *Axiomata*, with the understanding that this was for the duke's private use. In this work Erasmus stated that the bull *Exsurge Domine* was unworthy of Christ's Vicar, its spirit of hatred being incompatible with the spirit of Christ. Good men, he wrote, were little offended by Luther, and the whole affair should be settled not by Luther's biased adversaries but, rather, by impartial judges, so that peace might be restored within the Church. In private he added that Luther had, however, been too hot-headed and violent; and Spalatin promised to remonstrate with the reformer. Having this text in his hands, Duke Frederick found himself in a position to rebuff Aleandro – which he did when the latter called upon him. Some weeks later, however, the *Axiomata* were published by the friends of Luther without Erasmus's consent or even his knowledge. His position as a neutral party, a mediator, was once again jeopardized.

Erasmus returned to Louvain after three weeks. He immediately wrote to Cardinal Campeggio in Rome, carefully explaining that he was not opposing the Church, but that he nevertheless could not condone the shameful manner in which Luther was being treated; nor did he think that religious affairs should be conducted in a spirit of anger. In a short period of time he wrote five letters to Luther, admonishing him to serve the cause of reform with less hatred, demagoguery and violence. Similar letters were sent to Luther's friends. In the meantime he wrote, in collaboration with the Dominican Johann Faber, a booklet entitled *Concilium* which was published under Faber's name and sent to the emperor and his advisers. The *Concilium*, like the *Axiomata*, proposed that a commission of humanists be appointed to settle the question of Luther in a peaceful manner.

Thus Erasmus spent the second half of 1520 wholly occupied with the business of mediation, rather than with his usual work. As he continued in these good offices he became more and more estranged from Luther and his cause. Still more harm was done by Ulrich von Hutten, who besieged him with hysterical letters. In one such letter he insisted that it was Erasmus's duty to die for liberty, and lectured him that 'we Germans' must stick together in the present danger. Erasmus did not reply, but he did write a letter to a friend, saying that if things continued to go on like this he would soon declare himself a Frenchman. In another letter, to Richard Pace, he confessed that he had no taste for martyrdom – and that even if he had, he certainly would not care to die for Martin Luther. Hutten, who failed to grasp why Erasmus had not replied, wrote again, calling his former friend a coward who extricated himself from the service of every good cause.

Luther's most recent writings dismayed Erasmus no less than the letters he was receiving. *Babylonian Captivity*, published in 1520, he found atrocious. It is not difficult to guess what he must have felt when reading another of Luther's tracts, published the same year, in which the reformer advised his followers to 'take up arms' and 'wash your hands in the blood of these cardinals, popes and all the offscourings of the Roman Sodom'. In Louvain one heard a variation on the same theme, for the theologians were demanding the destruction of 'the heretic Luther, that pestilential fart of Satan whose stench reaches to the high heavens'.

Having made enemies on both sides, threatened by the Catholics and continuously exploited by Luther's friends, Erasmus realized at long last that his policy of reconciliation was doomed to failure, that 'indivisible Christianity', which he was upholding and from which the contesting parties were excluding one another, was becoming more divided each day. Since the Church was showing no flexibility or moderation, Luther took up the same intransigent stand. By this time no committee of learned men, nor indeed any other humanistic remedy, could be of any help. Erasmus decided to withdraw from the battle.

The last scene of the first act of the Reformation was played at the Diet of Worms, to which Luther was summoned in April 1521. The overwhelming majority of those present were eager to condemn the reformer, who refused to retract anything, and whose only alternative indeed was the humiliation of recanting everything and placing himself at the mercy of pope and emperor. Erasmus was invited to the Diet, just as he had been invited to the coronation of Charles V and nearly every other important event in the empire. He declined, although it was widely expected that he would attend and speak. On occasion historians, perhaps over-dramatizing the situation, have criticized him for missing 'the greatest moment of his life' and being 'a timid scholar, afraid of public activity' and thus necessarily destined not to succeed in changing the course of history when he might otherwise have done so.

Unfortunately, neither the Catholics nor the Protestants asked Erasmus to mediate; and they knew, their stands being what they were, that there was no room for mediation. The majority of the estates arrived with instructions to vote against Luther. No argument, no eloquence, no amount of oratory could have changed this situation. Mercurio Gattinara, chancellor of the Empire, wrote in his letter of invitation to Erasmus that he could guarantee his safety, but not that of Luther. The Dominican Faber, who had written the *Concilium* with Erasmus, did attempt to mediate at the Diet, but he was voted down. Erasmus himself would probably have been silenced less rudely than Faber was, but no less decisively. Thus, in remaining at home in his library Erasmus was not, as is so often claimed, hiding from reality; he was very nearly the only man facing it.

After the Diet Luther was spirited off by the soldiers of Duke Frederick and brought to the safety of his castle at Wartburg. At first it was rumoured that he had been murdered by his enemies, and Albrecht Dürer, who was then in Antwerp, made a long entry in his diary lamenting the untimely death of the reformer. 'O Erasmus of Rotterdam,' he wrote, 'where wilt thou abide? O Knight of Christ, seize the martyr's crown!' Similar pious invitations were extended by other Lutherans to Erasmus. Happily, Dürer himself continued to follow the path of his art, leaving for others the martyr's crown he was so eager to see on Erasmus.

Because of the progress of the Reformation and the flood of polemic that accompanied it, Erasmus devoted less time than usual to literary work between 1519 and 1521. The *Colloquia*, published in 1519 and destined to become his most famous work after *The Praise of Folly*, was still in unsatisfactory shape. In 1520 the charming Platonistic dialogue *Antibarbari*, composed 30 years before, was printed for the first time. One imagines him, having nothing else at hand, searching his baggage for half-forgotten manuscripts. In 1521 the *Paraphrases of St Matthew* was published, a beautifully written exegesis of the first of the Gospels. Later he was to continue this by composing similar works on all the books of the New Testament except the Apocalypse, all written for the general reader. The series proved extremely popular and was translated into English in 1543. An order of Edward VI, upheld by Mary Tudor and Elizabeth I, stipulated that a copy of the *Paraphrases* must lie open in every English church.

In 1521 war broke out between France and the Empire. This was a heavy blow for Erasmus, who, having written *The Complaint of Peace*, now declared that he must write its epitaph. He had seriously hoped that his pacifistic booklets, sold in tens of thousands of copies all over Europe and read and praised by its rulers, might have had some effect. Now he was forced to realize that, just as religious conflicts could not be resolved by committees of learned men, neither were books likely to have much effect on princes, not even when, as in the case of Charles V, they had been reared on them.

A few years earlier he had still dreamed of a golden age of mankind lying not far in the future. Now he wrote that he had suddenly awakened from the dream. He felt old, not so much from the strain of his work as because of the hateful quarrels and controversies. The whole age suddenly seemed black and wicked. Seeing the inevitable destruction of humanism by Lutheran and Catholic reaction, he pleaded: 'Let us resist not by taunts and threats, not by force of arms and injustice, but . . . by gentleness and tolerance.'

On the very day he wrote these lines Aleandro arrived for the second time in the Low Countries to carry out the task of ridding the area of heresy. He was filled now with hatred for Erasmus. A year before, in Cologne, he had invited his former friend to dinner, but Erasmus sent word that he would gladly come if he were not afraid of being poisoned. This brief exchange was well known throughout Germany, as was Aleandro's humiliation at the hands of Frederick the Wise, which he rightly attri-

buted to 'the intriguing of Erasmus'. A few months after this
Aleandro had sent a secret report to Rome about Erasmus's
having 'brought forth opinions on confession, indulgences,
excommunication, divorce, the power of the pope and many
other matters, which Luther has merely had to adopt – save that
Erasmus's poison is much more dangerous'.

Aleandro first went to Brussels, where he attended to the
burning of two Lutherans and heard the recantation of two
others. From the latter pair false testimony was extracted in
which they maintained that they had had contact with Erasmus,
who was called 'a secret Lutheran'. Under torture they also said
that Erasmus had encouraged booksellers to stock Luther's
pamphlets. Aleandro saw to it that this testimony was advertised
far and wide in order to frighten Erasmus.

He may have succeeded up to a point, for Erasmus decided to
move again. Wavering for a time between returning to England
and going back to Rome, he finally rejected both ideas and went
instead to Basle. He still had many friends in that city, including
his printer, Froben. The city was not threatened by war, and,
he thought, religious strife was unlikely there. In October 1521
as he was preparing to leave, having already packed all his
books, Aleandro suddenly appeared in Louvain and asked
Erasmus to meet him.

Erasmus knew the owner of Aleandro's hostel, the Inn of the
Wild Man, and so was not afraid of being poisoned there. He
and Aleandro spent several evenings together, and we possess
plentiful, if contradictory, information concerning their conversations. All things considered, Erasmus was in an advantageous position; Aleandro did not know that he was prepared
to leave Louvain, that he was in fact only waiting for the end of
their talks to do so. Neither could the inquisitor have known
that Franz von Sickingen, general of the army of the Meuse and
a great admirer of Erasmus, had taken upon himself the responsibility of guaranteeing the humanist's safety during his trip to
Basle. This was no idle gesture, for the general had some 20,000
troops under his command. Erasmus thus had the pleasure of
being as insolent as he pleased to Aleandro, who was further

handicapped by the secret instructions of Giulio Cardinal de' Medici to treat Erasmus with the utmost consideration and tact.

Their conversations ranged from polite chit-chat to outright invective, from outbursts of mortal hatred to reminiscences of their pleasant days together in Venice. Aleandro wept, complaining that he had not forgotten his old love for his friend – even though the friend had treated him badly, especially in the matter of defamatory and anonymously-written pamphlets. Yet, he continued, he forgave him everything and asked nothing more than that he write against Luther, if only one page. For this he promised him a fat bishopric, or, according to other sources, a somewhat leaner cardinalate.

Erasmus refused each offer and aroused Aleandro to fury by praising Luther, quite against his own convictions, in glowing terms. Aleandro replied with more threats, saying that the pope could easily destroy a 'lousy man of letters' just as he destroyed princes and kings. At the end of their conversations they drank together and exchanged memories of the past, which cheered Aleandro as much as it bored Erasmus. After their last evening at the inn Erasmus must have smiled with relief when he arrived home and saw his books packed and ready for his departure. On the following day, his fifty-second birthday, he left the town which had become 'too Catholic' for him. A few days later he arrived with his secretary and servant in Basle, where he would reside for the next eight years until it in turn became 'too Protestant'.

VI

'I Concede to None'

Erasmus moved into a comfortable house which is still shown to visitors in Basle. From the very first he liked the free and amiable atmosphere of the city. Good French wines were available, if at outrageous prices, and meat was sold even on fasting days. In Louvain, as everywhere else in the empire, the selling or eating of meat on Fridays or during Lent was punishable under the law – 'unlike exploitation and war-mongering', as Erasmus added. When the papal legate Campeggio, travelling through Basle, delivered a reprimand to Erasmus on behalf of Pope Clement VII for his unorthodox views on fasting, his reply was, 'My heart is Catholic but my stomach is Protestant'.

He chose Basle as a refuge from 'turbulence and disorder', but there is nothing to indicate that this change of locale robbed him of inspiration or lessened his activities in any way, as has sometimes been asserted. 'I cannot be other than that which I am,' he wrote to a friend shortly after his arrival, indicating that he would continue his fight under the increasingly difficult conditions of the religious struggle and, indeed, in the teeth of the cataclysm which now loomed on the horizon, threatening humanism with destruction.

The Reformation and the regression which accompanied it convinced him that he had to redouble his activities, especially in pedagogy and the propagation of simple Christianity, meekness, mutual understanding and moderation. Aside from a dozen

or so political and moral treatises, he now wrote hundreds of
letters to the princes and leading civil servants of Europe, and
to the pope. In spite of the unpleasantly obsequious tone and
naïve flattery of some of these letters, it is clear that Erasmus
was not seeking anything for himself; what he asked of the lords
of Europe was a conciliatory and humanistic attitude towards
the religious conflict, and an end to hostilities.

There was a change in his attitude about this time, although it
is not certain if he himself was aware of it for the time being.
In his earlier years he, like the Italian humanists, had seen the
Renaissance as an all-conquering entity which included the
rebirth of religion, learning and literature, a renewal of man's
entire spiritual, intellectual and social life. Shortly before or
after his move to Basle Erasmus began to distinguish between
these aims. This is not to imply that his faith as a Christian
underwent any change. On the contrary, it quite obviously
remained as strong and as uncomplicated as ever, and just as
averse to theological speculation. It remained now, as always,
a sort of spiritual armour in every conflict. During the last
fifteen years of his life he composed many religious treatises
and edited nearly the whole of patristic literature, an almost
superhuman accomplishment. Yet in many of his letters from
this time onwards he clearly separated Luther, his Catholic
adversaries, the whole religious conflict and even religion itself
from that humanism which he represented: 'They are not one
thing, but two different things.' And from then on he took care
to keep them separated.

This refusal to mix humanism with the warring of the
Churches or with religion itself was, in its final form, one of
Erasmus's most important legacies. Many years after his death
the movement, in various guises, made the separation complete.
It seems probable that he did not fully realize what he was
starting with this; but one cannot imagine that knowledge of
the ultimate results would have restrained him in any way.

Although he was depressed by events, his perseverance was
strengthened, if anything. According to his friend and biographer Beatus Rhenanus, his writing now progressed 'as a

fountain flows'. Of the most important 65 original works and translations which he wrote in his life, 35 were undertaken during these last 15 years in Basle and Freiburg. His best book after *The Praise of Folly*, the *Colloquia* – and some even prefer it to the *Folly* – was also written in Basle. During the last seven years of his life alone he was still to publish more than 20 works; and though by then he was so lame that he could scarcely walk, he still worked standing at his lectern, writing up to 16 hours a day. It was only during his last months that he dictated original work to his secretary.

He had many faithful followers by the time he arrived in Basle, and such friends or admirers as Thomas More, John III of Portugal, Louis II of Hungary, Chancellor Szydlowieczki of Poland, Cardinal-Archbishop Campeggio of Palermo and a host of others. But his enemies were also numerous, and attacks arrived from all sides. The most painful were probably those in which he was ridiculed as 'a lame old ass', 'a grumbling scholar with one foot in the grave', or which charged him with not being able to understand the spirit of the times or 'the noble fight for Christendom against Lutheran heresy'. One wonders what Erasmus thought when, at the same time these slanders were being hurled against him, the Turks were at the gates of Vienna, Rome was sacked and burned and, in neighbouring Southern Germany, peasant rebels were massacred by the thousand. One wonders if he still had any hope that the words he continued to put down in his elegant script would be read by posterity. Certainly he could never have dreamed that they would resound, stronger than ever, a hundred and fifty years later, and thereafter become an integral part of the conscience of western man.

The town council of Basle was delighted to find Erasmus in their midst, and promptly offered him citizenship. He declined, however, with the now-famous reply: 'I am a citizen of the world, known to all and to all a stranger.' Visitors arrived in a steady stream, and his house was always open to them; although it was not in keeping with local custom, he never permitted the gates to be closed. Many of the guests introduced themselves as Erasmians, but their host, though undoubtedly pleased, objected to the term: 'I find nothing in myself which should cause anyone to wish to be an *Erasmicus*, and in any case I dislike such partisan names.'

He devoted half of every day to writing or to keeping up with his correspondence, and the other half was wasted, as he somewhat unreasonably complained, with visitors. Interest in him was enormous, and so was the amount of gossip about him. He once complained that even the things he told his confessor were being published and spread abroad.

Besides his work his greatest pleasure was conversation with his friends. Beatus Rhenanus was living in Basle at this time, and the humanists of nearby Strasbourg often journeyed down to visit him. The famous jurist Zasius, professor in the University of Freiburg, was also living not far away, as was the humanist Botzheim, a canon in Constance. In 1522 Œcolampadius, the cleric who had helped Erasmus prepare the *Novum instrumentum*, arrived back in Basle where he was to teach theology in the university, having in the meantime run away from his monastery. Œcolampadius still adored Erasmus in spite of his conviction that 'everything Martin Luther says is as true as if an angel had announced it'. Hearing this, Erasmus not unnaturally concluded, 'Thus you intend to teach Lutheran rather than Catholic theology in the university.' 'By no means,' replied Œcolampadius, 'we want neither the Catholic nor the Lutheran Church. We want a third one.' It was a portentous remark.

The year 1523 brought with it both the Peasants' Revolt and the accession of Hadrian of Utrecht to the papal throne. As Pope Hadrian VI he attempted some measure of reform, but too little and far too late. He sent Erasmus two letters asking him to move to Rome and to write against Luther there. Then he dispatched a nuncio, who asked Erasmus to draw up a memorandum listing possible methods of extirpating the new Lutheran sect. Erasmus worked out an elaborate excuse for not complying. His private opinion, as he wrote to the humanist Spalatin, was that 'should Luther be vanquished neither God nor man would any longer be able to endure the monks'.

During the preceding two years there had been a certain truce in effect between Erasmus and the reformer. Luther and his friends agreed not to mention Erasmus and not to cause him trouble; and Erasmus did not mention Luther's name in his own writings. But he was more than ever displeased with Luther's antinomian views. Because of them he wrote to Zwingli in 1523 to say that he was stupefied by the reformer's 'absurd enigmas'. Zwingli, at the time an admirer of both Erasmus and Luther, may well have passed this information on to Luther in Wittenberg. At the same time, Œcolampadius, who was now lecturing in the University of Basle, received a letter from Luther in which the reformer said that God might help him in his lectures after all, for Erasmus disliked his teachings.[1] The letter continued to the effect that Œcolampadius should not be afraid of Erasmus, who had introduced the study of languages, but nothing more. The higher study of divinity, according to Luther, was not his field. When shown the letter Erasmus could only conclude that it was the prelude to war between them.

The open rift between the humanist and the reformer was caused by more than gossip, however. Their attitudes towards the Peasants' Revolt in Germany, for example, were as revealing as they were irreconcilable. The revolt of 1523–24, the result of the appalling misery of the peasants of southern Germany, was sparked by a misunderstanding of Luther's doctrine of 'Christian liberty'. The rebels fought cruelly and were opposed with still greater cruelty. Some 100,000 of them were put to the sword, hanged or impaled, including many who had nothing at all to do with the revolt. Erasmus maintained that 'against this revolt of misery and despair the princes know no remedy but cruelty, which does not cure the evil'. He repeated that violence begets violence, and that the abolition of feudal taxation, which he had proposed long before, could have prevented it. In another

---

[1] Which was untrue: Erasmus attended the lectures of Œcolampadius and praised them in several letters.

treatise he declared that there is nothing in the Gospels that grants any man feudal rights over another, but much that denies such things.

Luther's position was more difficult, dependent as he was upon the favour of the German princes and magistrates. Being at once a mystic and a realist, he had as the former no interest in such things as feudal taxation and as the latter no mercy to waste on the German peasantry. 'A Christian serf enjoys Christian liberty,' he wrote. 'Rather the death of the peasants than that of the princes and magistrates . . . O Lord God, if such a spirit also dwells in the peasants, it is high time that they were slaughtered like mad dogs.' In the time of final revenge he advised the princes: 'In the matter of dealing mercifully with the peasants: if there are innocent men among them God will know how to protect them, as he saved Lot and Jeremiah. If he does not save them it will be because they are not innocent...'

Erasmus had watched the Peasants' Revolt from the beginning with mounting horror and despair. He was scarcely prepared for those aspects of Luther which it revealed, and, as these became clear, the profound revulsion of a humane man was added to all his other objections.

It was at this time – the worst possible moment, as it happened – that Ulrich von Hutten arrived in Zürich. Ever the knight-errant, Hutten had embraced Luther's cause with ardour, and had published Erasmus's correspondence with him without permission and then called him a coward. A year before, Hutten had worked with Sickingen to start a holy war against the priesthood in Germany. They attacked Trier and were defeated, and Sickingen mortally wounded. Hutten wandered with his friend Busch to Basle, making up for his lack of money by occasional robberies along the high road. Erasmus refused to receive the two men on the pretext that Hutten's health did not permit him to go anywhere without a stove, while his own maladies would not permit him to enter a heated room. To take revenge Hutten wrote a pamphlet against him. Before publishing it, however, he tried to blackmail him into buying the manuscript. Erasmus refused and protested to the town council of Basle. Hutten was expelled and forced to seek asylum in Zwingli's house in Zürich.

In his *Expostulation* Hutten reviled Erasmus for duplicity and cowardice for not having joined the Reformation. Erasmus's reply was a work entitled *A Sponge to Wipe Off Hutten's Aspersions*; it was dedicated to Zwingli, because 'the antidote should go to the same quarter in which the poison was brewed'. Erasmus reiterated in the pamphlet that he had never been a partisan of Luther, that he had failed to join him not out of cowardice, as Hutten maintained, but because he never took sides 'in scholastic quarrels'. 'I am a lover of liberty,' he concluded. 'I cannot and will not serve parties.' He was of course right, but the general tone of the pamphlet was unworthy of him.

By the time the work came off Froben's press Hutten was already a broken man, crushed by poverty, illness and disappointment. He repented of having written the *Expostulation*, but he was turned out of Switzerland and died a few weeks later on the island of Ufenau in the Lake of Zürich. Now Erasmus found himself in the painful situation of one who has kicked a dying man. He regretted having written the *Sponge*, and let it be known that he was praying for Hutten's soul. Then he wrote an apology in which he explained that he had never reproached his adversary for his military life ('not to use a worse term for it') nor for his vices ('which not even his shameful disease could make him cease'). One would think that this apology itself required an apology. Erasmus's unwonted vindictiveness was amply repaid, however, when one of Hutten's friends, Otto Brunsfels, arose to heap fresh slander on him.

In the meantime Pope Hadrian VI had died, having accomplished nothing towards ending the religious controversy. He had aroused such resentment in Rome with his parsimony that on the night after his death a triumphal arch of olive branches and flowers was erected before the house of the papal physician. It bore the inscription, *To the liberator of our town, from the senate and people of Rome*. After the death of Hadrian, the last of the non-Italian popes, Giulio Cardinal de' Medici, a patron of the arts and a friend of Erasmus, was elected and took the title

Clement VII. He immediately sent a gift of 200 florins to Basle for the dedication, which Erasmus had just given, of the *Paraphrase on the Acts of the Apostles*. Unlike his predecessor, Clement VII did not try to force Erasmus to write against Luther. Almost as if in reward for this kindness, he soon received a manuscript from Basle, the *Discussion of the Free Will*, Erasmus's first attack on Luther.

It had been obvious from the beginning that the break had to come sooner or later. Luther's theological views represented, as far as Erasmus was concerned, the same armoury of scholastic doctrine he had hoped to see thrown out of the Church, except that the rusty syllogisms of the Middle Ages had been 'sharpened at the other end' by Luther, and had thus become more dangerous. Since Luther was by now anything but a persecuted man, having much of Germany solidly on his side, Erasmus no longer felt the same reluctance to attack him. That he did restrain himself to a great degree, even now, owed primarily to the fact that he was by no means eager to champion Roman orthodoxy or to provoke an unnecessary quarrel.

The first provocation had come from Germany in the form of a tract published in April 1524. It was a dialogue, anonymously written by someone in Luther's inner circle, for it was crammed with his views and favourite expressions. In it the devil was rejoicing that he had seduced the master of such beautiful Latin. Erasmus was represented as a coward who had, for hard cash, become a merciless persecutor of the evangelical cause. He was said to lick Aleandro's boots and 'to kiss the rump of the pope'. Johann Faber, co-author of the *Concilium* and the man who had tried to help Luther at Worms, was given similar treatment.

Luther's second assault was launched in the form of an insulting letter in which new allegations were added to the old ones of Hutten:

> Since we see that the Lord has not given you courage and sense to assail those monsters [meaning the papacy] openly and confidently with us, we are not such men as would extract what is beyond your

power and measure. . . . We only fear that you may be induced by our enemies to fall upon our doctrines with some publication, in which case we should be obliged to resist you to your face. . . . Heretofore I have controlled my pen . . . for although you will not side with us, and although you injure and make sceptical many pious men by your impiety and hypocrisy, still I cannot and do not accuse you of wilful obstinacy. . . . We have fought long enough; we must take care not to eat each other up. This would be a terrible catastrophe, as neither of us wishes to harm religion, and without judging each other both may do good.

It is impossible to know precisely what Luther intended by this letter, beginning as it does with slander and ending with an unwonted plea for peace. Having judged Erasmus by his own standards, Luther proceeds to plead that they should not judge one another. Erasmus was as well at a loss to decipher these sentences, conceived with so much passion and so little sense. In May 1524 he replied to Luther in a polite letter, assuring the reformer that he was not the only person zealous in the cause of religion, and assuring him that he had not yet lifted his pen against him.

But not for long. It was on this same day that he went to his lectern and began work on the *Discussion of the Free Will*, completing it in less than five days. Of the many hundreds of books written on metaphysics during the past millennium this remains one of the few which are still readable. This is owing partly to its wit, moderation, brevity and elegance, and partly to the fact that in it Erasmus came as close as anyone ever had to cracking the kernel of the problem of free will. Ignoring the general confusion which surrounded the question, he succinctly outlined the two antithetical theories, and in so doing separated once and for all the underlying principle of humanism from that of its adversaries.

Free will, that which enables men to concern themselves with matters of salvation, among other things, or to disregard them, was, along with the determinist denial of it, one of the most widely discussed issues within the Church. From the age of the Fathers down to the Reformation and beyond it was expounded and debated but never satisfactorily defined. St Jerome, St Thomas and nearly all the scholastics upheld the concept, which became a fundamental doctrine. The determinists put up varying degrees of opposition. One of Luther's theologians, Carlstadt, maintained for example that the will is free only to sin. This was moderate compared with the opinion of Wycliffe, or Luther himself, who denied the existence of free will altogether. Luther saw man as 'a saddle horse mounted by God, or by the devil', incapable in his weakness of throwing off either rider and thus proceeding inevitably to a predetermined fate, heaven or hell as the case might be. 'God's eternal hatred of man is not only hatred of the shortcomings of the free will, but a hatred which existed even before the creation of the world', wrote Luther in his answer to Erasmus's book.

Luther's negative and Erasmus's positive stand on free will represented not only two conflicting theological positions, but two ways of life. For humanists since the time of Petrarch faith in the liberty of the will had had little to do with their loyalty to the Church, but everything to do with their stand as Catholic thinkers. In *De libero arbitrio* Valla spoke of free will as the means of breaking through the barriers which scholastic theology had erected between God and man so that man might lay himself open to the divine and find again the 'original nature of innocence', i.e. God Himself. To St Bernardino of Siena free will was 'the king of the human mind and the emperor of the universe'. To Pico it was 'the pledge of human dignity' and 'the boundary between man's soul and the Infinite'. Humanism meant the exaltation of man, a belief in human perfectibility, in freedom, individuality, the efficacy of learning and human values. No one believed and upheld this more passionately or consistently than Erasmus. Thus for him Luther's vision of a race of men hopelessly wretched and unable to contribute to their own salvation meant a retreat to the Middle Ages, and not only in a theological sense.

The problem was to be discussed for centuries to come, and it has only recently been dismissed as a question falsely formulated in the first place, and one that is consequently irrelevant.

However correct this may be from the point of view of logic, one has yet to admit that there are men who think and act in terms of free will and men who do in fact have a deterministic point of view, and that the results are easily seen in their thinking and in their lives.

The *Discussion of the Free Will* begins with an essay on the principles to be followed in considering theological problems. Taking the Bible as his sole authority, Erasmus shows the manner in which many scriptural passages are difficult or even impossible to understand, especially those which seem to touch upon this issue. How much, for example, does salvation depend on grace, and how much grace can we obtain by our own deeds? The theologians, Erasmus says, are inclined to read their own interpretations into Holy Writ. Some appeal to 'solid reason' and others to their own infallible inspiration. The solution of these enigmas, he concludes, will evidently have to await the Last Judgement.

Elsewhere in the book he explains that even if there were no such thing as free will, and salvation did depend solely upon grace obtained through faith alone, it would still be foolhardy to proclaim such a doctrine. For why is obedience praised if in the working of good and evil we are tools in the hands of God in exactly the same way as the adze is in the hands of the carpenter? Morality depends, above all else, upon a consciousness of freedom. Then he skilfully turns the tables and enumerates those things, taken from the writings of Lutheran theology, upon which salvation does *not* depend.

Examining Luther's stand he admits that it does not deserve to be called heresy, as so many of the reformer's adversaries had already pronounced it. He states frankly that there are ample Bible texts to support Luther's views, and not a few to contradict them. However, he continues, there are still weighty arguments against his whole case. Thus, for instance, the Catholic believes in a God desirous of man's salvation, not his damnation; if we deny free will then damnation becomes entirely the responsibility of God. Yet Christ has shown us a God to love, not the wrathful Jehovah of the Old Testament with Whom Luther was so obsessed. Finally, without good works on the part of man the grace of God loses much of its meaning, in that it is no longer divine justice but rather divine capriciousness. There must, then, be some interconnection between grace and free will. By way of compromise Erasmus advises the acceptance of the doctrine 'of attributing salvation to grace first of all and to good works secondly'. In a letter he referred to More's opinion, 'so dear to me', which was similar. From Luther's point of view, however, the compromise would have been a pact with the devil.

The *Discussion of the Free Will* was printed in September 1524 and received with relief and joy by the humanists of England, Germany and Italy. Even Melanchthon applauded it and sided on this point with Erasmus against Luther. Everyone expected the reformer to make a quick reply, but Luther was occupied now with a controversy with one of his followers, Carlstadt, about the sacraments, and, even more, with providing the princes of Germany with advice and justifications for the massacres of the Peasants' Revolt.

Luther had married in the meantime, and Erasmus expressed the hope that this might take the edge off his temper. Not at all mellowed, Luther proceeded to write *The Bondage of the Will*, an angry polemic against Erasmus. In this he was encouraged, perhaps even prompted, by his new wife. The book was later to become a chief source of Calvin's doctrine of predestination. Erasmus's moderation, which Luther attributed to scepticism, fanned rather than cooled his anger, and the allegation that there are contradictory texts in the Bible roused him to fury.

He began *The Bondage of the Will* with a lengthy introduction in which he expounded his arguments for determinism. These were based on his idea of the sufficiency of God's grace and of man's inability to choose the good. 'God . . . foresees, preordains and accomplishes all things by an unchanging, eternal and efficacious will. By this thunderbolt free will sinks shattered in the dust.' He sent the treatise to Erasmus with a letter in which he expressed unshakable conviction in these views, and went on to call his adversary an atheist, an Epicurean and a sceptic.

Erasmus replied, complaining bitterly about the savagery with which Luther had attacked his book 'in spite of its courtesy'. He went on to ask:

How do your scurrilous charges that I am an atheist, an Epicurean and a sceptic help your argument? . . . It pains me terribly, as it must all good men, that your arrogant, insolent and rebellious nature has put the world in arms. . . . You treat the Evangelical cause so as to confuse all things sacred and profane, as if it were your chief aim to prevent the tempest from ever becoming calm . . . I would wish you a better disposition were you not so marvellously satisfied with the one you have. Wish me any course you will, except that of your temper, unless the Lord change it for you.

Erasmus's next book was the long *Hyperaspistes*, the first part of which was published in 1526 and the rest in 1527. When reading this book, one cannot avoid the impression that Erasmus's views had progressed far during the two years since he wrote the *Discussion of the Free Will*. He realized by now that the fight concerned an issue which could never be resolved, and he knew as well that his enemy would never grasp this fact. 'In sacred literature,' he stated without even bothering to argue the point, 'there are certain sanctuaries into which God wills that we shall not penetrate further.'

In the first part of *Hyperaspistes* Erasmus explained that the importance of the question of free will is overshadowed by the importance of the Reformation itself, the beneficial aspects of which were being crushed by Luther's extremism. He attacked the German for the rank nationalism on which he had launched his career, for the uncompromising and dogmatic pride which caused him to destroy friend and foe alike and for the brutish cruelty of his attitude towards those peasants on whom he had ridden to power. As in his earlier controversies with the scholastics, he made it plain here that the issue between them was not one of faith against faith, let alone of scepticism against faith, as Luther maintained, but simply a matter of humanity against inhumanity.

In the second half of the book he carefully refuted the reformer's arguments against free will, pitting against them his own views, which by now were clearly anticipating the 'natural religion' of the eighteenth century, much more a foretaste of Rousseau than of any subsequent Protestantism or Catholicism. In what was to become the most famous passage of the book, he dissociated himself from both extremes but admitted that he would remain within the Catholic Church in so far as he had to remain officially within anything:

> I have never been an apostate from the Catholic Church. I know that in this Church, which you call the Papist Church, there are many who displease me; but such I see also in your Church. One bears more easily the evils to which one is accustomed; therefore I shall bear with this Church until I find a better one . . . and he does not sail badly who steers a middle course between two evils.

The three books against Luther enjoyed great success, as did Luther's one against Erasmus. After a general choosing of sides in Germany some of the humanists severed their ties with Erasmus, and thereafter remained deaf to his arguments. At the same time, however, the more conservative Catholics could not bring themselves to forgive the services he had inadvertently rendered the reformer.

But there were also those who rejoiced. Among these were Thomas More and Lord Mountjoy, who had long appealed to Erasmus to stand up for Roman orthodoxy; the Spanish humanists Juan Luis Vives and Alonso de Fonseca; the German Willibald Pirckheimer, who had just returned to the Roman fold; and Georgius Wicelius, who had just left it but was nevertheless to preach Erasmian tolerance to Catholics, Zwinglians, Lutherans and Calvinists alike for nearly 40 years after Erasmus's death. Others who were elated at his stand were the Italian humanists Bembo, Sadoleto, Calcagnini; Gattinara, chancellor of the Empire; and an as yet unknown French physician, François Rabelais.

Luther no longer replied to Erasmus now, but his letters and recorded conversations are filled with invective against him. 'The author of *Hyperaspistes*,' he wrote, 'will fall between two stools and will be damned together with Lucian and Epicurus.' He called Erasmus 'a snake', 'a piece of filth' and 'an insane destroyer of the Church who inflames the baser passions of young boys and who regards Christ as I regard Klaus Narr'.

While Erasmus missed no opportunity to bring Catholics and Protestants together, if not to establish a common doctrine, then at least to search for a *modus vivendi*, Luther's vilification of him rose to an ever higher pitch. In a pamphlet he called Erasmus a Pelagian heretic for refusing to accept the doctrine of salvation by faith alone, and an Arian heretic for his satire on Pope Julius II. He ordered all Erasmus's books out of the Lutheran schools, and maintained that Erasmus had compared Christ with Priapus, and that he, Martin Luther, had seen the humanist walking arm in arm with the devil in Rome. After all this and much more Luther wrote to Erasmus to offer him his friendship. (Not the least curious aspect of Luther's nature was his habit of always forgiving those he had slandered.) Needless to say, Erasmus rejected the offer.

Of the books that Erasmus wrote at Basle the most important and enduring was the *Colloquia*. During his first sojourn in Paris, around 1498, he had written a textbook called *Outlines of Friendly Conversation* which was intended as a guide to Latin usage, a list of phrases for all occasions. Twenty years later the manuscript, which he had left with Caminade, fell into the hands of Beatus Rhenanus, who had it published. At first Erasmus was angry that what was, after all, a rough draft had been printed without his permission. When his annoyance abated, however, he revised the text and a second edition appeared in 1519, this time with several real dialogues added. In the next five years the book ran through 25 editions and was constantly enlarged and improved, most notably in the editions of 1522 and 1524.

In the *Colloquia* Erasmus borrowed slightly from Lucian and Poggio and, somewhat more extensively, from the Neapolitan humanist Giovanni Pontano. But on the whole the book was original, much more so in fact than the *Folly* had been. It reveals sides to Erasmus which had remained long hidden or were hitherto unknown: the scholar of strict realism, insatiable in his hunger for the visible world; the aristocrat who had never severed his ties with the popular vein; and the moralist devoid of pomposity who smiled with a quiet irony.

It was something of a surprise, as it had been with the *Folly*, to see the near-recluse emerge from behind his lectern and show himself still on familiar terms with such types as artisans, sailors, soldiers, prostitutes, beggars, alchemists, nuns, housewives and a host of others, and as capable as ever of bringing them to life on paper. Fifteen years earlier, after writing the *Folly*, he had remarked to a friend that he had intended to reiterate the ideas contained in the *Enchiridion*, only in more lively fashion. It seems safe to assume that he had much the same intention in mind with the *Colloquia*: to restate his religious, moral and political views in a more engaging and immediately accessible manner; to delight those who had already understood them and to reveal them to those who had not.

Like the *Folly*, the *Colloquia* shows unmistakable signs of having been written with pleasure and ease. It affords more insights into Eramus than any of his other works, perhaps, and is the only one which reminds us in any way of his origins. Many of the colloquies are almost of the Dutch *genre*; some few of them, for instance the one describing a group of drunkards on Palm Sunday, conjure up a vision of Brueghel's world. The variety of themes in the 63 dialogues is amazing. One depicts an alchemist wheedling money out of a hapless victim, and manages to be excellent satire both on pseudo-science and on human gullibility. Another depicts the hazards of soldiering and war; a third proposes that people with venereal disease should not be allowed to marry. Others ridicule the foibles of grammarians, and the hypocrisy of mendicant friars who become wealthy while preaching poverty. There are dialogues which attack the adoration of saints (as opposed to their veneration), and the making of pilgrimages as an excuse to go whoring. Still others deal with the cloister, false nobility, knights-errant, the inconveniences of marriage, spiritism and even feminism (in this case the fifteenth-century Florentine custom of educating girls in the same manner as boys).

The dialogue entitled 'Echo', between Echo and a young man, is a *tour de force* in a *genre* very popular during the Renaissance: Echo repeats the last two syllables of the young man's sentences, twisting their meaning or saying something entirely different each time. In the dialogue 'The Apotheosis of Capnio' Johannes Reuchlin is seen in heaven and the Dominican Egmondanus of Louvain is derided without mercy. 'The Shipwreck' gives a vivid picture of the dangers encountered by sailors on the high seas, and praises the humanity of the Dutch, who, though 'surrounded by savage nations', receive the shipwrecked with Christian compassion and provide them with food, clothing and shelter. Not a few of the dialogues conjure up the atmosphere of Lorenzo's circle at Careggi, of More's *Utopia* or of Rabelais's *Theleme*: a friendly stroll and a good meal during which gentle and learned people, agreeing in substance but not in particulars, discuss the affairs of God and man.

The modern reader is inevitably somewhat put off by the book's tendency to moralize, though this was undoubtedly one of its greatest attractions in its day. He may also object that Erasmus's *personae* are stock-characters, like those of Rabelais and the Italian *novella* writers. Nevertheless, Erasmus set forth the whole of the human comedy with pervasive realism; and if the means at his disposal were primitive he more than made up for it with his liberal spirit and the variety and liveliness of his characters.

The anti-clerical sentiments of the *Colloquia* were less pointed than those of the *Folly*, yet the book touched off a powder keg of scandal. The Reformation was making Rome hypersensitive, and, on the other side of the fence, Luther had never been one to brook a hint of criticism from any quarter. The comparatively friendly reception accorded the *Folly* was probably due to the fact that its criticisms of superstition, abuse, ritual, kings, knights, monks and popes were made without reference to identifiable people. In the *Colloquia*, however, individuals were attacked; some of the victims recognized themselves through the thin veils of pseudonyms, others by well-placed adjectives or the mimicking of their own styles. As complaints poured in Erasmus

merely shrugged and assured each victim that he had had someone else in mind. His pleas of innocence notwithstanding, all
Europe identified his characters almost to the last man.

Not even an application of the narrow standards of the sixteenth century would reveal anything heretical in the *Colloquia*.
It contains no mockery of religion, but merely an attack on its
false application. Erasmus was far too proficient a writer to
permit any fatal excesses in that direction. Egmondanus, utterly
humiliated by his inclusion in the section called 'The Apotheosis
of Reuchlin', denounced Erasmus in 1522 for his stand on
pilgrimages, fasting and indulgences. That the book was condemned by the Sorbonne was due chiefly to the zeal of Erasmus's
fellow scholar at the Collège de Montaigu, Noel Beda. Against
the will of King Francis I the book was later burned in Franche-
Comté and other provinces. Like the pope himself, Francis I
was all but powerless against the Sorbonne. Luther, in a gratuitous
abetment of the Inquisition, denounced the dialogue on idolatry
(which happened to be in complete agreement with his own teachings) as impious. He declared that on his death-bed he would
forbid his sons ever to read the *Colloquia* because of its mockery.

The target of rage from both sides, Erasmus was still the
spokesman of the best minds of Europe, and the number of
people prepared to listen to him can hardly be said to have
diminished. According to the records of bookshops in Oxford,
Salamanca and Venice for three separate years between 1520
and 1528, his works accounted for one-twelfth to one-tenth of
all books sold. When it was rumoured in France at the end of
1526 that the Sorbonne intended to ban the *Colloquia* the book
was hastily reprinted in 24,000 copies, approximately the number
of families living in Paris at that time. During the 18 years
between its first printing in 1518 and the author's death in 1536
it was reprinted one hundred and two times, often in new
editions. It was the uncontested publishing success of the sixteenth century.

It was used far into the seventeenth century as a textbook, as
well as for entertainment. The first translation, into Spanish,
was made in 1528. Clément Marot put two of the dialogues into

French verse, and thereafter the mass of translations began, including nearly all the languages of Europe. Neither More's *Utopia*, Montaigne's *Essays* nor Rabelais' *Gargantua* and *Pantagruel* was so widely influential or left such a lasting impression on its own age as did the *Colloquia*; nor were their messages so readily and distinctly understood. Its liberalism, cloaked in realistic dialogues which purported to be stylistic exercises, was a breath of fresh air, much needed and much appreciated. Its ideas remained a source of enlightenment for several strata of society. Developed further by Rabelais, Montaigne and various Protestant sects, including the Unitarians and the Anabaptists, these ideas continued to sustain intellectual resistance to the reign of oppression which was descending upon Europe.

During Erasmus's years in Basle the volumes of the Paraphrases of the New Testament continued to come off Froben's press one by one. In his exegesis he expounded, to a public still largely unfamiliar with the idea, a Christianity which demanded inner commitment, a faith to guide men in their actions. Here again he provided a précis of the *philosophia Christi*, with emphasis this time on the enlarged role of religious instruction, the regulation of clerical privilege, the curtailment of the monastic orders, the use of the vernacular in the mass and the emergence of a Church of moderation. A few years later Princess Mary, daughter of Henry VIII, was to translate the *Paraphrases of St John* into English, and it, among other books of the series, was to have a marked influence on the Henrician Church.

Erasmus continued the editing of patristic literature, which he had begun in 1516, with the first of his nine-volume edition of St Jerome, and at the same time (1522) he completed the highly-popular treatise *On the Writing of Letters*. The most important work of this period, after the *Colloquia*, was the *Dialogue on the Ciceronians*, written in 1528. Though it shares few of the literary merits of the *Colloquia*, the book, as an essay on style and a satire on some of Erasmus's contemporaries, was to have a pronounced influence on Latin literature.

It has already been mentioned that the humanists were often concerned with language, grammar and style to the exclusion of other and equally important matters. Lorenzo di Valla believed that it was philology which would lead in the end to an understanding of the ultimate and original meaning of past thought, and that language was the most important manifestation of the human spirit, 'the basis of intellectual life and the texture of society'. Humanists accepted Valla's thesis that grammar, style and uniform spelling were prerequisites of correct thinking.

From the beginning, however, Petrarch had favoured Cicero above all other Roman writers as the arbiter of Latin usage, probably because his was the largest surviving body of classical Latin prose and was attractively rhetorical to boot. Petrarch's preference gradually gave rise to an unfortunate cult, that of the Ciceronians. It was Angelo Poliziano who first objected to the custom of slavishly imitating Cicero, maintaining that a writer's style should 'emerge from the continuous process of study, of comparison of styles and the unending effort of composition'. He advised those whose method was outright imitation of the past that they would do well to tear themselves away from 'that miserable superstition' which forced them to suppress their own modes of expression simply because they were original. It might be, he added, that he himself would never surpass the divine Cicero, nor even reach him, but he was able to express himself quite well as it was, and the phrases he used were his own.

Poliziano's arguments were ignored by the Ciceronians, who indulged in endless and empty rhetoric, employing tales from mythology as philosophical proofs and maintaining that the classical heritage consisted of Cicero's vocabulary and syntax and nothing else. The humanist Hermolao Barbaro, patriarch of Venice, proudly declared in the preface to his translation of Aristotle (1484) that his intention had been to render the text of the *Stagirite* in the best Ciceronian Latin; as for the meaning of the text, he continued, it concerned him not at all.

It was Pico della Mirandola who first took Barbaro to task for this, in a friendly enough letter, explaining that writing means much more than a laborious search for words, that it is a 'science of things' rather than a 'science of names'; here he sided with the scholastics of the past who, 'though they stammered', possessed 'the spirit' – as opposed to those humanists who wrote with marvellous fluency but had nothing to say.

By 1520 this situation, especially in Italy, and to a lesser extent in France and Germany, was worse than ever. In the *Dialogue on the Ciceronians* Erasmus's character Nosoponus, who had once been a cheerful man but was now crabbed after 14 years of reading nothing but Cicero, was by no means an exaggeration. There were plenty of scholars in Rome who resembled him, and the contemporary reader could scarcely fail to recognize in him the humanist Longiolus, whom Erasmus had elsewhere singled out as 'the solemn grammarian' who fostered a childish paganism in the name of stylistic purity.

Nosoponus explains his projects to the other characters in the dialogue, two of whom are Hypologus, an interested bystander, and Bulephorus, who upholds the Erasmian point of view. In 14 years Nosoponus has written three books: a dictionary of Cicero's vocabulary, a thesaurus of his tropes and metaphores and a treatise on the cadences to be found in his prose. He lives in a room without a window, has no intention of marrying or of taking part in public affairs, and succeeds in writing one sentence each night, assembling it from bits and pieces of Cicero after hours of toil.

Through the character of Bulephorus Erasmus derides all this with gusto. He ridicules the Ciceronians for calling God the Father 'Jupiter optimus maximus', the Blessed Virgin 'Diana' and the Holy Ghost 'the Celestial Zephyr'. He heaps scorn on them for their inability to describe such simple actions as walking out of a room or eating a meal without piling up references from Graeco-Roman mythology. The founders of humanism, he explains, agreed on the use of Latin as a living language which would absorb new words. To limit Latin to the usage of a former age was tantamount to signing its death warrant. 'Times have changed: our instincts, needs and ideas are not those of Cicero.' And further:

The Ciceronians who play this game are dilettants walking in a land of make-belief. They talk about the senate, about consuls, quirites and Caesar as if they were with us today, alive and real, substance and not shadow. . . . Why pretend that antique virtue is restored by the trick of dubbing modern degeneracy with ancient names? Let us face reality as we know it, and fit our Latin to it as the expression of a modern world of politics, thought and sentiment.

He pointed out that Cicero did not deal even with the whole of Roman culture, much less that of later ages; and he complained that those who filched his words neglected to take his spirit at the same time. He reiterated that the author's first duty is to express his thoughts as clearly as he can; that his intelligence and sense of proportion alone should obviate any affairs with out-of-date paganism, stylistic conformism and mannerism; and that ultimately there is no fixed vocabulary and no authoritative usage of the Latin language, nothing to follow in fact except common sense, good taste and one's own conscience. The school of the Ciceronians, he concluded, offered nothing but an antiquated style in which neither modern culture nor modern ideas had any place.

It is hard to explain the paroxysms of rage which followed the publication of the dialogue. Erasmus foresaw the results: having attacked Luther's religious romanticism and alienated a great part of the already-fanatical younger generation (though he still commanded the allegiance of German humanism), he had now assailed the stylistic conformism of the Roman humanists and made enemies of nearly all of them. The literary historian Julius Caesar Scaliger, with the help of the inquisitor Beda, published a pamphlet in which Erasmus was described as a parasite, a drunkard and the son of a whore. In it he called Cicero's style the summit of Latin, any criticism of which must be considered 'the profanation and destruction of the Latin tongue'.

Rather than reply, Erasmus let it be known that he would remain silent until he discovered who the real author was – for obviously the pamphlet was 'too intelligently written to be the work of Scaliger'. After this humiliation Scaliger was so dejected that he wrote to Erasmus begging for peace; but again he received no reply. Étienne Dolet, a humanist of Lyon, insulted Erasmus as an 'old buffoon and a toothless drybones', asserting that Cicero supplied all that was necessary to the demands of the present since 'human character and social life are not variable quantities'. He likewise received no reply from Erasmus, who seemed by then to have become bored with 'the insufferable apers of Cicero'. Dolet did receive a letter from Scaliger, however, who berated him for his encroachment upon his preserve.

Today it is not easy to understand how Erasmus, who was so obviously in the right in his stand, could have raised such a furious storm of hatred with it. He was recognized as the best stylist of his time, and he employed a large and elastic vocabulary, free for the most part of medievalisms and latter-day over-embellishments as well as imitation of the ancients. The storm was to continue, however, for a full two decades after his death, with the humanists of France and Italy largely against him and those of Germany and England generally siding with him. The dispute was settled for all time in 1556 by the humanist Muretus, who came out on the side of Erasmus's views. From that time onwards until its death as a literary language Latin followed the path which Erasmus had pointed out, as is amply shown by the writings of Descartes, Spinoza and most other authors during the seventeenth century.

Such frequent mention has been made of Erasmus's conciliatory efforts during the first years of the Reformation that the reader may well suspect that tolerance had become an established custom by the beginning of the sixteenth century. Such, unfortunately, was not the case. Like pacifism, tolerance had been held to be unchristian during the Middle Ages, a lack of steadfastness and courage in the face of evil.

The seeds of the idea had been contained in the *Laws* of the Greek neo-Platonist Pletho, who predicted the approaching end of monotheistic religions and the unity of mankind under Platonist rule. It was first broached directly by Marsilio Ficino in his book *Of the Christian Religion*, though even here it was treated in a theoretical manner. Ficino saw man and nature both as admirable things, and he acknowledged that in all philosophies, religions and cults some spark of divine truth is invariably present. The idea of tolerance was the natural result of this view. Erasmus had never read Ficino, but he acquired these ideas through the works of Ficino's disciple, Pico.

After 1521 Erasmus and a few others grasped the fact that the rupture of Christianity could not be repaired by force, disputation or, probably, by any other means. The conservative forces within the Church, already strong under Leo X and Hadrian VI, gained still more power under Clement VII; and while they still hoped to annihilate Luther and his followers in the near future, Luther for his part still dreamed of marching triumphantly into Rome. Thus the reformer, like his Catholic opponents, was intent upon re-establishing the unity of Christianity at any price – short of making any concessions – and was hardly interested in peace or tolerance. Erasmus, having realized the impossibility of restoring unity, was no longer interested in anything but peace or tolerance.

His unprecedented plea for tolerance was based on the best in the humanist and Christian traditions. He never tired of repeating that the keystone of religion is peace, and that all fanaticism is opposed to the spirit of the Gospels. He asked the contesting parties to consider not those matters which divided them, but the much larger number of issues in which they were agreed. He stressed that a return to the simple teachings of the early Church and to its spirit of gentleness was vital if the word of Christ was to survive. 'You will not be damned for not knowing whether the Holy Ghost precedes the Father and Son as from three premises or from two', he wrote in the preface to his edition of St Hilary, '. . . but you will not escape damnation if you do not attempt to acquire . . . charity, patience and meekness.' In a small tract which he had written some time earlier he commented upon Matthew, xii: 18–20 ('Behold my servant, whom I have chosen . . . a bruised reed shall he not break, and smoking flax shall he not quench . . .'):

Here one hears no mention of tortuous syllogisms, nor of threats and thunderbolts; no mention here of troops armed with steel, nor of bloodbaths and burnings. But you hear of gentleness, of kindness towards the weak in whom there is still some hope of the fruits of goodness. . . . Who then does not see that when the Christian commonwealth has fallen into a state of decay, it must be defended and saved with the same means which helped it to be born, to grow and to establish itself?

One of his chief aims had long since been to discredit by every means at hand the attitude of the medieval Church towards heresy. He was eager to refute the Thomistic explanation of the parable of the tare 'which should be pulled out when it can be clearly distinguished'. Erasmus declared that there were no grounds whatsoever for arriving at so grossly laboured an interpretation of the sacred text. In a short time he composed three extremely lucid and impassioned treatises: *Against the Theological Faculty of Paris, Refutations of the Errors of the Inquisitor Beda* and *Against the Holy Inquisition.* In these he denounced the burning of heretics, witches and books, and the institution of the Inquisition itself. It was an act of incredible daring, considering the times.

Another aim was to convince the warring parties that the issues at stake could only be settled by a general council of Catholics and Protestants, convening to agree on essentials and then dispersing with the guarantee that each could think as he pleased in non-essentials. He argued that no such council could meet with success, however, until both sides had cooled their tempers and submitted to thorough moral reform. Meanwhile both sides should try to live in peaceful coexistence, for which he had given the rules in his *Advice to the Senate of Basle.* Finally, anticipating the religious wars which would come soon after his death, the last of which would lay waste to Europe during three decades, he begged the princes to banish all thought of such enterprises from their minds.

Erasmus still had strong allies in both camps. In 1526 the Diet of Speyer produced the so-called 'recess', a resolution stating that each party could keep the gains it had acquired, and that rulers were free to act as they pleased in religious questions. The decision was not unfavourable to the Lutherans at that point, though it was a stunning blow to those who held out for freedom of conscience. Yet for a time, especially in Germany, quite a few statesmen and even some princes favoured the Erasmian solution. Mercurio Gattinara, chancellor of the Empire, who had previously shown a cool politeness towards Erasmus, now appeared to realize that the humanist had been right all the time in his conciliatory policies. On 1 October 1526 Gattinara wrote to Erasmus to say that he saw Christendom divided into three parts: those who remained loyal to the Roman pontiff no matter what he might command, those who followed Luther, and those who sought nothing but the glory of God and the welfare of the people. His own party, he continued, was that of Erasmus, and he was proud to belong to it.

From this time onwards Gattinara did his best to create a policy of peace and moderation. Unfortunately he had little power in the loosely knit Empire, more than ever divided among warring factions and estates. Prince Joachim II of Brandenburg, who went over to the Protestants, and Duke George of Saxony, a Catholic, were both more powerful. They too hoped for the restoration of Christian unity in the Erasmian sense; especially in the case of the duke, who surrounded himself with 'conciliatory heads' such as his chancellor, Simon Pistorius, and the humanists Petrus Mosellanus and Georgius Wicelius, who were and remained determined champions of tolerance. Erasmus likewise had great influence over Ferdinand, who from 1521 onwards had charge of the German possessions of his brother, Charles V, and over his minister, Faber, who was in regular correspondence with him in Basle, seeking his advice.

'In the cities where the tumults have increased,' he wrote to Faber in 1526, 'each party keeps to its own quarter and everyone is left to his conscience until time brings opportunity for agreement. . . . Some of the abuses which gave rise to the disturbances should be corrected, and the rest should wait for a general council.' To the duke of Saxony he wrote: 'One must not ask what one believes the heretic to deserve, but one must act to serve the interests of the Christian Republic.' And later: 'Tolerating the sects may appear a great evil to you, but it is still much better than a religious war; if the clergy should succeed in entangling the rulers, it will be a catastrophe for Germany and for the Church . . . ruins and misery everywhere, and destruction under the false pretext of religion. . . .' Some of these remarks were to become famous a century later, during the Thirty Years War.

Events which weighed as heavily on Erasmus as the German situation were the incursions of the Turks, the fate of Berquin and the steady advance of the Swiss Reformation. The German Peasants' Revolt was far from the only calamity to take place during the third decade of the sixteenth century. In 1525 Pope Clement VII, who had been a good second-in-command to his cousin Leo X, joined the king of France in his war against the emperor. The battlefields, previously extending from Artois to Burgundy, now reached as far as Northern Italy. Erasmus's proposal that the pope should be forbidden to enter into military alliances had fallen on deaf ears.

Now he voiced his fear that the Turks, who could only be deterred by the joint action of Christian states, would attack and do irreparable harm. Seven years earlier he had written to Colet: 'The princes conspire with the pope, and perhaps with the Turks, against the happiness of the people.' The sentence has, for some reason, been quoted from time to time as proof of Erasmus's political naïveté.

In 1526 Suleiman the Magnificent, in secret alliance with the pope, as it happened, and with the French king, asked for right of passage for his troops across Hungary to attack the Empire. Louis II of Hungary and Bohemia, brother-in-law of the emperor, refused the request. The emperor, Charles V, had no troops to spare owing to the French war and the necessity of policing his own strife-torn domains. On 31 August 1526 the Hungarian army was massacred by the Turks at Mohács. Its leaders, King Louis and Archbishop Tomori, died on the battle-field. The larger part of Hungary was eventually occupied by the Turks and was to remain under them for the next 160 years.

In 1527 Rome was sacked by the Lutheran mercenaries of the Catholic emperor, thus marking the date which is generally considered the end of the Renaissance. The year 1528 brought religious disturbances to Basle, causing Erasmus to move once again, this time to Freiburg. Upon his arrival there he learned that Berquin had been burnt at the stake in Paris and that the 'recess' had been revoked by the second Diet of Speyer (both these events occurred in April 1529). The second Diet of Speyer signalled the beginning of the persecution of Zwinglians and Anabaptists in Germany, and the first preparations for full-scale war between Catholics and Protestants.

Louis Berquin, a French reformer, a talented writer and an admirer of Erasmus, had excellently translated several of Erasmus's works into French, albeit with certain radical and inflammatory interpolations of his own. He had also published a book against Luther's calumniators. Erasmus had warned him earlier about the spurious additions, not as an outraged author but rather out of concern for the translator's safety. In 1523 Berquin had been summoned before the doctors of the Sorbonne and forced to witness the public burning of his defence of Luther. Two years later his translations, including the French version of *The Complaint of Peace*, met the same fate. Erasmus wrote to Berquin thanking him warmly for his efforts, but again requested him to desist before they both found themselves in serious trouble.

In 1526 Berquin sent Erasmus a list of charges which the Sorbonne had brought against him; the inquisitors of Paris were brave, he sneered, only when up against such small fish as he: they would never dare attack Erasmus. Shortly after this he was imprisoned. Erasmus wrote to Francis I concerning the charges of 'impudence and incredible ignorance', and to the Parliament of Paris as well. Thanks to these letters Francis gave the order to free Berquin. He was arrested again, however, in

April 1529, while the king was away from Paris. He was hastily condemned and burnt at the stake. It was one more example (John Hus and Giordano Bruno provide others) of clerical authority usurping the civil, of the priests having their way against the wishes of king and magistrates.

Berquin not only refused to recant, which would probably have saved his life, but showed great courage throughout, addressing an impassioned speech to the crowd assembled to watch the burning. Erasmus immediately added a letter to the new edition of his *Collected Letters*, then in preparation, paying tribute to Berquin. A few months later he contrived a vicious but fully-deserved satire on the Parisian inquisitors, Beda, Quercus and Sutor, adding it to the *Colloquia*. It was reported that Beda was seized with a fit and fainted after reading the dialogue. 'But it neither killed him nor resurrected Berquin,' wrote Erasmus unhappily.

Erasmus's relations with the Swiss reformers were different from those he had with Luther. Ulrich Zwingli was and always remained to some extent humanistic in his thinking. Though unyieldingly dogmatic, he was nevertheless a rationalist in many ways, and one who permitted himself no subservience to authority. He did not judge people according to their potential value to his cause, and in this as in other things he lacked Luther's crude opportunism as well as his political acumen.

In 1515 Zwingli had read those lines of Erasmus which declare that Christ is the only mediator; it was the great revelation of his life. Later he memorized passages from the *Novum instrumentum*, including portions of the commentaries. At the time Erasmus arrived in Basle Zwingli was a priest in Zürich. Although they quarrelled and Erasmus disapproved of Zwingli's rigidly dogmatic stand, the Swiss reformer continued to hold him in respect. Later, when he learned that Erasmus had left Basle because the Zwinglians had taken over the town, he was reported to have fallen silent for a few minutes. 'It is impossible,' he finally said, 'not to love Erasmus.'

During 1524 religious tension mounted almost day by day in Basle, and in order to check the flow of hate-filled religious pamphlets the town council introduced censorship. They asked Erasmus to oversee the censor's office, but he refused, not surprisingly, and urged them to moderation. If they were displeased with the old way of administering the sacrament of the Holy Eucharist, for example, let them get the assent of the rest of the Swiss Confederation and apply to the pope on behalf of the whole country, he advised.

The following year the university appointed new lecturers on Holy Scripture to work side by side with Œcolampadius; at the same time they dismissed four professors, all Catholics. A fiery-tempered young man by the name of Guillaume Farel arrived with the new lecturers. A violent hater of Erasmus, he was later to become Calvin's aide-de-camp. Basle now reverberated with religious controversy, especially over the confession of sins. It is likely that this prompted Erasmus to write the tract *Exomolegesis* (*On Ways of Confessing*), in which he agreed with the Protestants that neither Christ nor the Apostles had instituted the custom, although it had been sanctioned by the Fathers. He added, however, that confession was often helpful to people, especially in difficult times, and ought therefore to be retained.

In the meantime Œcolampadius wrote a tract in favour of the Zwinglian doctrine of the Lord's Supper. This was published in Strasbourg, and the town council of Basle asked Erasmus whether they should permit the sale of the book in the town. In a written statement he pronounced it 'learned, eloquent and carefully worked out', adding that he would gladly call it 'pious' as well, except that it was in disagreement with the teachings of the Church and its piety was therefore questionable. The book was consequently banned in Basle, to the great dissatisfaction of the Protestants. But the Catholics were equally displeased; even Erasmus's friend Zasius wrote to him complaining that Œcolampadius, being a Protestant, could no more be called learned than Satan could.

As dissension grew the perplexed council again called on

Erasmus, this time to ask what religious reforms they should institute in order to restore peace. His reply, *The Advice of Erasmus of Rotterdam to the Senate of Basle in the Lutheran Matter*, is not to be found in his *Collected Works*, though it is a profoundly interesting document, and one of the first to propose that different religious practices should be permitted to flourish side by side. It also advocated the toleration of books which advance opposing religious views, so long as 'the authors argue temperately, without slander or vituperation'. All in all the *Advice* is a plan for religious coexistence, presupposing the existence of many denominations and equal rights for all of them. In both Protestant and Catholic countries such compromises as were eventually reached, like that at Worms in 1540, or the Peace of Augsburg, were hardly based on principles of religious freedom.

The first application of Erasmus's *Advice* occurred far from Basle in the dukedom of Transylvania where, in 1554, the Diet of Torda adopted it both in letter and in spirit with altogether successful results. In most of Europe religious freedom was not to be codified until the nineteenth century, and in some places, Spain for example, it has for the most part still to be done.

Œcolampadius also addressed a petition to the council, explaining that Basle had to become the city of Basileus, i.e. of Christ the King, and that there was no Christ except that of the Zwinglians. The petition included a curiously naïve vow not to praise the beauties of the city either in speeches or in poems until it became 'the bride of Christ'. It also contained some entirely inapposite passages praising Erasmus to the point of adulation, but warning the council at the same time not to heed his advice, which was 'merely human'.

Two years later, when the Zwinglians had won over Zürich and Bern, Œcolampadius took it upon himself to organize the religious revolution in Basle. Utenheim, the bishop of mildly Protestant leanings, had just died, and his successor was a conservative. In October 1527, 400 Zwinglians tried to convince the town council to forbid Catholic worship, but the members stubbornly insisted that everyone was free to worship as he pleased. The Protestants, incensed, organized a demonstration during which paintings were removed from the churches and burned in the squares. The council entreated the citizens to remain at peace with one another, but by now no one was listening.

Finally, in February 1528 a mob gathered before the town hall and forced the council to expel its Catholic members. Catholic worship was suppressed, the remaining statues and sacred paintings were destroyed and Œcolampadius was installed as virtual dictator of Basle.

Erasmus, knowing that if he remained in the city it would be taken to mean that he agreed with the iconoclasts who had suspended the constitution, decided to leave; 'subverted', as he put it, 'by the Œcolampadian whirlwind'. Learning of his impending departure, Œcolampadius was unable to understand why Erasmus should want to leave a town in which no one threatened him, and he asked for an interview. The meeting took place in the garden of Froben's house. Erasmus had meanwhile notified Faber, the minister of Ferdinand of Austria, that he intended to move to Freiburg, a little university town some 40 miles north of Basle and a possession of the Habsburgs. Faber replied, as expected, with delight.

Thus the scene which took place in Louvain at the Inn of the Wild Man was now re-enacted in Basle. As they were seated in Froben's garden Œcolampadius protested against a passage in the *Colloquia* which described a long nosed man with the head of a sheep and the heart of a fox; he had easily recognized himself in the description. Erasmus assured him that it was his own secretary that he had had in mind, and that Œcolampadius was imagining things. Then Œcolampadius tried to convince him that it was justice which had been established in Basle, that peace would soon follow; thus, he concluded, Erasmus had no reason to leave. Erasmus retorted that there were many kinds of justice but only one kind of peace, and it was advisable to establish first the latter, which is necessary to human happiness, than the former, which remained open to definition. Œcolampadius replied that in spite of the differences between them the friendship he felt for Erasmus remained unshaken. After this the two men parted for ever.

At first Erasmus planned to leave secretly, afraid that the Zwinglians would stage a demonstration against him. He changed his mind, however, and took his departure openly on 13 April 1529. A few friends accompanied him to the docks. On the bank of the Rhine a great crowd had assembled to bid him farewell. The spectacle so cheered Erasmus, who had hardly expected it, that then and there he composed a poem thanking Basle for its hospitality.

Faber, the Austrian Minister of State, placed a handsome house at Erasmus's disposal, one built a few years earlier as the Freiburg residence of the emperor. The inevitable fly in the ointment was one Professor Othman Nachtigall, who shared the royal residence with Erasmus. Most inappropriately named, Nachtigall was an unpleasant and loquacious man. Erasmus soon moved out and bought a house of his own at a cost of several hundred guilder.

The Catholic University of Freiburg was highly honoured to have the humanist in the town, and immediately requested him to permit the professors and students to consult him from time to time. Four years after his arrival in Freiburg Erasmus was to agree to become professor of theology, and was duly elected to the university senate. Very ill by then, he accepted the post on condition that no heavy duties should be assigned to him.

He liked Freiburg, partly because of its pleasant situation and partly because it was comparatively peaceful (although he did grumble occasionally about being 'in belligerent Germany'). He took comfort in the fact that escape would be easy: 'France is near, should I want to flee from here.' In 1531 he visited Besançon, at that time a part of the Empire. According to his own testimony he made the journey solely to quench his thirst for good Burgundian wine. The emperor saw to it that he received a royal welcome, and, together with numerous casks of wine, he brought a secretary back to Freiburg with him.

This ambitious young man was Gilbertus Cognatus (Gilbert Cousain), who from the beginning took his new position with great seriousness. Soon he was to publish his own first book, entitled *On the Duties of a Secretary*, in which he described the choice of a secretary as being no less important than that of a wife. Cognatus was a Protestant, which caused considerable scandal in Catholic Freiburg. Erasmus reacted by saying that he had no intention of permitting fanaticism to enter his study.

The year 1529 brought fresh troubles for Erasmus. It was during his move to Freiburg that he learned that Berquin had been burnt at the stake; and when news came, too, that Sir Thomas More had become Chancellor of England he seemed no less distressed. More, who evidently guessed Erasmus's thoughts, wrote in a letter soon after his appointment: 'I am unexpectedly thrown into the stream of affairs. . . . My friends here exult vehemently and congratulate me . . . you perhaps will pity my fortune.'

And so he did. Erasmus had long lamented that his friend, having entered political life, would be lost to literature. He was not quite correct, though, for More continued to write up to the very day of his arrest. Erasmus's fears were justified, however. Although he had once praised Henry VIII's moderation and 'conjugal virtues' to the high heavens, he was also aware of the monarch's undisciplined nature. He knew all about the events which had been taking place within the English court. In a letter to Amerbach in 1530 he admitted to 'the worst forebodings of further troubles and of a great slaughter'.

After his arrival in Freiburg he learned that the second Diet of Speyer had reworded the 'recess' of 1526 to deprive all but Catholics and Lutherans of the rights it set forth. In the meantime the Diet refused to vote any help for Ferdinand of Austria in his defence against the Turks. The immediate result was that religious tension reached a peak in most of the Empire. A second consequence was that towards the end of the same year Suleiman, as skilful a politician as he was a general, appeared with his army beneath the walls of Vienna without meeting any serious resistance along the way. He withdrew at leisure after ravaging

Lower Austria, and strengthened his grip on Hungary and the Balkans. From then on until his death seven years later Erasmus was to be chiefly preoccupied by the religious conflagration and the Turkish threat to Europe.

Since he had spent most of his time in the years leading up to 1529 in fighting the Inquisition and defending the rights of Protestant dissenters, he might reasonably have expected to enjoy at least tacit approval on the part of Luther. At the beginning of the Reformation Luther had vowed to maintain tolerance, and he had expressed complete agreement with Erasmus's interpretation of the parable of the tares. After Speyer, however, the situation changed and only Lutherans were allowed the rights which previously they had shared with Zwinglians, Anabaptists and all the other sects, now outlawed. As a result of this the two major powers, Catholics and Protestants, now saw each other in sharper focus as enemies, and immediately began preparing for a final confrontation. In the meantime they occupied themselves with the persecution of the smaller groups.

Before the end of 1529 civil war broke out between the Catholics and Protestants of the Swiss Confederation. It was halted only briefly by an armistice. The doctrine of the Eucharist proved to be an insuperable source of antagonism between Luther and Zwingli, on the other hand, and at the 1529 conference at Marburg Luther parted from his Swiss colleague with almost papal hauteur: 'Your spirit differs from ours.' After this encounter Luther reversed his views on tolerance. Ferreting out a likely passage from the Old Testament, Leviticus, xxiv: 16 ('And he that blasphemeth the name of the Lord, he shall surely be put to death, and all the congregation shall certainly stone him . . .'), he used it to uphold the Thomist injunction to root out heretics, without of course referring to the 'papist theologian'.

Eventually Luther advised Duke Albert of Prussia to expel the Zwinglians from his realm, and he signed the infamous document urging Johann Friedrich, the tolerant elector of Saxony, to introduce capital punishment for heresy. This codification of intolerance by the Lutheran ecclesiastical authorities was reinforced by the formation of the League of Schmalkalden, in which the Lutheran dukedoms, counties and towns of Germany were brought into military alliance against the emperor and against their Catholic counterparts. At the same time the Catholics and Pope Clement were far from looking at the situation in a conciliatory manner.

Thus where there had previously seemed some small hope of compromise, Erasmus now saw only irremediable antagonism, division and preparation for war. 'Just look at the Evangelical [i.e. Lutheran] people!' he wrote bitterly from Freiburg. 'Have they become any better? Do they yield less to luxury, lust and greed? Show me a man whom the Gospels have changed from a drunkard to a temperate man, from a brute to a gentle creature, from a miser to a generous person. . . .' Yet bitterness never retained the upper hand in him for long, and his native optimism always re-emerged under the soothing effects of hard work.

Resistance to the sectarian struggles was far from dead, however, especially in Germany where the two major contenders had tried to monopolize the churches, schools, printing presses and universities, indeed all life public and private, and had filled it to the brim with theology and hatred. Each party claimed to be the one and only repository of Christian truth – though it was obvious that the essentially medieval theological structure of the Church was badly shaken by the Reformation, and equally obvious that the Lutherans had not yet managed to formulate a creed of their own. To the thoughtful it was also clear that the massacre which both sides were yearning for, far from bringing victory to either, would merely give rise to new and fiercer hatreds. And with large groups of Zwinglians, Anabaptists and others on the scene, it was no longer within the power of either Luther or the pope to reunite Christianity.

To all this was added the most shameless political bargaining on both sides, a traffic in human lives while the Turks stood at the gates of Vienna. Erasmus was far from alone in his revulsion; many people, Catholics and Protestants alike, had reached the point where they were beginning to wonder if the future held anything but a prolongation of the bickering over theological details, for they had been brought up to enjoy the benefits of the printing-press, the new custom of wide-ranging discussion and the whole flowering of civic and intellectual life which was the legacy of the Renaissance. Thus there is nothing surprising in the fact that many still sided with Erasmus, including quite a few young people who realized that while they could not hope to halt the flood they might perhaps outlast it and build something better once it had passed.

One of these young men was Georgius Wicelius (1501–73) a priest who had left the Church in 1524, had married and been rewarded by Luther with a parish of his own. In 1531, seeing 'the disastrous consequences of faith without works', he broke with the reformer. In March 1533 Erasmus received a letter from him which said 'only Erasmus and his disciples can restore harmony in the Church'.

Julius Pflug (1499–1564), a Catholic and later bishop of Naumburg, wrote to Erasmus in 1531: 'All who desire look towards you. God has given you alone the authority and power to cure the evils from which we suffer.' Insisting on thorough reform of the Church and the right of the clergy to marry, Pflug was at odds with the authorities throughout his life. We shall return later to the role he played at the Council of Trent, where he was one of the leaders of the Erasmians.

During the summer of 1530 Charles V convoked the Diet in Augsburg 'in order to restore a good peace and Christian truth'. The announcement produced a stir of optimism, especially among the townspeople, though they should have known by now that 'Christian truth', so often mentioned, was not only a meaningless expression but also a dangerous one. At the Diet Philipp Melanchthon, well known for his moderation and his sympathy with Erasmus, was to defend the Lutheran cause.

Erasmus heaved a sigh of relief, hoping against hope that some compromise might at last be reached. A few months before the Diet met he applied himself to the task of writing letters to the rulers of Europe, suggesting ways in which they might come to an agreement. He wrote letters to Faber, now bishop of Vienna; to Nicholas Granvella, an Erasmian and successor to Gattinara as chancellor of the Empire; and to Charles V himself. In his letter to the emperor – which has been lost – he urged acceptance of the policy of coexistence, and suggested that reform, like charity, ought to begin at home. He proposed that the Eucharist be administered in both ways, that priests be permitted to marry and that laws such as those he had suggested to the Basle town council be drafted to enforce tolerance.

Historians have seldom agreed as to what extent, if any, Erasmus influenced the emperor at this point. At the Diet Melanchthon defended the Augsburg Confession, which he had worded so as not to offend the Catholic theologians. But the emperor rejected the document. He did declare, however, that he would not move against the Lutherans until the pope introduced reforms within the Church. Since Clement VII was totally unprepared for this in every way, it was a victory for Luther.

Scholarly disagreement centres first of all on whether Erasmus had expected to be summoned by the emperor to Augsburg, and secondly whether the emperor was acting at Augsburg on Erasmus's advice. Some writers have maintained that there was no connection between Erasmus's letter and the declarations of Charles, that for all his sympathy with the *philosophia Christi* the emperor was unable to comprehend anything outside the framework of orthodox Catholicism, i.e. neither Lutheranism nor even Erasmian tolerance of it. Others have believed that Erasmus's influence has been underestimated: for if the emperor had not been brought up on *The Education of a Christian Prince* he would probably have sent Luther to the stake as far back as the Diet of Worms, as Emperor Sigismund had done to Hus a century before. It must be admitted in any case that even if Charles misunderstood Erasmus's advice or was acting on motives of his own, the reforms he demanded of the pope were nothing if not Erasmian.

The year 1531 saw the renewal of hostilities between the Catholic and Protestant cantons of Switzerland, and the cities

of Basle, Bern and Zürich. Zwingli was killed in the débâcle at
Kappel, and a few weeks later Œcolampadius succumbed to a
fever in Basle. Erasmus committed what was for him an act of
incredible callousness and poor taste by writing that he saw
'God's wonderful hand in the death of those two preachers'
whose 'fall has wrought great changes in the minds of many'.
The statement was worthy of Luther at his worst. It was hardly
true, however, and the two preachers had in fact been much
closer to Erasmus both spiritually and intellectually than any of
the other reformers were.

It must be regarded as a curious psychological phenomenon
that Erasmus, who saw his life's work subverted, possibly
for ever, by Luther, displayed so much patience towards him.
He ventured to criticize his indomitable nature, and once,
going as far as he ever would, he called him 'the teacher of errors
and the leader of tumults' – mild stuff indeed compared with
the slanders he received in reply. He would never have written
about his arch-enemy the things he did about the two men who
had always shown him their respect and gratitude.

No picture of Erasmus's attitudes towards the various sects
would be complete without mention of his surprising relationship with the Anabaptists. Originally an anarchistically-minded
German group, the Anabaptists had endured terrible persecu-
tions at the beginning of the 1520s. By the end of the decade
they had renounced all forms of violence, even acts of self-
defence. In his exposition of the 82nd Psalm Luther compared
them to the Turks, advising his flock: 'Such people should not
be tolerated . . . and should be stoned.'

Erasmus commiserated with the aspirations of the Anabaptists,
not only in their contempt of force and dogmatism but also in
their peculiar form of individualism and their dislike of the
exclusive concept of Church and hierarchy. He wrote about
them with tenderness and compassion, though he disagreed
with many of their beliefs. Reading his remarks, one is almost
inclined to suspect that had he been 40 years younger Erasmus
might well have gone off to join them – although he was always
the advocate of the middle way, while the Anabaptists were in

a sense the ultimate reformers: like their Unitarian descendants they abolished all theology, the idea of a church and even the symbols of metaphysical thought, in order to lead the uncomplicated existence of the early Christians. The leader of the Anabaptists in Southern Germany, Hans Denk, and his followers regarded Erasmus 'from a polite and reverential distance' as their 'spiritual leader and as a saint'.

The victory of the Turkish armies at Mohács in 1526 and the subsequent march on Vienna and threat to the rest of Europe weighed heavily on Erasmus. At once a pacifist and a believer in the 'indivisible Christian Republic', he was also influenced in his reaction to it by his close ties with the Hungarian Erasmians[2] and the court of Queen Mary at Buda.

His Hungarian ties began as early as 1509 when he met the humanist Jacobus Piso, Hungarian ambassador to the Vatican. At their first meeting Piso presented him with a volume of his, Erasmus's, correspondence. Piso had collected these letters assiduously during years of travelling on diplomatic missions. Erasmus, who at that time did not yet appreciate the humanists' custom of publishing their own correspondence, consigned the whole collection to the fire. Later he was furious with himself for having done so. Piso heard about it, however, and sent him a few Roman coins found in the vineyards of Pannonia – a more durable gift.

Piso eventually became tutor to Prince Louis (later King Louis II of Hungary and Bohemia), and educated his charge 'with the *Enchiridion* in one hand and *The Education of a Christian Prince* in the other'. When Louis married Mary of Habsburg, sister of Charles V and Ferdinand, at the age of sixteen, Piso stayed on to educate them both. As already mentioned, Erasmus's books were read aloud in the royal court at Buda, which became an island of enlightenment in a country in which the nobles were preoccupied with feuds and the serfs condemned by law, after the revolt of 1514, 'to eternal slavery'.

[2] See p 95

One of the Erasmians at Buda was the Italian Girolamo Balbi. In the monastery at Steyn Erasmus had argued with his friend Cornelius about Balbi. Cornelius had considered him the only true poet of the age, while Erasmus contended that he was only one among many. Shortly before Erasmus first went to Paris Balbi had taught literature there. It was Fausto Andrelini who had driven him out with slander and intrigue, and had then occupied his chair in the university. In later life Balbi had become a diplomat for the Hungarian government. At the Diet of Worms in 1521 he was spokesman for the Hungarian delegation, which had come primarily to ask for help: the previous year Suleiman had succeeded his father, Selim, and was offering Hungary peace and alliance if he were granted free passage across the country to attack the Empire. The Hungarians refused Suleiman only to find themselves let down by the Empire.

At Worms Balbi had delivered a speech based on Erasmian principles and interspersed with quotations from Acncas Sylvius. He blamed the disunity of Europe, the fratricidal conflicts (especially the war between France and the Empire) for the Turkish incursions, and maintained that a tiny fraction of this furious activity, redirected, would suffice to check the sultan. He stressed that he was not asking for a crusade against Constantinople, which was a hopeless cause for the time being, but merely that the estates and princes give their attention to the fact that Buda and Vienna were in mortal danger. The Diet, unfortunately, was interested in nothing but condemning Luther, and Balbi's pleas were heard without interest.

In May 1526 Francis I, Henry VIII and Clement VII allied themselves in the League of Cognac against Emperor Charles V. Before this the Hungarian Bishop István Brodarics had visited Rome to beg for help, not knowing that the pope had made a secret agreement with the Turks. Another Erasmian, Tamás Nádasdy, pleaded the same cause at the Diet of Speyer. It is significant that while Suleiman was already moving his armies against Hungary only the Erasmians showed the slightest interest in the fate of the country. The Hungarian nobility continued to occupy itself with internal strife. A part of the

Hungarian army even looked on with pleasure as, a few weeks after the Diet of Speyer, the rest of the army and King Louis himself were massacred by the Turks.

The queen and her almost totally Erasmian court sailed up the Danube to Pozsony (present-day Bratislava) near the Austrian border. From there Bishop Brodarics wrote to Pope Clement: 'Your Holiness may not only hear our curses but also see our total decay, and with our decay, the decay of Christendom.' Before the queen and her court could continue on into Austria the anti-humanist palatine Báthory had the servants dragged from the ships and impaled along the banks of the Danube.

Queen Mary moved to Linz, and later to Augsburg, with a few of her supporters. Among these were the Lutheran János Henckel, and the Catholic Miklós Oláh, both staunch Erasmians. They continued to look for allies who could speak more forcefully than they for a united stand against the Turks. It was probably owing to naïveté that they did not immediately single out Erasmus as their chief ally, although they had long since been in correspondence with him.

The following year, 1530, he wrote the political pamphlet *Advice in the Final Hour on the Necessity of War Against the Turks*, arranging to have it published simultaneously in Basle and Paris. From the title one might think that he had made a startling about-face. Scrutiny of the contents of the book, however, shows that it was written in full conformity with his previous views and with the best humanist traditions of the past. It was during the fifteenth century that the popular epithet 'Dog-faced, pagan, Godless Turks' was countered, at least in Italy, by the view that the Turks were, at worst, merely Turks. Ficino and others professed respect for Islam, and Cusanus hoped for a peaceful settlement with the Turks. But no humanist had ever recommended capitulation before their onslaught. On the contrary, Poggio and his mortal enemy, Filelfo, canvassed together for a European coalition to withstand their attacks, and Aeneas Sylvius did the same after the fall of Constantinople.

Erasmus, following humanist tradition in the matter, rarely

referred to the Turks as pagans, but out of consideration for their monotheistic religion generally called them, in neo-Platonist fashion, 'half-Christians', adding that many a Christian was not even that. On the other hand, as a humanist he could not resist calling them barbarians, the name given all those outside the sphere of Graeco-Roman civilization.

He had always opposed crusades, not only because of the military impossibility of recapturing Constantinople, but also because 'so many crusades degenerated into predatory expeditions' or that 'the money [for them] was stolen before they began'. He added to this: 'It is not our aim to murder as many Turks as we can but to save as many as we can. . . . What would Christianity profit if the bishops, cardinals and the pope were to get to the countries of the east? Do you believe that they would call for Jesus Christ to come and reign there with them? Hardly.' But he did have a remedy against the Turks which he recommended time and again: 'Do you want to appear terrifying to the Turks? Then live in concord amongst yourselves.'

In this sense *Advice in the Final Hour* added very little to what he had already said. The treatise began with the statement that Christianity was in decline. Wars had devastated Europe, famine was raging in Italy, and the French disease, the *morbus gallicus*, had become so widespread that courtiers and other 'fine people' despised everyone who had not yet contracted it. No new steps could be taken until morals were changed. Having said this, he reviewed the history of the Turkish advance into Europe, concluding that the Turks had won their victories not so much because of their bravery as because of the disunity of the west, the rivalries within the Byzantine imperial family and because of Christian deceit, greed and megalomania.

Luther had previously divined that the Turks were a plague sent by God to punish Christian sins, and thus according to him all who fought against them were rebelling against the will of God. Erasmus was convinced that Catholics and Protestants were on the verge of civil war (which did come in 1539) and that this was the reason for Luther's lack of interest in the Turks. He refuted the reformer's stand by claiming that, if he were right, it would also be unchristian to cure illnesses, for they are as well sent by God. Not to withstand the Turks, he concluded, was a form of that Moslem madness which made men sit unperturbed beneath a crumbling roof until Allah ordained that it should fall down on them.

At the end of the pamphlet he assailed those who, instead of trying to achieve a united front, went about shouting 'War against the Turks!' and never stopped talking about the atrocities of the Turkish armies – which, he added, resembled nothing so much as those committed by Christian mercenaries. Finally he expressed the hope that now that the French king was making peace with Charles V, and perhaps even with Henry VIII, it might happen that the rulers would finally unite themselves against the menace from the east.

The pamphlet was written to create an effect at the Diet of Augsburg, but it failed to attract attention except among those who already agreed with it – and of course among the Austrians and Hungarians, who already were dangerously threatened.

In Freiburg during 1529 and 1530 Erasmus wrote *On the Education of Boys* and *On the Civility of Boys*, the last in his long series of pedagogical works. Although most of his books had touched in one way or another on pedagogy, the first to deal explicitly with the process of teaching had been *A Method of Study*, written in 1511 at the behest of John Colet for St Paul's School. Erasmus's other strictly pedagogical works were *On Plenty* (1512), the revision of Lily's *Grammar* (1513), the translation of the two books of Gaza's *Greek Grammar* (1516 and 1518, respectively), the first draft of the *Colloquia* (1519), *On the Writing of Letters* (1522) and *The Correct Pronunciation of Latin and Greek* (1528). In 1531 he finally published his *Annotations* to Valla's *Elegantiae*, having carried the manuscript about with him ever since he had written it at Steyn some 40 years before.

Erasmus's views on pedagogy were, for the most part, logical extensions of those things we already know about him, and need little further elucidation. Learning was to him 'an instrument of life, with only practical goals'; yet these practical goals were in reality subordinate to the true aims of Renaissance pedagogy: to communicate to the pupil 'all the treasures of the mind', to teach him to respect and yearn for perfection and 'to transform the raw material of youth into the visible image of God'. Not unnaturally, the middle-school education based on these principles was, compared with present-day education, extremely literary; certainly it consisted of little outside the realm of what we now call the humanities. Its basis was the intellectual and spiritual reconciliation of antique wisdom with Christian doctrine, and its end was the creation of a learned, humanistic and enlightened laity.

Professional instruction, indeed all instruction not leading directly to this goal, was left to the universities. The ascetical and fanatical features of the medieval Christian personality were to be eradicated, and the Renaissance cult of narcissistic, absolute individualism was to be replaced by a desire to serve God and society. At the same time all this was being attempted the imitation of antiquity was supplanted by an emphasis on classical wisdom as the chief social virtue, the prompter of logic and the guide to Christian ethics, a cicerone in the ways of philosophic thinking and correct expression.

Erasmus did not hesitate to advocate a wholly secular education and to reject the idea of religious schools. In his opinion it would be better to have no schools at all than church schools only. He blamed both the Lutherans and the Catholics for trying to make allies of religion and ignorance, Savonarola's method as it happened; and he was in complete agreement with Philipp Melanchthon and François Rabelais that classical, especially Greek studies were indispensable in the development of the mind. He remained faithful throughout to that tenuous thread of optimism extending from Socrates to, say, Pico; and he was wont to attribute stupidity and wickedness to unfortunate circumstances or defective training rather than to any innate incapacity on the part of men. The generosity of this, as well as his highly idealized view of antiquity, may account for the fact that he so easily united the old and the new in himself without a trace of inner conflict, and could look down on the farce of neo-paganism, for example, with a smile.

He constantly pointed out the evil effects of too much dis-cipline: 'If a boy can be controlled only by flogging, either have him sent away from school or else turn out the master.' No mother should be allowed to strike her child; upon seeing a child thrashed Erasmus once remarked that his fingers twitched in their desire to box the mother's ears. 'Harshness drives boys to join monasteries, and girls are broken in spirit by it. . . . A boy who is not influenced by fear of God, regard for his parents, shame or conscience, is not likely to be moulded by physical pain.'

In his controversy with the Parisian inquisitor Beda he went still further, attempting to analyse the phenomenon of youth turning away from the faith. He suggested that attempts should be made to prevent this, but, if they failed, it was best not to compel or to interfere further. 'The past age did not achieve anything by its use of coercion; let us try persuasion.'

He held that girls should be instructed in the same subjects as boys and in the same manner, that 'a woman's life can be enriched in the same way as a man's', thus rejecting the time-honoured view that learning is harmful if not fatal to feminine virtue, or at best unbecoming to it. He often cited the exemplary households of Thomas More and Willibald Pirckheimer, in which the equality of the women and girls was accepted as fact. Learning, he said, should begin with play, and parents should take great care with children under four lest they fall prey 'to the anarchistic society of infants of similar age'. He maintained also that parents continue to be responsible for their children throughout their education, for: 'The choice of a tutor does not mean that the father has abdicated.'

Erasmus was aware of the conditions existing in the schools, and knew well that many headmasters and teachers were 'drunken, broken down and imbecilic'. 'They teach in miserable hovels, as though they were turning out pigs instead of citizens. Such is the seed-pot of the state.' Together with Colet he had dreamed of a new type of school and the creation of an alto-gether new sort of master who, backed by upright officials, a devoted clergy and an enlightened ruler, would form one of the four pillars of national well-being. In *A Method of Study* he portrayed this new teacher, calling his profession 'one of the highest to which the Christian can be called'. He criticized the disdain in which most families held the tutor, 'whose pay is less than that of the cook', and castigated the decadence of a society in which 'the teacher is chosen with less care than a lapdog'.

Most of this can be traced back to Plutarch, Aristotle, Plato and, to a lesser extent, Seneca and Quintilian. All of it was expounded and developed by the Italian humanists, especially Petrarch and Leonardo Bruni d'Arezzo, and was put into practice in Vittorino da Feltre's famous school at Mantua. After 1440 or so the ideas of humanist education were generally accepted in Florence and, somewhat later, in the other cities of northern Italy. The education of girls was conducted along the same lines as that of boys. Corporal punishment was abolished and infinite care was taken, as almost never before in history, that the best possible education should begin at the earliest possible age. Teachers were idolized, and since it was believed that 'man is not born but made', pedagogy became a chief concern of the literate classes – which in the cities of northern Italy included an unprecedentedly large part of the population.

All of Erasmus's basic pedagogical theories had been voiced at least a hundred years before his time. His original contributions were important, but they consisted largely of practical innovations. His recommended pronunciation of Latin and Greek, which in the case of the latter language was still followed in most of Europe until recently, is an outstanding example. In the matter of Latin style he had provided the best model in his own prose, clarifying his position in the *Ciceronians* and summing it up still more strikingly in *On the education of Boys*. He realized that the reaction against 'Gothic barbarism' had gone to the other extreme and was degenerating into overblown rhetorical fancifulness, and he observed: 'This is apparently the law of human progress, that upon attaining a certain point in its course a movement only escapes detrimental exaggeration by recoiling in the opposite direction.'

He made many minor improvements on Italian pedagogy. We shall name only a few of the most characteristic. In opposing the Italian nationalists, for example, who asserted their superiority over all the other nations of Europe, he wrote 'The love of one's fatherland may be advantageous to the individual . . . yet our philosophy demands that we look upon the world as the common fatherland of all.' Many of his precepts concerning the teaching of languages, such as constant oral practice and vocabulary revision, have generally been thought of as twentieth-century innovations. His thoughts on psychology are often striking: he insisted on a personal bond between pupil and teacher ('Men are not cattle and the school is not a workshop'); he advised teachers to instill a desire for praise into their pupils towards the attainment of a 'proper self-respect', for man has 'an inborn love of fame'. These and dozens of perceptive remarks on child-rearing could be listed almost *ad infinitum*, and one wonders where Erasmus, who spent so little of his life in contact with children or families, acquired his insights. The most obvious answer is that he simply reflected on his own childhood and thought how it might and should have been.

He lagged behind the Italians in only two respects. Though he had corrected the proofs of Gaguin's *History of France* and was undoubtedly familiar with the works of Raffaele de Volterra and Filippo Villani, who had written a history of Florence, Erasmus openly despised modern historical writing and banished it from his pedagogy as a hotbed of chauvinism. The other matter, his perfectly correct refusal to regard 'the vigour of the athlete as a compensation for ignorance' led him to the unfortunate conclusion that physical education hinders the growth of the mind.

In his general preoccupation with his own health, however, he developed a commendable love of cleanliness and order and a distaste for dirt, whether in city streets, markets or communal dormitories, and he stressed the beneficial effects of long walks, clean linen, habitual bathing and moderation in food and drink. Curiously enough, he was attacked for this from various sides. The Catholic rigorists reproached him for 'having betrayed the

Christian norm in his pagan concern for the body', while his Italian friend, the humanist Sadoleto, protested against 'the proposal of washing oneself every day, a disgusting northern idea incompatible with human dignity'.

Until recently many historians sought to maintain that Erasmus brought humanist pedagogy to northern Europe. The reader will remember, however, that Hegius, Wessel and Agricola had already introduced the new methods in Holland during Erasmus's childhood. The new pedagogy arrived in the schools of Vienna in the 1430s with Aeneas Sylvius himself, and the humanist Conradus Celtis was teaching it in the University of Vienna while Erasmus was still in the monastery. Reuchlin and others introduced humanist methods in the schools of Germany at about the same time, and there is little need to mention the well-known work of Grocyn, Linacre and Colet in England.

Erasmus's accomplishment was the perpetuation and strengthening of humanist pedagogy, not its initial exportation to the north. His merit lay in having summed up the general aims and methods of the new theories in his works, and in a manner so concise and thorough that it was unequalled by anyone else.

Pedagogy was the one field in which Erasmus can be said to have achieved decisive victory during his lifetime, and in which his work was not successfully contested by his enemies after his death. His textbooks were too obviously superior to all others to be discarded by the schools. Erasmian pedagogy flourished most conspicuously in England, perhaps, where the chief advisers of Edward VI and Queen Mary were strongly in favour of its aims. Erasmus's version of Lily's *Grammar* was authorized in 1540 'to be used in the King's Majesty's dominions' and was reprinted more than 200 times in the sixteenth century alone. *A Method of Study*, *On the Education of Boys*, the *Colloquia* and *On Plenty* also stood without serious competition. Erasmus was never without ardent followers in England, including besides the first great English humanists such men as Henry Bullock, Roger Ashcam, John Cheke and Bishop Pilkington. The line was to continue down to the Cambridge Platonists of the seventeenth century and, to a lesser extent, beyond.

The situation was similar in Hungary, where Cardinal-Archbishop Oláh eventually founded the theological seminary of Nagyszombat (later the University of Budapest) and introduced Erasmian methods in it. The same process took place in Catholic Poland and, a few decades later, in the Protestant dukedom of Transylvania.

The situation in Germany around 1530 looked much gloomier. In the Lutheran areas the Catholic churches were expropriated, as were the institutions attached to them. No schools were opened to replace those which had been closed. At the University of Wittenberg, where Luther was in residence, theology was considered the only subject worthy of attention. In the meantime in many Catholic countries, including Spain and France, scholastic pedagogy received an infusion of new life when it was employed as a weapon against the Protestants.

The process by which these setbacks eventually gave way to the re-establishment of Erasmian pedagogy in each country is, unfortunately, far too complicated to deal with here at any length. At the Council of Trent, convened in December 1545, two months before Luther died, Erasmus's works were condemned; but thereafter Melanchthon, Pflug, Wicelius, Pistorius, Capito, Faber and many others, Lutherans and Catholics alike, began slowly to revive his methods in the schools of Germany. Few objected: both civil and ecclesiastical authorities were still embroiled in the religious struggle. Scholastic pedagogy proved, after prolonged flogging, to be a dead horse, and there was nothing at hand to replace it except the books and methods of Erasmus. The same process was to repeat itself in other countries.

In 1531 Erasmus's health took a turn for the worse. He sometimes suffered great pain, walked with a heavy limp and often had to be carried on a litter. Nevertheless he continued his work, and in that year alone published, besides the already-mentioned *Annotations* to Valla, an edition of Aristotle and the *Apophthegmata*, a collection of 'winged words' which was in a sense a continuation of the *Adagia*. It was an imposing selection of

erudition, including maxims of the Seven Sages, Greek philosophers, Athenian statesmen, Persian kings, Scipio, Cato,
Caesar and Hadrian. The only contemporary to be honoured by
inclusion was, oddly enough, Alphonso of Aragon, king of
Naples, who could certainly not have been considered remarkable among Renaissance tyrants for his list of clever sayings.
The *Apophthegmata*, though only a compilation, became very
popular, and was to go through a dozen printings and be twice
translated into English during the next decade.

The year 1532 brought fresh troubles. In May Sir Thomas
More resigned the chancellorship of England, giving ill health
as an excuse; but it was clear that the rift between More and
Henry VIII over the validity of the latter's marriage had more
to do with his decision than his health. More immediately wrote
to Erasmus reassuring him that the step had not been forced
on him by the king. Yet the two men understood each other
well, and Erasmus knew that More was only trying to allay his
fears.

Deeply concerned, Erasmus wrote an open letter to Faber,
bishop of Vienna, in which he praised King Henry's magnani-
mity and largesse and reassured the reader that it was More who
had begged the king to be relieved of his duties. He took care
to see that many hundreds of copies of the letter reached England, hoping that 'the most human of all princes' would be
impressed enough with the flattery to spare More's life.

In a pamphlet he proposed that the king should be permitted
by the pope to live in bigamy; which was of course one way of
solving the problem, if not the most likely. Though he knew
both Englishmen well enough, Erasmus failed on this occasion
to interpret the situation correctly: More, far from capitulating
to the king, was not unwilling to die for his views, i.e. for
Roman orthodoxy; and the king, having decided to abandon
his former servility to Rome in favour of open rebellion against
it, necessarily had to insist on full support and total conformity,
especially on the part of his own chancellor.

Erasmus's health declined rapidly during 1532. In November
he wrote that he had little hope of seeing in the new year.

When Warham, archbishop of Canterbury, died and Aleandro was created cardinal he declared with resignation: 'My friends decrease, my enemies increase in power.' No original work of his was printed by Froben that year, but only the first edition of Basil – one more volume in the monumental series of patristic literature. Ill health may have been the reason that he now broke with the habit of a lifetime and no longer answered all the letters he received. On 30 November 1532 he received a letter from François Rabelais, but it may be that he was not even shown it by his secretary, for it is difficult otherwise to believe that he would not have replied. 'I call you my father,' wrote Rabelais, 'and I would call you my mother as well if, in your kindness, you would permit it. . . . All that I am and all that I am worth I owe to you.'

In 1533 his health unexpectedly improved, and a measure of good news arrived. Johann III, duke of Cleve-Jülich (and later, briefly, father-in-law of Henry VIII), introduced Erasmian reforms in his domain. These met with general approval and restored peace to the country. Erasmus did not live long enough to see the *philosophia Christi* swept away after a short but effective life there. Reassuring news came, too, from Bishop Faber that the efforts to make peace between the two warring kings of Hungary were showing signs of success. But again Erasmus was not to live long enough to see the results, in this case the peace-treaty of Nagyvárad, which in any case would eventually be broken.

Invitations continued to pour in from all quarters. The Fuggers, the bankers of Europe, asked him to spend his remaining years with them in Augsburg. Francis I of France, Ferdinand of Austria, Sigismund of Poland and all the humanists of Cracow sent him invitations. Early in 1531 Charles V had appointed his sister, Mary of Hungary, regent of the Lowlands by the Sea. Mary's chancellor, Miklós Oláh, wrote a letter to Erasmus asking him to return to his native country. He must have gathered detailed information concerning Erasmus's past in Holland, for he wrote that he could live at the court 'without being bothered'; he said that they had already put in a supply of his favourite

Burgundian wine and that, when the queen recovered her Hungarian realm, they would give him all the wines of Tokay to sample as well. Erasmus replied that he was considering the matter.

He still worked incessantly, adding a few last pieces to the *Colloquia*, editing the works of the Church Father Hayno, translating Ptolemy and composing a little book entitled *On the Sweet Concord of the Church*. Though this booklet was violently assailed by many of his contemporaries of all persuasions and has generally been disregarded by his biographers, it is nonetheless a document of importance, similar in some ways to the *Enchiridion* – an *Enchiridion* written not by a young man hoping to conquer the world with his ideas, but by an old man who realized that he had failed to do so, who suffered the nightmare of believing himself a failure in a cause which he knew to be right.

In the last analysis the *Concord* shows not Erasmus the humanist, the author, the philologist or the theologian, all aspects of the man which we have tried to display in these pages; rather it shows the prophet who had once pointed in his books to the earthly paradise he saw on man's horizon. In the *Concord* he cast a last glance at the ranting conservatives of the old Church and the intransigent zealots of the new. And seeing that the future would bring more religious strife instead of the Utopian meadows of the neo-Platonists, he made his last and most modest plea: 'Tolerate one another.'

In the *Concord* he reviewed for the last time all the issues at stake: images, relics, saints, the mass, confession, fasting, free will and the rest. He still insisted that praying to statues as opposed to using them as aids to prayer was idolatry, and he warned his Catholic friends to beware of it. But he also condemned the Lutheran and Zwinglian burning and pillaging of churches, pleading that images should be tolerated as 'symbols of silent poetry'. He asked that those who appealed with a sincere heart to the saints be left in peace, as should those who prayed not to the saints but only to the Father, the Son and the Holy Ghost.

He pleaded again for the weeding out of superstition, but said that it was more important to abandon intolerance first. He came out strongly against 'the calumniators who twist the language of piety', the 'hot-tempered who shout Heresy! and Burn them at the stake!' At the end of the book he enjoined men for the last time to live in concord, expressing the hope that after a few more years there might yet be a general council in which Catholics and Protestants would come to terms. And he made it clear once and for all, in case anyone still doubted it, that Erasmus of Rotterdam was now far away from all the contesting parties.

It was an innocent book, full of meekness, goodwill and moderation, and perhaps for that very reason it provoked a storm of hatred greater than any of his previous books. Luther attacked it in an open letter, calling Erasmus a heretic and a sceptic who wanted in his blindness to bring Christ and Satan together. The Catholic reaction was even stronger: the University of Louvain condemned the book; the papal nuncio Vergerio sent word from Germany to Rome that Erasmus was now 'Luther's fellow'.

In Spain the treatise, together with a translation of the *Enchiridion*, was pronounced heretical for its tolerance and for its criticism of the Inquisition. Erasmus's old enemy, Edward Lee, now England's ambassador to Spain, published a list of his heresies and sent it to various religious institutions. Hysteria broke out. In some monasteries Erasmus's name came to be used in place of Satan's. A Spanish prelate declared that when reading the works of Erasmus every pious Christian must feel an irresistible urge to strangle the author. A few months later Erasmians all over Spain were rounded up for interrogation and, in many cases, imprisoned. The country which for over a decade had provided some of his most ardent disciples now abandoned him.

The following year he published *On Preparing for Death*. He worked as well on a book on the art of preaching, one he had meant to write for many years. Living on the thresholds of hope and despair, he complained in his letters that his voice had been drowned in the cacophony of the age, and that he expected, as in a Greek tragedy, God's appearance after all human resources had been exhausted. On one occasion he looked through the bundles of his letters and noted that nearly all the correspondents were dead now: Aldus, Ammonio, Andrelini, Bombasius, Colet, Froben, Pirckheimer, Mountjoy, Warham. The previous year Pierre Gilles had died, so much younger than he. 'If Christ favours me, He will soon bring an end to my troubles', he wrote.

In September 1534, after a long and disastrous reign, Pope Clement, 'the seventh of his name, who had no clemency for us', died and was succeeded by Alessandro Cardinal Farnese, Pope Paul III. Erasmus hastened to write a long letter to the new pope, though he had little hope of receiving a reply. He expressed his wishes for the peace of the Church, advising the pope to follow a policy of neutrality and to summon a general council with all the parties participating. Unexpectedly, the pope answered, explaining that he was all for peace and that he counted on Erasmus's aid in securing it. A few weeks later, as a pledge of sincerity, Erasmus was offered a cardinalate. By now he was far too frail for such duties, and in any case he had little hope of living long enough to bring about the council he was advocating. In an amiable letter he declined the offer, referring to his age, his infirmity and his wish to die, as he had lived, a free man.

During the winter and spring he continued to work on Ecclesiastes, published in four large volumes, 'a forest of a work', as he said. It covered a large field of practical theology, was erudite and elegant, but somehow revealed the exhaustion he now felt. Originally he had planned to dedicate the work to his old friend, John Fisher.

After this he left Freiburg for Basle, where things had long since calmed down. It is likely that he wanted to supervise the printing of his Ecclesiastes there and then move on. 'I think that on account of my age, of habit and of what little erudition I possess, I have now got so far that I may safely live anywhere.' He had various plans. One was to visit Besançon again, where he liked the freshness of the air and the good local wines. Another

possibility was the invitation of Queen Mary, to move to
Brussels where the whole court of humanists was eagerly
awaiting him. Ioannes Secundus, the best Latin poet of the age,
had already written a poem to mark his arrival:

> Erasmus comes home with white hair to his country
> Verity and Noblesse return with him to us . . .

A few days after his arrival in Basle he learnt of the beheading
of Fisher and More. At first he refused to believe the news,
which was generally doubted in Europe (even Luther discredited
it for a while). But then he received a detailed account from
Chapuys, the imperial ambassador in London.

'In More I seem to have died, so much did we have one soul',
he wrote in August 1535. Shortly afterwards he published a
letter on the death of both men. It purported to be the work of
one Guglielmus Nucerinus, but was in all probability written
by Cognatus under Erasmus's direction. After an account of the
trial and execution, taken from eye-witness sources, and a
description of the lives and virtues of the two victims, the
writer asserted that he would have liked to persuade the king
to be less severe towards the lights of England. At the same
time, he continued, he would have urged More and Fisher not
to defy the storm, 'for time heals many things which the power
of no king can ever mend'. Erasmus included a commemoration
of Fisher's death in the preface to Ecclesiastes. His friends and
readers had expected much more from the great adversary of
injustice: a violent attack on Henry VIII, or at least a few harsh
words.

We have no way of knowing why Erasmus reacted as he did.
He was still capable of carrying on his habitual work, but it
may be that the illness which was soon to kill him, or perhaps
simply the calcifying effects of old age, had rendered his brain
incapable of grasping fully this sudden and unexpected turn of
events. Or perhaps, even, it was the mute and petulant anger of
an old man against a friend who had refused to heed his good
advice, who had 'mixed himself in politics' and sacrificed himself for that same medieval Church they had once hoped to

change. On the other hand we might equally well attribute his strange silence to the peculiarly realistic way in which he looked at the world, to his acquiescence to the will of God, to his expressed conviction that words can in no wise revive the dead, or to the nearly Goethean equilibrium with which his hypochondriacal spirit now faced death – perhaps More's and Fisher's as well as his own.

Whatever his motives, they caused no small degree of misunderstanding and harm. A few decades later More was regarded as a Catholic martyr and his name began to be wielded as a tool of propaganda by the Catholics, though the Church was to wait four centuries before canonizing him. At the same time, Erasmus, condemned by the Council of Trent, was called a traitor to the Church and a pillar of Protestantism.

In the editions of More's works which were published on the Continent his correspondence with Erasmus was omitted; in the preface their friendship was played down and commentaries were written to the effect that the two men had become estranged in the 1520s. Some of these tales are still widely believed, though there is not the slightest evidence to support any of them in their works or letters or in any documents originating during their lifetime.

From their first meeting in 1499 Erasmus and More had agreed in their basic aims: the reconstruction of society and Church through the spread of humanism. They had also disagreed from the first in many things: Erasmus had already attacked Aquinas in his *Antibarbari*, while More held the theologian in esteem; Erasmus was trying desperately to free himself from his monastic vows, and More was considering becoming a monk. But both men were 'made for friendship', as Erasmus said of More, and in the warmth of their relationship they respected in one another even those ideas they could not share.

Erasmus never ceased to praise More as the embodiment of the ideal humanist layman, and he was proud of their friendship to the point of boasting about it. He also seems to have been aware that More was the deeper and more strikingly original thinker. More, on the other hand, accepted from the first the fact that it was Erasmus who was destined to lead the humanist movement, not he. They continued to defend one another against their common enemies, even when More came out in favour of burning heretics in his *Dialogue Concerning Heretics* and repented of his earlier criticisms of abuses within the Church.

Erasmus's personality, lacking More's imaginative powers, was admittedly less attractive, less complex and by no means as remarkable. Yet his thinking was closer to the real needs of the time and further away from its prejudices (though in his *Utopia* More came close to bridging this gap between them). Both lived lives of inner conflict and paradox. The man who a few years earlier had been alarmed by his king's blind submission to the papacy, now died to uphold the rights of that same papacy. There is perhaps a certain irony in the fact that he who gave Utopian socialism its name should have become a Catholic saint. Erasmus's own end, however, was hardly less ironical, for he was considered the forerunner of Protestantism, was attacked by Luther and defended by the pope; and now he was awaiting his death in Basle – a Catholic seeking refuge in a Protestant stronghold.

Hieronymus Froben, son and heir of Johannes, built a large and beautiful room for Erasmus in his own house, '*zum Luft*', and prepared quarters nearby for his servant and secretary. Erasmus immediately settled down to work, continuing the series on patristic literature which he had begun in 1516: the much neg- lected and pre-eminently Christian undertaking for which neither his contemporaries nor posterity was to show him gratitude.

In 1516 he had started with the nine enormous volumes of St Jerome and then continued with Cyprian (1520), Arnobius (1522), Hilary (1523), Irenaeus (1526) and Ambrose (1527) and had completed the eleven volumes of Augustine by the time he left Basle for Freiburg. In Freiburg he added to the series Lactantius (1529), Chrysostom (1530), Alger (1530), Basil (1532) and Haymo (1533). During the last year of his life he began the edition of Origen, but was not to complete it. He wrote a beautiful preface to Origen, paying his last homage to the neo-Platonist Church Father whom he had inherited as his guiding light from Pico della Mirandola before the beginning of the century.

Towards the end of 1535 he suddenly remembered that the customs official, Christopher Eschenfelder, whom he had met in 1518 at Boppard-am-Rhein, had long ago requested him to dedicate the paraphrase of a certain psalm to him. Erasmus had forgotten which one it was, but he chose Psalm 14, adding to it a treatise, *On the Purity of the Church*. He wrote this in 1536, while in great pain. The treatise was immediately published, bearing a dedication 'To the publican, Christoforus Cinicampus'.

In February he made slight changes in his will, written some nine years before. He had long since sold his library to a Polish nobleman by the name of Lasko, on the condition that the books would not be turned over until his death. The gifts he had received from the rulers of Europe were to be left to his remaining friends: the beautiful goblet presented to him by Alexander Stuart was to go to Beatus Rhenanus, the carnelian ring to the printer Amerbach. He left a considerable sum of money to his devoted servant-pupils Quirinus Talesius and Carl Utenhove, and to his querulous housekeeper Margarethe, to whose Xantippe, as he said, he played Socrates. Nor did he forget the poor, leaving sums of money for impoverished students and for girls without dowries. Apart from this there was not much more than his wardrobe: a number of black, brown and green robes lined with fur, waistcoats of silk and damask and scarlet shirts.

During the spring bad news continued to come in: in Spain the persecution of the Erasmians went on unabated, Charles V was preparing for war with France and the pope's proposals for negotiation were flatly rejected by Luther. Erasmus was still toying with the idea of accepting the invitation of Queen Mary and leaving Basle. 'If only Brabant were nearer', he lamented on 28 June 1536. He had a fortnight to live.

During the last two weeks of his life he was forced to stay in bed, but even then he continued dictating to his secretary as long as his strength lasted. On 6 July, exactly one year after the execution of More, he received the last sacraments, fully conscious and aware that death was near. He lingered five days longer, and on the last day his friends assembled around the bed, heard him murmur incessantly: '*Domine, libera me! Domine, miserere mei!*' His last words, according to Beatus Rhenanus, were, touchingly and ironically, in the Dutch of his childhood: '*Lieve God*'.

The funeral was much more splendid than that which Erasmus had asked for in his will. Philipp Melanchthon, having been about to visit him in Basle, was inconsolable. Luther remained true to form and spread it abroad that Erasmus had died 'without Cross and without God'. Johannes Faber and Cardinal Campeggio put forward proposals for his beatification. Julius Caesar Scaliger, formerly one of Erasmus's most outspoken enemies, now composed a poem in which he lamented having denied himself the friendship of his greatest contemporary. The most eloquently simple lines, however, were probably those of Paulus Jovius:

He passed away among the Helvetians, in Basle, in the seventieth [*sic*] year of his life, while Emperor Charles invaded Provence and began his war against the king of the French.

NORTH

SEA

SCOTLAND

ENGLAND

London

KINGDOM
OF
DENMARK

HOLSTEIN

BREMEN

POMERANIA

MECKLENBURG

Amsterdam
Rotterdam

NETHERLANDS

MÜNSTER

BRUNSWICK

BRANDENBURG

POLAND

Antwerp
Brussels

LIEGE

Rhine

Cologne

HESSE

SAXONY

SILESIA

THE

LUXEMBURG

EMPIRE

K. OF

Prague

Paris

L'UPPER
PALATINATE

BOHEMIA

PALATINATE

FRANCE

BURGUNDY

LORRAINE

Strasburg

Rhine
BADEN
WÜRTEM-
BERG

MORAVIA

Dijon

FREE COUNTY
OF BURGUNDY

BAVARIA

Munich

AUSTRIA

Vienna

Basel

SWISS
CONFEDERATION

Salzburg

Lyons

Geneva

SAVOY

TYROL

CARINTHIA

HUNGARY

Avignon

MILAN

VENETIAN

CARNIOLA

EXTENT OF TURKISH
INCURSION INTO EUROPE

Genoa

REPUBLIC

DALMATIA

SPAIN

Florence

PAPAL
STATES

Rome

NAPLES

Naples

EDGAR HOLLOWAY

SICILY

0   100   200   300 MILES

0   100   200   300 K.M.

Western Europe, *c.* 1547

Epilogue

Notwithstanding the wealth of material on Erasmus's life and times, the history of his legacy was still largely ignored until as late as 1930. Once its presence as an undercurrent in the past was surmised, however, writers ran the danger of finding it everywhere. After his death Erasmus, who had stood out so clearly against the background of his own time, virtually disappeared; and when he was later resurrected it was not as one but as several men. After 1680 it was Erasmus the prophet and the author of the *Enchiridion* who came to light. By 1750 he was the satirist, a pillar of the Enlightenment who, with a sneering smile on his thin lips, resembled no one so much as Voltaire.

As for the *philosophia Christi*, it vanished for all practical purposes a few decades after its author's death. It reappeared after 1700 in the Reformed and Lutheran Churches and, after 1900, in the Catholic Church; it remains in both but is, one is tempted to add, largely unrecognized for what it is.

There are obvious parallels between the fate of Erasmus's thought and that of humanism itself; both stories, unfortunately, have yet to be written. There are in fact only three works of distinction which are helpful in tracing the Erasmian heritage through nearly four and a half centuries since his death. They are the regrettably short essay of W. Kaegi, *Erasmus und das 18te Jahrhundert* (1936); *Erasme et l'Espagne* (1937) by M. Bataillon; and *Humanism and Reformation Politics in the Reigns of Henry VIII and Edward VI* (1965) by J. K. McConica. McConica's work is the first to discuss humanism not as a local but as a European movement; it would be hard to praise its general evaluation of Erasmus highly enough. All three monographs, however, cover only a fraction of the history of humanism, and though it has not of course been the intended purpose of the present book to fill this gap, nevertheless, a few remarks on the subsequent fate of Erasmus's heritage may not be out of place.

During the last years of his life Erasmus often prophesied that wars and massacres would come after his death, and that his enemies were lying in wait to expunge his memory. Wars and massacres did indeed follow, but erasing his memory proved to be a larger task than his enemies had counted on. At least 750,000 copies of his books, not including his translation of the New Testament, were sold during his lifetime. There was scarcely a library which did not have several of them on its shelves. In 1540 Froben undertook to publish his *Collected Works* in nine volumes, while separate printings of the *Adagia*, the *Colloquia* and the *Enchiridion* appeared in many parts of Europe – the *Folly*, oddly enough, was no longer very popular. In the same year a wooden statue of Erasmus was erected before his alleged birthplace in Rotterdam (probably the house of his grandparents). During the Spanish occupation of the Low Countries it was destroyed by the mercenaries of the duke of Alba. At that time his books were burned, and those who possessed them were often imprisoned and tortured.

Humanists who knew or who were in correspondence with Erasmus remained an exclusive intellectual fraternity after his death, extending from Spain to Lithuania. Rabelais, his most obstreperous disciple, and Montaigne, one of the most sceptical, both praised him highly and did much to sustain his memory. Clément Marot translated parts of the *Colloquia* into French verse. The best French poet of the sixteenth century, Pierre de Ronsard, echoed Erasmus's views on peace and tolerance. Faber, bishop of Vienna, did his best to continue the work Erasmus had begun, and along with Pflug, Wicelius, Pistorius and Cassander, he still attempted to mediate between Catholics and Protestants. Pflug published his *Three Dialogues on Religion,* exhorting Catholics, Lutherans, Zwinglians and Calvinists to unite, to keep only the doctrines of Christ and to leave the rest, especially hatred, by the wayside. Cassander, occupying the newly-established chair of humanities at Louvain, avenged Erasmus there by preaching tolerance from his cathedra.

Even new forces arrived on the scene: in Basle the humanist Castillo advised his readers to disregard the dogmatism of both sides; and another refugee from Italy, Mino Celsi, composed an eloquent defence of heresy, referring repeatedly to 'the great Erasmus, never praised highly enough'. There were even a few full-scale victories. In Poland, for example, humanism remained firmly entrenched for many decades. The previously-mentioned Transylvanian Diet of Torda in 1554 codified, for the first time anywhere, the Erasmian conception of religious freedom. The ideas of Erasmus also made themselves felt within the Henrician Church. The precepts of the *philosophia Christi* arrived at an opportune moment for the advisers of Henry VIII, who were searching for a formula differing from both Roman orthodoxy and the radicalism of Lutheran heterodoxy. Erasmian exegesis flourished during the reign of Edward VI, and to a lesser extent under Mary and even Elizabeth; what Erasmus would have thought of the view of the English Church is another question.

Catastrophe came with the Council of Trent. There was an Erasmian contingent at the session of 1546, and its members urged the acceptance of Erasmus's New Testament as the official translation. Cardinal Quinones, Bishop Pflug of Naumburg, Grawe of Vienna and Dudith of Pécs proposed that the whole of Erasmus's theological thought should be adopted. The majority, however, voted in favour of the *Vulgate*, and Erasmus's translation was condemned as heretical. At a later session of the council Pope Paul IV branded Erasmus 'the leader of all heretics' and wanted his books burned. Surprisingly, this proposal was voted down by the assembled bishops.

The Council of Trent ended any lingering hopes of a reconciliation of Catholics and Protestants, and it signed the death warrant of the *philosophia Christi* throughout most of Europe. Wicelius, still pleading for tolerance, was called 'the stinking

cadaver of a bygone age'; Cassander was called 'a dirty peace-
monger' and 'an old fool who still dreams of Christian unity'.
In the sixth, seventh and eighth decades of the century – the
reigns of Mary in England, Philip II in Spain, the last of the
Valois in France, Calvin's theocratic reign of terror in Geneva
and the freshly-blooded Inquisition of Paul IV – the moderate
party slowly withered and died. Soon there were few left who
could remember the time when quite different modes of reform
had been advocated within the Church.

Catholic Poland, and two new countries, the Protestant dukedom of Transylvania and the republic of the United Provinces
of the Netherlands, alone refused to join in the universal rule of
intolerance. According to Huizinga, William of Orange was an
Erasmian, and as such was far above religious hatred. Most of
his advisers were liberal humanists, devoid of Calvinist fanaticism. No aristocracy, says Huizinga, except that of Venice, has
ever ruled so long and so well and with so little violence as those
Dutch magistrates. It is in any case certain that they were
determined enough to withstand the Protestant pastors who
pestered them with their prejudices and demands for the codification of bigotry. Thus the execution of witches and heretics
ceased in the Netherlands hundreds of years earlier than anywhere else in Europe. The symbol of all this (for it was taken as
such) was the famous *brazen image* of Erasmus in Rotterdam,
which showed him walking in a long gown, reading a bulky
codex.

In February 1600 the seventeenth century got off to a portentous start with the burning of Giordano Bruno on the Campo
dei Fiori in Rome before a crowd of elated priests and applaud-
ing nuns. After this came the Thirty Years War, fought for a
variety of motives under the pretext of religion. Erasmus's books
were still widely read, but not as they once were as guides in
human affairs. Now they were merely a source of consolation.
During the Thirty Years War the *Enchiridion* and *The Lament of
Peace* were continually printed in various languages. The most
famous edition was that brought out in Basle in 1634, entitled:
Lament of Peace, Hunted Down and Expelled from Every Quarter,

written by Erasmus of Rotterdam in the Latin Language and put into German by a Lover of Peace. The translator no doubt had his reasons for remaining anonymous.

The rebirth of Erasmianism coincided with that of the European conscience after 1680, when the philosophies of Descartes, Spinoza, Locke and Leibnitz and the new discoveries, especially in mathematics, engendered a more reasonable view of nature, society and the meaning of life. A broader, less parochial and more historically-oriented way of thinking made the religious quarrels of the past and the narrow path of piety stale on the European palate. For the time being the bitter memories of massacres and war resulted in a longing for moral regeneration, tolerance, peace and a more humane perception of religion. In many respects it was the beginning of the sixteenth century all over again. Erasmian fermentation was taking place in the movements of the age: German pietism, the 'Platonist Renaissance' in England and the Enlightenment.

The relation of Erasmus to his readers now underwent a change. For more than a century his personality had been obscured to the point that he had become a mere phantom. Now interest in his life and activity was regenerated, and instead of a long-dead writer he was thought of as a brother-in-arms. A contemporary poet, significantly, put these words into his mouth: 'I was writing in darkness, time was my hope.' This fresh attitude can be felt in Bayle's essay, which ends with the laconic sentence: 'It would be superfluous to remark that he was one of the greatest men ever seen in the Republic of Letters: it is a truth little contested.'

To mark the 'resurrection of Erasmus' a splendid edition of the *Folly* was published in Basle in 1676. In Oxford a new English translation appeared in 1683, followed by the monumental ten-volume edition of the *Collected Works* in Leyden, prepared for the press in 1703 by the Swiss J. LeClerc, a rebel within the Reformed Church.

The so-called Arminian rebellion against predestination 'and the other destitute subtleties of Calvin' inside the Reformed Church was lead by H. Gropius. Its aims were practical piety and a gentler view of God and man, 'under the good auspices of our captains St Paul and Desiderius Erasmus'. The theologians Turretini in Geneva and Werenfels in Basle started a movement for the unification of the Protestant churches and for the abandonment of dogmas and catechisms. 'Among Biblical scholars', wrote the theologian Usteri, 'Erasmus and Gropius occupy first place.' The Swiss Platonist Wegelin published a dialogue in which Luther and Erasmus discuss free will in the afterworld, the humanist driving the reformer to the wall with his superior arguments.

Such was the general trend of the time. Only the Catholic Church refused to yield to it, though it showed signs of wavering. In his *Diarium italicum* of 1702, the French traveller Bernard de Montfaucon described his visit to a monastery near Venice. He was shown the library in which, above the shelves on the right, were the statues of Catholic theologians, and above those on the left famous heretics. The monks told Montfaucon that Erasmus's statue was moved from time to time: no one seemed to know to which category he belonged.

Erasmus's influence on the Enlightenment is well known. Many of his ideas triumphed and became public property. This meant, among other things, that his books were thoroughly pilfered, and their contents incorporated into the ideas and slogans of the Enlightenment. Many of them were no longer connected with his name. Still, the leaders of the Enlightenment were not stinting in their praise. Diderot, for example, wrote: 'In [Europe] we are indebted to him principally for the rebirth of the sciences, criticism and taste of antiquity.' And Voltaire wrote: 'Erasmus, though he was a monk for a long time, or rather because he had been one, in most of his writings heaped on the monks an amount of ridicule so great that they will never recover from it.' In his *Dialogue Between Lucian, Erasmus and Rabelais in the Elysian Fields* he depicted Erasmus as the sort of man who could have written the *Folly*, but never the *Enchiridion*. Yet he was sensitive enough to appreciate the difficulties the humanist had had in maintaining his stand during the Reformation, and he characterized him beautifully in the dialogue by

making him say: 'The greatest pleasure is to show the way to
our friends who have lost it.'

The nineteenth century, which looked upon Erasmus with
respect, seems to have had no great understanding of him – with
the notable exception of Renan. Nietzsche politely listed him,
together with Petrarch and Voltaire, among the 'three great
banners of enlightenment'. In general he was regarded by the
last century as an eminent personage who, for vague and largely
undisclosed reasons, ought to be esteemed. Apart from a few
dissertations on points of detail, the nineteenth century produced
no important books on him at all. Froude's work is, in spite of
its fame, virtually useless; the essays of Durard du Lair and L.
Amiel represent him as a free-thinker and an atheist. All this
was probably caused by the view, once generally accepted by
historians (after Sismondi, and with the exception of Burckhardt), that the Renaissance was a play of two acts: at the
beginning the humanists arrived and prepared the ground for
the reformers by liberating the human mind; in the second act
the reformers appeared, dismissed the humanists and successfully
liberated the soul. The curtain dropped, presumably, to the
cheering of the multitudes.

The persistent presence of humanism in our own time is a
complicated and controversial affair. During the past 80 years
something resembling the mentality of the humanists of former
days has reappeared. The latter-day humanists, a loosely knit
fraternity, are strikingly similar in their stand to their fifteenth-
century predecessors. They have generally taken a definite
position in all the social, moral and political questions of our
time, retaining, *mutatis mutandis*, many of Erasmus's ideas and
even many of his traits.

Erasmus's pacifism, for example, continues to survive in them
almost in its original form, and so do his tolerance and his belief
that man can be changed by education and led aright by reason,
and that international conferences, 'benefiting from the advice
of learned men', can restrain the self-destructive impulses of

mankind. Modern humanism has also retained Erasmus's contempt for ideological quarrels and, perhaps above all, his belief that man is his own end and not a means – be it to the ends of totalitarian dictatorship or those of technocracy.

Thus humanism remains with us still, and is still the peculiarly European phenomenon that it was in Erasmus's time. The names of those who have embodied it most outstandingly – men such as France, Russell, Unamuno, Mann, Madariaga, Camus and Moravia, to mention only a few – serve to show that it still flourishes chiefly in those lands in which it first appeared and developed. As an attitude towards man and his predicament it is still allied as strongly as ever to Erasmus. Those who fail to grasp the significance of this enduring link stand little chance of understanding Erasmus himself.

Like the former statue in Rotterdam, Erasmus's tomb in Basle has become something of a shrine for those who pay allegiance to him. It was there that the leaders of French and German socialism, Jaurès and Bebel, met to pledge solidarity and peace shortly before World War I. A quarter of a century later, on the four-hundredth anniversary of Erasmus's death in 1936, scholars and writers from all over Europe gathered in Basle to commemorate the event. It was on this occasion that Huizinga reminded those present in the shadow of two totalitarian dictatorships that Erasmian tolerance and pacifism were still the only hope of civilization. On the same occasion Georges Duhamel, foreseeing the impending cataclysm, concluded simply 'Maître Erasme, priez pour nous!'

Table of Events

1306   Birth of Petrarch (Francesco Petrarca), poet, author, generally considered father of modern humanism (d. 1374)

1331   Birth of Colluccio Salutati, chancellor of the Florentine Republic, disciple of Petrarch; upheld the primacy of will and a philosophy based on Socrates, Christ, St Francis of Assisi as against scholastic views (d. 1406)

1369   Birth of Leonardo Bruni d'Arezzo, disciple of Salutati, author, humanist, admirer of Roman ethics for its ability to resolve thought into concrete concepts for benefit of community; translator of Aristotle's *Poetics* (d. 1444)

1380   Birth of Gianfrancesco Poggio Bracciolini, humanist, author, philologist, rediscoverer of 'lost' manuscripts of classics; author of *Facetiae*, immortal collection of ribald anecdotes (d. 1459)

From about 1400   Famous school of Vittorino da Feltre (1373–1446) in Mantua

15th century   Foundation of more universities than during previous or following 200 years; learning ceases to be monopoly of clergy; new private libraries besides old libraries possessed only by institutions; general interest in classical antiquity in Northern Italy; education becomes central problem of society; this trend spreads all over Europe in second half of century

1405   Birth of Aeneas Sylvius Piccolomini, poet laureate, humanist, author, diplomat, antipapal legate to Emperor Frederick III, bishop of Trieste, archbishop of Siena, from 1458 Pope Pius II; author of best autobiography of fifteenth century (d. 1464)

1407	Birth of Lorenzo di Valla, humanist, philologist; denied the claim of the Church to secular power and wealth, wrote brilliant analysis of Latin style, was first to exert textual criticism on the *Vulgate* (d. 1457)
1433	Birth of Marsilio Ficino, humanist, theologian, translator of Plato
from 1440 (*circa*)	Platonic Academy in Florence
1449	Birth of Lorenzo de' Medici
1450 (*circa*)	Papal Library (later: Vatican Library) founded by Pope Nicholas V
from 1450 (*circa*)	Invention of printing from movable type reaches most countries and major cities in Europe in second half of century
1451	Birth of Christopher Columbus and of Amerigo Vespucci
1452	Birth of Leonardo da Vinci and of Girolamo Savonarola
1453	Constantinople captured by the Turks
1454	Birth of Angelo Poliziano, poet, humanist, one of the leading spirits among Florentine Platonists
1455	Birth of Johannes Reuchlin and of Jacques Lefèvre d'Étaples, humanists
1458	Aeneas Sylvius, humanist, ascends papal throne as Pius II
1460	Birth of Quentin Matsys
1462	Birth of Pietro Pomponazzi, humanist, author of *De Incantationibus* and of *De Fato* (d. 1525)
1463	Birth of Giovanni Pico della Mirandola, Florentine humanist, hero of Erasmus; Louis XI, king of France
1464	Pope Pius II dies in Ancona, from where he intended to lead a crusade against Turks
1465	Charles the Bold, heir of Burgundian throne, organizes league of French princes against France; Cosimo de' Medici dies
1466	Birth of John Colet
1467	Second war begins between Charles the Bold and Louis XI

1469	Birth of Niccolò Machiavelli; Lorenzo de' Medici becomes prince of Florence
1470	Birth of Pietro Bembo, poet, humanist, later bishop of Bergamo and cardinal under Paul III
1471	Birth of Albrecht Dürer
1472	New war begins between Charles the Bold of Burgundy and Louis XI of France
1473	Birth of Nicholas Copernicus
1475	Birth of Michelangelo Buonarrotti
1477	Birth of Jacopo Sadoleto, humanist, Erasmian, secretary to Pope Leo X, cardinal; Charles the Bold slain in battle of Nancy
1478	Birth of Thomas More; Marsilio Ficino publishes his *Theologia Platonica* in Florence
1480 (*circa*)	National Library in Paris
1483	Birth of Martin Luther; birth of Julius Caesar Scaliger, literary historian
1484	Birth of Ulrich Zwingli; first complete editions of Plato's works in Latin published in Florence; Pope Innocent VIII promulgates bull against witches
1485	Birth of Beatus Rhenanus, humanist, Erasmus's first biographer
1488	Giovanni Pico della Mirandola proclaims his Nine-Hundred Theses in Rome; intends to unite all philosophical and theological schools, is accused of heresy; birth of Ulrich von Hutten
1490 (?)	Birth of François Rabelais; (?) beginning of Aldine Press in Venice
1492	Granada, last stronghold of Moors, taken by Spanish; Lorenzo de' Medici dies in Florence, deaths of Emperor Frederick III in Vienna, Pope Innocent VIII in Rome; Maximilian I becomes emperor, Rodrigo Cardinal Borgia elected Pope Alexander VI
1493	Birth of Philippus Aureolus Theophrastus Paracelsus von Hohenheim, physician, Erasmus's doctor
1494	Both Giovanni Pico della Mirandola and Angelo Poliziano die in Florence; Charles VIII of France invades Italy;

LIFE OF ERASMUS

1469?	Erasmus born on 27 October, probably in Gouda
1469?–78?	Childhood in Gouda; attends elementary school from 1473
1478?–83?	Attends school of the Brethren of the Common Life at Deventer; humanism reaches Deventer in person of Agricola
1483?	Erasmus's mother dies in Deventer; Erasmus returns to Gouda, where his father dies soon after; forced by his guardians to attend another school
1483?–86	Attends school of the Brethren at 's Hertogenbosch
1486	Becomes a novice in the Augustinian monastery at Steyn near Gouda
1486–93?	Takes monastic vows (1487); prepares for holy orders; studies the classics, has hopes of becoming a poet; ordained a priest by the bishop of Utrecht (25 April 1492)
1492 or 1493	Leaves monastery to enter the service of Henri of Bergen, bishop of Cambray
1492?–95	Travels as a member of bishop's entourage; obtains the bishop's leave to study theology; travels to Paris (autumn 1495)

1494 (cont.)	Girolamo Savonarola installs theocratic rule in Florence; Sebastian Brant's *Narrenschiff* (Ship of Fools) published in Basle
1497	Birth of Hans Holbein
1498	Girolamo Savonarola condemned to death and executed in Florence
1499	Marsilio Ficino, humanist, translator of Plato, dies in Florence; Louis XII's first campaign against the dukedom of Milan
1500	Second campaign of Louis XII of France against the dukedom of Milan; Caesare Borgia, Captain of the Church fights princes of Central Italy
1503	Pope Alexander VI dies; after short pontificate of Pius III. Giulio Cardinal della Rovere elected as Pope Julius II
1506	Pope Julius II begins series of Italian wars, takes Perugia and Bologna
1508	Pope Julius II, Emperor Maximilian, Louis XII of France, Ferdinand of Spain and Vladislas II of Hungary join the League of Cambray against the Venetian Republic
1509	Birth of Jean Calvin; death of Henry VII; humanists hope for a liberal and enlightened reign of Henry VIII; Pope Julius II, now in alliance with Venice and Ferdinand of Spain, attacks Ferrara, French protectorate in Italy
1510	Pope Julius II fights French armies in Italy, loses Bologna; Turks capture Rhodes
1511	Birth of Michael Servetus, theologian, reformer, victim of Calvin in 1553
1512	French victory over Julius II and Spanish allies at Ravenna; French occupy the Romagna, lose it and nearly all Italian

1495–99	First stay in Paris; associates with Gaguin, desires to become a humanist; studies theology, makes his living as a tutor; visits Bergen during summers of 1496 and 1497: travels to Holland in March 1499	
1499	First visit to England; with More in London; with Colet at Oxford; Christmas in London	
1500–02	Second stay in Paris; returns in February 1500; second half of year spent in Orleans; back in Paris December 1500; studies Greek, earns a measure of fame; last visit to Holland (spring 1501); visits Tournehem and St Omer, associates with Vitrier (autumn, 1501)	ADAGIA
1502–04	First stay in Louvain, translates Greek authors	ENCHIRIDION
1504–05	Third stay in Paris; little information on Erasmus during this period	
1505–06	Year in London with More and Colet	
1506	Departure for Italy (July); Paris, Turin, Florence; winter in Bologna	
1507–08	Leaves Bologna for Venice (late in 1507); works there with the printer Aldus, associates with Bembo, Aleandro; leaves Venice (autumn, 1508); visits Padua, Ferrara, Siena	
1509	He spends winter in Siena with his pupil Alexander Stuart; Aldine edition of *Adagia* brings fame all over Italy; goes in spring to Rome, associates with humanists, bishops; leaves for England in July	
1509–14	Five years in England; no information on Erasmus from his arrival until spring, 1511, when he visits Paris to publish *Folly*; lectures on divinity in Cambridge from August 1511 to January 1514; revises there	IN PRAISE OF FOLLY A METHOD OF STUDY ON FLUENCY

1512 (cont.)	possessions few months later; Julius occupies Bologna once more
1513	Julius II dies; Giovanni Cardinal de' Medici becomes Pope Leo X, follows policy of peace and reconciliation; England at war with Scotland and France; Battle of Flodden
1514	England concludes peace with France and Scotland
1515	*Epistolae Obscurorum Virorum* published in Mainz
1517	More's *Utopia* published in Antwerp; Martin Luther proclaims his ninety-five theses in Wittenberg
1519	John Colet dies; Charles V Holy Roman emperor (until abdication in 1556)
1520	Luther's *On the Babylonian Captivity of the Church* published
1521	Long war between the Empire and France begins; Luther excommunicated by Pope Leo X, condemned by Diet of Worms; persecution of Lutherans begins
1522	Johannes Reuchlin, humanist, dies; Leo X succeeded by Hadrian VI
1523	Ulrich von Hutten dies, Pope Hadrian VI dies; Giulio Cardinal de' Medici becomes Pope Clement VII
1524	German Peasant Revolt; Luther condemns the Peasants; Pope Clement VII in secret alliance with France and Turks against the Empire
1525	France loses Battle of Pavia, King Francis I captured by Charles V
1526	Suleiman the Magnificent defeats Hungarian army at Mohács, country lost to Turks; German Diet of Speyer orders so-called 'recess', not unfavourable for Lutherans
1527	Sack of Rome by Imperial armies

1509–14 (cont.)	Lily's Grammar for Colet, translates classics, writes educational works, studies Greek New Testament and St Jerome; spends first half of 1514 in London	JULIUS SHUT OUT
1514–16	First stay in Basle; leaves London in summer, 1514; voyage along the Rhine to Basle a triumph; is seen as leader of humanists, light of theology, herald of a Golden Age; arrives in Basle August 1514, works there at Froben's press preparing edition of New Testament; writes educational works and polemics against war; short visit to England in April 1515; journey to the Netherlands in spring of 1516, stays with Pierre Gilles in Antwerp; short trip to England in summer	WAR IS SWEET TO THE IN-EXPERIENCED NEW TESTA-MENT EDITION ON THE EDU-CATION OF A CHRISTIAN PRINCE
1517	Spends first half of year in Antwerp; last visit to England in spring, moves in July to Louvain	LAMENT OF PEACE
1517–21	Second stay in Louvain; disputes with theologians; welcomes Luther's theses but has reservations; sees More in Bruges, Henry VIII in Calais (summer, 1520); tries to help Luther in Cologne (November 1520), where Frederick the Wise seeks his advice; is blackmailed by Catholics and Lutherans alike to take their side; flees theologians of Louvain in October 1521	ON LETTER WRITING
1521–29	Long stay in Basle; tries to mediate between warring orthodoxies, preaches tolerance and peace, continues educational work, edits Church Fathers; controversy with Hutten in 1523; open break with Luther in 1524; attacks Holy Inquisition in 1527; attacks neo-paganism and rhetorical degeneration of humanist contemporaries in 1528; mediates between Catholics and Zwinglians in Basle until Zwinglians take over city by force, when he emigrates to Freiburg (April 1529)	A DISCUSSION ON FREE WILL CICERONIANUS

1529   Treaties of Cambray and Barcelona restore peace between
                Empire and France for few years; Turkish armies ravage
                Lower Austria; recess of Speyer revoked by German Diet;
                German Catholics and Protestants preparing for civil war;
                open break between Luther and Zwingli at Marburg;
                persecution of Zwinglians and Anabaptists by Lutherans
                and Catholics alike; Erasmus's French translator, Berquin,
                burned at the stake; Sir Thomas More becomes lord
                chancellor, publishes *Dialogue Concerning Heretics*

1530 (*circa*) Persecution of Erasmians in Spain

1531   Cities of Basle and Zürich lose war with Swiss Confedera-
                tion, Ulrich Zwingli slain at Kappel; Henry VIII declares
                'royal supremacy'

1532   Sir Thomas More resigns the chancellorship

1533   First volume of Rabelais's *Pantagruel* published in Lyons;
                Francesco Pico, humanist, murdered by his nephew in
                Mirandola

1534   Alessandro Cardinal Farnese becomes Pope Paul III, offers
                Erasmus cardinal's hat

1535   Execution of Sir Thomas More and Bishop John Fisher

1536   New war between Empire and France begins; Calvin pub-
                lishes *Institutio Religionis Christianae*; Jacques Lefevre
                d'Étaples dies

1539   Religious war in Germany

1540   Wooden statue of Erasmus erected before his alleged birth-
                house in Rotterdam; first volumes of Erasmus's *Collected
                Works* published by Froben in Basle

1529–35   Six years in Freiburg; Erasmus ailing; THE EDUCA-
writes 'On Sweet Concord of the Church', TION OF BOYS
his conciliatory attitude infuriates Catholic
and Protestant; desires Christian unity as
deterrent against Turks; continues to edit
Church Fathers

1535–36   Last year in Basle
12 July   Death of Erasmus at Basle
1536

Bibliography

AGRICOLA, RUDOLF, *Lucubrationes*, ed. Alardus, Cologne, 1539

ALLEN, PERCY S., *The Age of Erasmus*, Oxford, 1914

—— *Erasmus, Lectures and Wayfaring Sketches*, Oxford, 1934

ANGELERI, C., *Il problema religioso del Rinascimento*, Florence, 1963

BATAILLON, M., *Erasme et l'Espagne*, Paris, 1937

BAYLE, PIERRE, *Dictionnaire historique et critique*, Paris, 1702

BERGER, S., *La Bible au seizième siècle*, Paris, 1879

BERNOULLI, CH., *Biographia magni Erasmi*, Basle, 1797

BLUDAU, A., *Die Biebelübersetzung des Erasmus, etc.*, Leipzig, 1902

BORNKAM, H., *Melanchthon*, Lüneburg, 1947

—— *Luther im Spiegel der deutschen Geschichte*, Heidelberg, 1955

BROD, MAX, *Johannes Reuchlin und sein Kampf*, Hamburg, 1966

BRUNI D'AREZZO, LEONARDO, *Vita de Messer Francesco Petrarca*, Florence, 1847

BURCKHARDT, JAKOB, *Die Kultur der Renaissance in Italien*, ed. Phaidon, Vienna, n.d.

BURIGNI, ABBÉ J. L. DE, *Vie d'Erasme*, Paris, 1757

BUXTORF-FALKEISEN, CARL, *Baslerische Stadt und Landesgeschichte des 16. Jahrhunderts*, Basle, 1866

CAMERARIUS, JOACHIM, *Melanchthon*, Cologne, 1566

Caroli ducis Burgundiae, De laudibus, De morte, etc., chroniques relatives à l'histoire de la Belgique sous la domination des ducs de Bourgogne, Brussels, 1873

CELSI, MINO, *In haereticis*, 2 vols., Christlingau, 1577

Charles Quint et son temps, ed. Centre Nationale de la Recherche Scientifique, Paris, 1959

COLET, JOHN (transl. and ed. by J. H. Lupton), *On the Sacraments of the Church*, London, 1867

—— *On the Hierarchies of Dionysius*, London, 1869

—— *Lectures on Romans*, London, 1873

—— *Lectures on I Corinthians*, London, 1874

COMMINES, PHILIPPE DE, *Mémoires*, ed. de Mandrot, 2 vols., Paris, 1901–03

CORSI, GIOVANNI, *Vita di Marsilio Ficino*, Lucca, 1722

CROSSENSIS, BARTHOLOMAEUS, *Oratio de Erasmo Roterodamo*, Wittenberg, 1557

DERMENGHEM, E., *Thomas Morus et les Utopistes de la Renaissance*, Paris, 1927

DUHAMEL, GEORGES, *Erasme ou le spectateur pur*, Paris, 1937

DUMBAR, G., *Analecta Daventria*, Deventer, 1719

DÜRER, ALBRECHT, *Schriftlicher Nachlass*, Munich, 1908

ECKHART, MEISTER, *Predigten*, ed. Pfeiffer, 2 vols., Leipzig, 1857

Epistolae aliquot eruditorum . . . quante sit insignis cuisdam syco-phantae virulentia, ap. Mich. Hillen, Antwerp, 1520

Epistolae obscurorum virorum, 2 vols., Cologne, 1515–17

ERASMUS, DESIDERIUS, *Opera omnia*, ed. Clericus, 10 vols., Lugduni Batavorum, 1703–06

—— *Opus epistolarum . . . denuo recognitum et auctum*, ed. P. S. Allen, H. M. Allen, H. W. Garrod, 12 vols., Oxford, 1906–57

—— *Iuilus exclusus*, ed. Cratander, Basle (1515?)

—— *Axiomata*, in: Opuscula Erasmi, ed. Ferguson, New York, 1923

—— *In Aleandron*, etc., in: Martin Luther, Werke, Erlangen edition, Opera latina, vol. IV, pp. 308 ff

—— *Apologia . . . quae respondet duabus invectivis Ed. Lei*, Antwerp, 1520

—— *Apologia*, Antwerp, 1520

—— *Apologia*, Louvain, 1521

ERASMUS, DESIDERIUS, *Apologia*, Basle, 1522

—— *Apologia*, Antwerp, 1524

—— *Consilium Senatui Basiliense in negotio lutherano datum*, in: Basler Chronic durch C. Wurtisen, vol. VIII, pp. 385 ff, Basle, 1883

FICINO, MARSILIO, *Opera omnia*, 2 vols., ed. Henricpetrina, Basle, 1576

FLAKE, OTTO, *Ulrich von Hutten*, Berlin, 1929

FLITNER, A., *Erasmus im Urteil seiner Nachwelt*, Tübingen, 1952

FRANKL VILMOS, *Henckel János, Mária királyné udvari papja*, Budapest, 1872

GAETA, F., *L. Valla; filologia e storia nell' Umanesimo italiano*, Naples, 1955

GAGUIN, ROBERT, *Epistolae et orationes*, ed. L. Thuasne, 2 vols., Paris, 1903

GANSFORT, W., *Opera*, Groningen, 1614

GARIN, EUGENIO. *Giovanni Pico della Mirandola*, Florence, 1937

—— *L'Umanesimo italiano*, Bari, 1952

—— *L'educazione in Europa, 1400–1600*, Florence, 1954

—— *La cultura filosofica del Rinascimento italiano*, Florence, 1961

GARLANDIA, MAGISTER IOANNES DE, *Equivoca et synonima*, Argentorati, 1487

GILSON, E., *Etudes de la philosophie médiévale*, Strasbourg, 1921

GIOVIO, PAOLO, *Viri illustres*, Venice, 1543

GODET, M., *La Congrégation de Montaigu, 1490–1580*, Paris, 1912

HEGIUS, ALEXANDER, *Dialogi*, Deventer, 1503

HESS, SALOMON, *Erasmus von Rotterdam*, Zürich, 1790

HUIZINGA, JOHAN, *Erasmus of Rotterdam*, transl. Hopman, New York, 1923

HYMA, ALBERT, *The Devotio Moderna or Christian Renaissance, 1380–1520*, Grand Rapids, Mich., 1925

—— *The Youth of Erasmus*, Ann Arbor, Mich., 1930

IMBART, DE LA TOUR, P., *Erasme*, 'Revue des Deux Mondes', Paris, 15 May 1913, pp. 369 ff

Inventarium über die Hinterlassenschaft des Erasmus, MS, University of Basle, No. 102–106/a

JORTIN, JOHN, *The Life of Erasmus*, 2 vols., London, 1758–60

KAEGI, WERNER, *Erasmus im achtzehnten Jahrhundert*, in: Gedenk-schrift zum 400. Todestage des Erasmus von Rotterdam, Basle, 1936

Karl V, ed. P. Rassow, F. Schalk, Hamburg, 1960

KISCH, G., *Humanismus und Jurispudenz*, Basle, 1955

—— *Erasmus und die Juristen seiner Zeit*, Basle, 1960

KOEHLER, W., *Huldrych Zwingli*, Stuttgart, 1952

KOLLÁNYI [*sic*] FERENC, *Oláh Miklós és Rotterdami Erasmus*, 'Uj Magyar Sion', Budapest, 1882

KRISTELLER, P. O., *The Philosophy of Marsilio Ficino*, New York, 1943

—— *Renaissance Thought*, New York, 1961

La Grande Encyclopédie, ed. D'Alember, Diderot, vol. XIV, 1765

LA MARCHE, OLIVIER DE, *Mémoires*, 4 vols., Paris, 1883–88

LANDINO, CRISTOFORO, *Quaestiones camaldulenses ad Federicum Urbinatum principem* (Florence, 1480?)

LECLER, J., *Toleration and Reformation*, London, 1960

LEE, EDWARD, *Annotationum in Nov. Test. Erasmi Rot. libri II*, Paris, 1520

LUTHER, MARTIN, *De captivitate babylonica ecclesiae praeludium*, Werke, Weimar edition, vol. VI

—— *Tischreden*, Werke, Weimar edition, vol. II

MAIER, D., *Die Willensfreiheit bei Lorenzo di Valla etc.*, Bonn, 1914

MAJOR, E., *Handzeichnungen des Erasmus*, Basle, 1934

MANCINI, G. M., *Vita di Lorenzo di Valla*, Florence, 1891

MANN PHILLIPS, MARGARET, *Erasme et les debuts de la Réforme française*, Paris, 1933

—— *Erasmus and the Northern Renaissance*, London, 1949

MASAI, F., *Pléthon et le Platonisme*, Paris, 1956

McCONICA, JAMES KELSEY, *Humanism and Reformation Politics in the Reigns of Henry VIII and Edward VI*, Oxford, 1965

MESTWERDT, P., *Die Anfaenge des Erasmus*, Leipzig, 1917

MICHELET, JULES, *Renaissance*, Paris, 1898

MILES, L., *John Colet and the Platonic Tradition*, Lasalle, USA, 1961

MONTFAUCON, BERNARD DE, *Diarium Italum*, Paris, 1702

MORE, THOMAS, *Utopia*, transl. R. Robinson, London, 1951

—— *The Confutation of Tyndale's Answer*, 2 parts, London, 1532–1533

NOLHAC, PIERRE DE, *Pétrarque et l'humanisme*, 2 vols., Paris, 1907

—— *Erasme en Italie*, Paris, 1909

PETRARCA, FRANCESCO, *Opera omnia*, in aedibus Aldi Romani, Venice, 1501

PICCOLOMINI, AENEAS SYLVIUS (Pope Pius II), *Opera quae extant omnia*, ex officina Henricpetrina, Basle, 1571

PICO DELLA MIRANDOLA, GIOVANNI, *Opera omnia*, apud Aldum Manutium, Venice, 1503

PIRENNE, HENRI, *Histoire de la Belgique*, 5 vols., Brussels, 1902–21

—— *Economic and Social History of Medieval Europe*, London, 1936

PLÉTHON, GEMISTHE, Νόμοι, ed. Alexandre, Paris, 1858

POGGIO BRACCIOLINI, GIANFRANCESCO, *Opera omnia*, Argentorati, 1513

POLIZIANO, ANGELO, *Opera omnia*, in aedibus Aldi Romani, Venice, 1498

PORTER, H. C., *Introduction to the Cambridge Letters of Erasmus*, Toronto, 1963

POST, R. R., *Geboortejaar en opleiding van Erasmus*, Mededelingen der Koninklijke Nederlandse Akademie von Wetenschappen, Nieuv reeks. dl. 16. No. 8, 1953

RABELAIS, FRANÇOIS, *Oeuvres*, ed. Moland, Paris, n.d.

Renaissance Philosophy of Man, ed. E. Cassirer, P. O. Kristeller, J. H. Randall, Chicago, 1948

RENAN, ERNEST, *Avérrhoès et l'Avérrhoisme*, 3rd edition, Paris, 1866

RENAUDET, AUGUSTINE, *Préréforme et humanisme à Paris 1494–1517*, Paris, 1916

—— *Erasme, sa pensée religieuse*, Paris, 1926

—— *Etudes Erasmiennes*, Paris, 1939

—— *Mélanges*, Geneva, 1952

—— *Erasme et l'Italie*, Geneva, 1954

—— *Humanisme et Renaissance*, Geneva, 1958

RHENANUS, BEATUS, *Des. Erasmi Rot. vita*, in: Opera omnia Des. Erasmi Roterodami, vol. I, apud Frobenium, Basle, 1540

RODOCONACHI, E., *Le pontificat de Jules II*, Paris, 1928

—— *Le pontificat de Léon X*, Paris, 1931

ROPER, WILLIAM, *The Mirrour of Vertue in Worldly Greatness; or the Life of Sir Thomas More*, Paris, 1626

RUYSBROECK L'ADMIRABLE, *Oeuvres de*, traduction du flammand par les Bénédictins de Saint Paul de Wisques, 3 vols., Brussels et Paris, 1917–20

SALUTATI, COLLUCCIO, *De saeculo et religione*, ed. Ullman, Florence, 1957

SANCTO AMORE, LIBERIUS DE, *Epistolae theologicae in quibus varium scholasticorum errores castigantur*, Irenopolis, (1680?)

SCALIGER, JULIUS CAESAR, *Poetices libri VII*, ap. Petrum Santandreanum, Antwerp, 1594

—— *Epistolae et orationes*, ex officina Plautiniana, Lugduni Batavorum, 1600

—— *Adversus D. Erasmum, etc.*, Tolosae, 1621

SEELEN, IO. HENR. DE, *Controversiae de N. T. inter Des. Erasmum et E. Leium consideratio*, Lubeck, 1730

SIMON, RICHARD, *Histoire critique des principaux commentateurs du Nouveaux Testament*, Rotterdam, 1693

SMITH, PRESERVED, *Erasmus, a study of his life, etc.*, New York, 1923

STAEHELIN, R., *Huldreich Zwingli*, 2 vols., Basle, 1895–97

STUNICA, J. LOPEZ, *Annotationes contra Erasmum* (Alcalà de Henares), 1519

—— *Erasmi Roterodami blasphemiae et impietates, etc.*, Rome, 1522

—— *Conclusiones principaliter suspectae et scandalosae quae reperiuntur in libris Erasmi Roterodami etc.*, Rome, 1523

TATEO, F., *Poggio Bracciolini e la dialogistica del Quattrocento*, 'Annali della Facoltà di Lettere e Filosofia', Bari, VIII, 1961

TERRASSE, C., *François Ier*, Paris, 1932

THIENEMANN TAMÁS, *Mohács és Erasmus*, Budapest, 1924

TOFFANIN, G., *Storia dell' Umanesimo*, Naples, 1933

TORRE, A. DELLA, *Storia dell' accademia platonica di Firenze*, Florence, 1927

TRENCSÉNYI-WALDAPFEL IMRE, *Erasmus és magyar barátai*, Budapest, 1941

ULLMAN, B. L., *Gesammelte Studien*, Basle, 1952

USTERI, J. M., *Zwingli und Erasmus*, Basle, 1885

VALLA, LORENZO DI, *Opera*, ed. Eugenio Garin, Bottega d'Erasmo, Turin, 1962

VASOLI, C., *La civilta dell' Umanesimo*, Genoa, 1956

VOLTAIRE, FRANÇOIS MARIE AROUET DE, *Nouveaux Mélanges*, Paris, 1765

VOSS, G. J., *De historicis latinis*, Lugduni Batavorum, 1651

WALSER, E. VON, *Poggius Florentinus, Leben und Werke*, Leipzig, 1914

WEISS, R., *Humanism in England during the Fifteenth Century*, 2nd edition, Oxford, 1957

WERTHEMAN, A., *Schaedel und Gebeine des Erasmus*, Basle, 1930

WHITFIELD, J. H., *Petrarca e il Rinascimento*, Bari, 1949

WIEDEMANN, TH., *Johann Eck*, Regensburg, 1865

WOODWARD, W. H., *Desiderius Erasmus concerning the Aim and Method of Education*, Cambridge, 1904

Index

Note—*Numbers in italic refer to illustrations*

Abélard, Pierre (Petrus Abae-
lardus), 21, 34, 62, 71
Adagia (*Adagiorum collectanae*—
(Erasmus), 81-2, 84, 94, 98-
101 *passim*, 105, 110, 115,
121-2, 129, 140, 154
Aldine edition of, 119-20, 126,
5b
*Advice in the Final Hour on the
Necessity of War Against the
Turks* (Erasmus), 236-8
Advice to the Senate of Basle
(Erasmus), 219, 225
Against the Holy Inquisition (Eras-
mus), 219
*Against the Theological Faculty of
Paris* (Erasmus), 219
Agricola, Rudolf, 4, 23-5, 27,
65, 103, 107, 243
Alanus ab Insulis (Alain de Lisle
or de Lille), 21
Parables, 21
Albert, duke of Prussia, 229
Albert of Mainz, *see* Hohen-
zollern
Alberti, Leon Battista, 36
Alcalá de Henares, University
of, 170, 181

Complutum Polyglot Bible: 181
Aldine editions
of Dante and Italian writers,
116
of Erasmus's works, 116-21,
5b
of Greek and Latin classics,
116
Aldus Manutius (Aldo Manu-
zio), 116-21, 165, 249
Aleandro, Girolamo, 118-20,
172, 187-9, 192-4, 202, 246
Alexander the Great, 18, 19, 150,
153
Alexander VI, Pope (Rodrigo
Borgia), 4, 12, 44, 87, 124
Ambrose, St, 86, 89, 108, 252
Amerbach, Bonifacius, 228, 253
Ammonio, Andrea, 128, 137-9,
142, 167, 249
Anabaptists, 93n, 213, 222, 229,
230
Erasmus's relations with, 233-4
Andrelini, Fausto, 52, 63-4, 65,
74, 80, 104, 105, 137, 235,
249
Annotations to the *Elegantiae* of
Valla (Erasmus), *see* Valla

Antibarbari (Erasmus), 45-7, 50, 54, 191, 251
Antioch, Synod of, 148
Antipolemos (Erasmus), 150
Antwerp, 5, 85, 96, 187
Erasmus in, 142, 166, 168
Apophthegmata (Erasmus), 244-5
Aretino, Pietro, 103, 106
Ariosto, Lodovico, 42, 103
Aristotelianism, 23, 35, 67
Aristotelian theology, 38
Thomistic Aristotelianism, 35-36
Aristotle, 18, 19, 29, 47, 59, 66, 67, 71, 116, 214, 241
Metaphysics, 18
Arras, bishop of, 96
Asolani, Andrea, 117, 118, 120, 121, 165
Augsburg Confession, 232
Augsburg, Peace of, 225
Augustine, St, 29, 89, 90, 148, 177, 252
Auxiliary Saints, cult of the fourteen, 1
Averroes (Abu Bekr Mohamad ibn Rushd al Kordobi), 19, 59, 71
Averroism, 35, 123
Avicenna (Abu Ali ibn Sina), 19, 71
Canon of Medicine, 19
Axiomata (Erasmus), 188, 189

Bade (Badius), Josse, 100, 105, 135, 140, 147
Bákocz, Cardinal Tamás, 129
Balbi, Girolamo, 63, 235
Barbaro, Cardinal Hermolao, 214-15

translations of Aristotle, 214
Basil, St, 139, 246, 252
Basle, 3, 5, 11, 126, 195, 258
censorship in, 224
its constitution suspended, 226
Erasmus in, 146-66, 183, 193-227, 249-54
Erasmus's death in, 254
Erasmus's remains exhumed in, 185
religious disturbances and tension in, 222, 223-6
University of, 198, 199
Bataillon, M.
Erasme et l'Espagne: 256
Batt, James, 45-6, 47-8, 61, 64, 84, 85, 86, 88, 96
Bayle, Pierre, ix, x, 260
Dictionnaire historique et critique: ix
Beaufort, Lady Margaret, mother of Henry VII, 73, 102, 136
Beda, Noel, 52, 212, 216, 219, 223, 240
Bembo, Cardinal Pietro, 65, 110, 116, 117, 120, 208
Berckman, Francis, 140
Bergen-op-Zoom, 43, 47
Erasmus in, 61, 64
Bernard de Clairvaux, St, 29, 32, 34, 71, 150
Bernardino of Siena, St, 108, 204
Beroaldo, Filippo, 62
Berquin, Louis, 221-3, 228
Bessarion, Cardinal, 68
Bible, the, 13, 27, 77, 79, 89, 92, 99-100 153, 157, 162, 165, 205
Biblical exegesis, 99

Ecclesiastes, Erasmus's work on, 249, 250
Isaiah, 78, 139
Old Testament, 82-3, 146, 159, 181
Pentateuch, 78
trilingual editions of, 170, 181
Vulgate, 83
see also: New Testament; Novum instrumentum; Alcalà
Bludau, A., 161, 162
Boerio brothers, 105, 113, 115, 122
Boerio, Giovanni Battista, 105
Bologna, Erasmus in, 113, 115-17, 122
Bombasio, Paolo, 115-16, 129, 138, 249
Borgia, Cesare, 4, 124
Borgia, Lucrezia, 4, 110, 117, 123
see also: Este, Alfonso d'
Borgia, Rodrigo, see Alexander VI
Borselen, Anna van, 64, 84-6, 96
patron of Erasmus, 64, 84-6
Botticelli, Sandro, 67, 113, 3a
Brant, Sebastian
Ship of Fools, 57, 103, 135, 146
Brethren of the Common Life, 12-15, 25-7, 32, 46, 51, 92
Deventer School of, 12-15, 23-5
frater houses of, 13
's Hertogenbosch School of, 25-6
Briard of Ath, Jan, 169
Brodarics, István, 235, 236
Brunfels, Otto, 201

Bruni d'Arezzo, Leonardo (Leonardus Aretinus), 36, 102, 110, 111, 241
Bruno, Giordano, 68, 110, 178, 223, 259
Brussels, 5, 43, 250
Buda, court of, 95, 234-6
Budé, Guillaume, 95
Bullock, Henry, 137, 241
Burgundy, 5, 6-9
Buridan, 46, 55, 59
Burigni, Abbé J. L. de
Vie d'Érasme, ix

Caesar, Gaius Julius, 18, 19, 216, 245
Calcagnini, Celio, 123, 208
That the Sky Stands Still and That the Earth Moves, 123
Calvin, Jean, 39n, 52, 91, 93, 152, 162, 172, 178, 206, 224, 259, 260
Cambray, 86
League of, 123, 128
Cambridge, 136-7
Erasmus as professor at, 102, 105, 135-42
Erasmus's income at, 136
Queens' College, 102, 131, 135, 137
plague at, 138
post created for Erasmus, 135
Caminade, Augustine, 81-2, 209
Campanella, Tommaso, 68, 110, 178
Campeggio, Cardinal Lorenzo, 189, 195, 197, 254
Canterbury, archbishop of, see Warham

Capito, 173, 244
Carlstadt, 204, 206
Carmen Alpestre vel potius equestre
 (Erasmus), 106-7
Cassander, George, 257, 258,
 259
Cassoviensis, Antoninus, 171
Cato Censorius (Cato the Elder),
 Disticha Catoris, Erasmus's
 work on, 141
Charles the Bold, duke of
 Burgundy, 6-9, 12, 39,
 149
Charles V, Holy Roman Em-
 peror, 95, 142, 188, 190,
 192, 222, 231-5 passim
 Erasmus as councillor to, 147,
 153
 and Erasmianism, 170
 and war with France, 221,
 238, 253, 254
 and Lutherans, 187
Charles VIII, king of France, 52,
 63, 118, 151
Cicero, Marcus, Tullius, 17, 33,
 62, 84, 85, 98, 153, 214-17
 De officiis: Erasmus's editing
 of, 84, 85
Ciceronians, 214-16
Clement VIII, Pope (Giulio de'
 Medici), 4, 115, 126, 129,
 180, 194, 218, 230, 235, 236
 death of, 249
 Erasmus reprimanded by, 195
 and Luther, 232
 becomes Pope, 182, 201-2
 and war against Holy Roman
 Emperor, 221
Clement of Alexandria, St, 148
Cognac, League of, 235

Cognatus, Gilbertus (Gilbert
 Consain), secretary of Erasmus, 227-8, 250
 On the Duties of a Secretary,
 228
Colet, John, 55, 65, 83, 88, 91,
 92, 94, 108, 114, 131, 182,
 7a
 death of, 187
 Erasmus's letters to, 98, 135-6,
 139, 173, 221
 and Erasmus's visits to England, 73, 75-9, 101-2, 137,
 139, 167
 and St Paul's School, 78, 101,
 238
Collected Letters (Erasmus), 223
Collected Works (Erasmus), ix,
 225, 257, 260
 see also: Opera Omnia
Colloquia (Erasmus), 110, 121,
 191, 197, 209-13, 223, 238,
 243, 247, 257
 burned in French provinces,
 212
 condemned by Sorbonne,
 212
 and Œcolampadius, 226
 successful reprints of, 212
 translations of, 212-13
Columbus, Christopher, ix, 19,
 56, 60, 106, 185
Commines (or Comines),
 Philippe de, 7, 8
Complaint of Peace: The (Erasmus), 192, 222
 burning of French version of,
 222
Complutum Polyglot Bible: see
 Alcalà

Concilium (Erasmus and Faber), 189, 191, 202

Constance, Council of, 13, 92

Constantinople, 6, 8, 39, 60, 237
  fall of, 236

Cop, Wilhelm, 98-9, 106

Cornelius (Cornelius Gerards), 26, 30-1, 38, 100, 235

Correct Pronunciation of Latin and Greek: The (Erasmus), 238

Cricius, Andreas, 171

Cusanus, Cardinal Nicholas, 57, 149, 236

Dagger of the Christian Knight: The (Erasmus), *see Enchiridion*

Dante Alighieri, 31, 39n, 42, 108, 114, 116, 149
  De monarchia, 149

De contemptu mundi (Erasmus), 40-1

De copia (Erasmus), 139

Denis the Carthusian
  Opera Omnia, 58

Denk, Háns, 234

Descartes, René, 217, 260

Desiderius, Erasmus adopts additional name of, 101

determinism, 203-5, 206

Deventer, 2, 10, 12, 24-7 *passim*, 137
  Erasmus at school in, 12-16, 23-5

devotio moderna, 13, 23, 27, 29, 51, 57, 58, 76, 91-2, 95, 111, 159, 170

Dialogue on the Ciceronians (Erasmus), 213, 215-17

Diderot, Denis, ix, x, 103, 156, 261
  La Grande Encyclopédie, ix

Diet of Augsburg, 231-2, 238

Diet of Torda, 225, 258

Diet of Worms, 190-1, 202, 225, 232, 235

Diets of Speyer, 219-20, 222, 228-9, 235, 236

Dionysius (pseudo-Dionysius) the Aeropagite, 14, 59, 69, 77

Discussion of the Free Will (Erasmus), 202, 203, 205-6, 207

Dolet, Étienne, 217

Dorp, Martin van, 133, 160, 162

Dudith, András, 258

Duhamel, Georges, 176, 263
  Érasme: ou le spectateur pur: 176

Dulce bellum inexpertis (Erasmus), 149-50, 151

Durard du Lair, H., 262

Dürer, Albrecht, 95, 167, 168, 191, *10b*
  Knight, Death and the Devil

Ebrardus, Latin grammar of, 21

Edward VI, king of England, 192, 243, 258

Egbert ter beck, 14, 15

Egmondanus, Nicolaus, 180, 187, 211, 212

Elizabeth I, queen of England, 192, 258

Enchiridion militis christiani (Erasmus), 88-95, 96, 98, 126, 163, 183, 210, 247, 248, 256, 257, 259, 261
  and Erasmianism, 170
  and Luther, 173

England, 8, 13, 128, 138
  Erasmus in, 72, 73–80, 83, 101–
    105, 130–42, 158, 160, 167–8
Enlightenment, the, 103, 122,
    156, 256, 260, 261
Enzinas, Francisco de, 166
Erasmianism, 147, 170–2, 198,
    258, 260
  in France, 172
  and Luther, 176
  in Poland, 171–2, 258, 259
  in Spain, 170
  and the Vatican, 172
Erasmians, 231, 232, 248, 253,
    258, 259
Eschenfelder, Christopher
    (Christophorus Cinicam-
    pus), 183, 253
Este, Alfonso d', duke of Ferrara,
    123
Este, Cardinal Hyppolito d', 129
Este, family of, 95
Eucharist, the, 90, 93, 224, 229,
    232
Eugene IV, Pope, 13
Euripides
  Hecuba, Erasmus's translation
    of, 105, 117
  Iphigenia, Erasmus's transla-
    tion of, 105, 117
Exomolegesis (Erasmus), 224

Faber, Johann, bishop of Vienna,
    152, 244, 246, 254, 257
  and Erasmus at Freiburg, 227
  Erasmus's letters to, 220–1,
    226, 232, 245
Faber, Johann, the Dominican
  Concilium, joint authorship
    with Erasmus, 189, 191, 202

at Diet of Worms, 191, 202
attacked by Luther, 202
Farel, Guillaume, 224
Farnese, Cardinal Alessandro,
    see Paul III
Feltre, Vittorino da, 110, 241
Ferdinand, archduke of Austria,
    142, 152, 171, 220, 226, 228,
    234, 246
Ferrara, court of, 73, 95
  Erasmus at, 123
Ficino, Marsilio, 53, 66, 67–71,
    91, 108, 110, 111, 114, 126,
    149, 156, 217, 218
  Of the Christian Religion: 218
  influence on Colet, 76, 77
  and Islam, 236
  translation of Plato, 33, 68
  head of Platonic Academy,
    Florence, 20, 69
  Theologica Platonica, 69
Filelfo, Francesco, 36–7, 63, 103,
    236
Fisher, John, bishop of Roches-
    ter, 62, 73, 167, 182, 187,
    249, 7b
  creates post for Erasmus at
    Cambridge, 135
  Erasmus and execution of,
    250–1
  and humanism, 102
  and Novum instrumentum, 165
Flodden, 129, 142
Florence, 49, 63, 113
  Erasmus in, 113–15
  Council of, 17, 68, 92
Fonseca, Cardinal Alonso de,
    170, 208
Fox, Richard, bishop of Win-
    chester, 73, 102

France, 6–9, 11, 13, 15, 141
    Erasmus's views of the French, 141
    war with the Holy Roman Empire, 192, 221, 238, 253
France, Anatole, 134, 263
Francis I, king of France, 12, 142, 187, 235
    and Berquin, 222–3
    his admiration for Erasmus, 152, 172
    presents canonry to Erasmus, 147
    invites Erasmus to France, 168, 246
Francis of Assisi, St, 36, 39n, 108
Francis of Paula, St, 8, 51
Frederick III, Emperor, 39, 44, 2
Frederick the Wise, elector of Saxony, 174, 188–92
free will, problem of, 203–9
Freiburg, Erasmus in, 197, 222, 226, 227–49, 252–3
    professor of theology in, 227
French–Burgundian wars, 6–9, 11
Froben, Hieronymus, son of Johannes, 249, 252, 257
Froben, Johannes, 146–8, 160, 193, 226, 249
    Erasmus's publisher in Basle, 5, 140, 161, 174, 201, 213
Froude, James Anthony, 133, 262

Gaguin, Robert, 53–5, 62, 64, 65, 95, 242
    Compendium of the Origins and Deeds of the French, 54–5
    Erasmus's addition to, 55

History of France: 242
Garlandia, Magister Ioannes de, 16, 21–2
Gattinara, Mercurio, 191, 208, 220, 232
Gaza, Theodore of, 168, 238
    Greek Grammar, Erasmus's translation of, 168, 238
Gerard, Erasmus's father, 1–3, 9, 25
Gerards, Cornelius, *see* Cornelius
Gerber, Nikolaus, 159, 164
Germany, 13, 172–3
    Erasmus in, 145–6
    support for Luther in, 202
Gerson, Jean, 32, 34, 55
Gigli, Silvestro, bishop of Worcester, 167
Gilles, Pierre, 166, 168, 249
Goclenius, Conradus, 3
Goethe, J. W. von, 103, 122
    Wilhelm Meister: 122
    Xenia, 122
Gouda, birthplace of Erasmus, 1–2, 5, 9, 10, 25, 85, 143
Granvella, Nicholas, 232
Grawe of Vienna, 258
Great Schism (1378–1429), 13
Great Soviet Encyclopaedia, 133
Greek, 16, 17, 18, 21, 79, 103
    Erasmus and studying, 79–84, 96, 115, 123
    Erasmus teaches at Cambridge, 135
    Erasmus's translations from, 96, 102–3
    of Homer, 17
    philosophy, 19, 86n
    see also: New Testament; *Novum instrumentum*

Grey Thomas,, 57, 62, 64, 65
Grimani, Cardinal Domenico, 126, 129, 146, 158, 161
Grocyn, 73, 137
Groote, Gerard, founder of *devotio moderna*, 13
Gropius, Hugo, 260, 261
Gutenberg Bible, 158

Hadrian VI, Pope (Hadrian of Utrecht), 126, 180, 182, 218
  death of, 201
  offers Erasmus professorship at Louvain, 96
  becomes Pope, 198
Handbook of the Christian Soldier: The (Erasmus), *see Enchiridion*
Hebrew, 16, 18, 21, 82, 103, 159, 161
  manuscripts, burning of, 146
  Old Testament in, 181
Hegius, Alexander, 23, 25, 27, 243
Henri of Bergen, bishop of Cambray, 49, 51, 56, 57, 60, 61, 64, 84, 86, 96, 112
  Erasmus as secretary to, 43–8
  end of relationship, 64
Henrician Church, 93n: 212, 253
Henry VII, king of England, 73, 74, 81, 102–5, 128
Henry VIII, king of England, 12, 137, 149, 165, 213, 235, 238, 246
  and Erasmus, 128, 130, 142, 228, 250, 258
  grants audience to Erasmus, 187
  and More, 245
  as prince, 74, 81

succeeds his father, 128
  and war with France, 141
heresy, 13, 35, 229
  Erasmus posthumously branded as heretic, 258
  Manichean, 38
  Pelagian, 39
Hermanus, William, 30-1, 44, 45, 55, 61, 84, 85
  Erasmus edits his poems, 55
Hess, Salomon, ix
  Erasmus von Rotterdam, ix
Hochstraten, Jacob, 146, 186-7
Hohenzollern, Cardinal Albert von (Albert of Mainz), 129, 145, 164, 172-3, 186
Holbein, Hans, the Younger, 132, 137, 167, *6, 7a, 7b, 8a, 9, 12*
Holland, county of, 1, 5, 11
  Erasmus in, 85-6
  patria of Erasmus, 109, 149
Holy Roman Empire, 6, 8
  and war with France, 192
  and the Turks, 228-9
Homer, 17, 83, 116
Horace, 46, 78, 119
Huizinga, Johan, x, 107, 119, 122, 133, 259, 263
  Erasmus of Rotterdam, x
  The Waning of the Middle Ages, x
Hundred Years War, 5
Hungary, 8, 234-6, 246
  and Erasmian influence, 171, 234-6
  and war with the Turks, 221-222, 234, 235-6
Hus, Jan, 34, 57, 91-3, 158, 175, 223, 232

Hutten, Ulrich von, 145-6, 179, 183, 186, 189-90, 220-1, 202
  Expostulation, 201
  The Letters of Obscure Men, attributed to, 179
Hyperaspistes (Erasmus), 207, 208

Ichtuophagia (Erasmus), 51
Imbart de la Tour, T., 107, 109
Innocent VIII, Pope, 44, 71
Inquisition, the, 34, 35, 52, 70, 71, 93, 212, 219, 229, 248
Institutio principis christiani (Erasmus), 153-6, 168, 232
Italy, 17, 109-11
  Erasmus's visit to, 105-6, 112-129
  humanism, 34, 109-11

James IV, king of Scotland, 4, 122, 129, 142
Jerome, St, 83, 86, 87, 89, 94, 96, 140, 161, 204, 252
  Erasmus and, 143, 147, 158, 168, 213
Jovus, Paulus, ix, 254
Julius II, Pope (Giulio della Rovere), 44, 123, 125, 150, 209
  asks Erasmus for treatise, 128
  grants dispensation to Erasmus, 104
  opposition to, 126
  as warrior, 113, 115, 141, 149
Julius Shut Out (Erasmus), 141-2

Kaegi, Werner
  Erasmus und das 18te Jahrhundert, 256

Kempis, Thomas à, 17-18, 27, 57
  Imitation of Christ, 17

Lament of Peace (Erasmus), 259-260
Landino, Cristoforo, 68, *3b*
Lascaris, Ioannes, 52, 118
Lateran Council, 129, 167
Latin, 16, 21, 32, 33, 35, 38, 42, 43, 81, 139
  of Cicero, 17, 214-17
  classics, 17, 23
  dog-Latin, 16, 18, 42
  adages selected by Erasmus, 81
  and Erasmus's books, 139
  poems by Erasmus, 41-3, 45, 50, 55
  transcriptions by Erasmus, 139
  medieval, 17
  style, 38
Lecler, J., x, 260
Lee, Edward, archbishop of York, 182-3, 248
Lefèvre d'Étaples, Jacques (Faber Stapulensis), 62, 108, 174
Leo X, Pope (Giovanni de' Medici), 1, 57, 118, 129, 150, 169, 172, 173, 218, 221
  death of, 182
  meeting with Erasmus, 126
  Exsurge Domine, papal bull of, 187-8
  and *Novum instrumentum*, 157, 158, 160-1
Leonardo da Vinci, ix, 4, 36, 113, 178
  Mona Lisa: 113
Libanus, 96, 98
  editio princeps, Erasmus's translation of, 96

Lily, William
  Grammar, 238, 243
Linacre, Thomas, 73, 137, 243
Lombardus, Petrus, 34, 77
London
  Erasmus in, 74-5, 80, 101-2,
    142, 147
Louis XI, king of France, 6-8,
  51, 54, 59
Louis XII, king of France, 141,
  142
Louvain, 43, 118, 195, 258
  Erasmus in, 60, 88, 96-8, 130,
    169-70, 180, 183-7, 189,
    190, 193
  Luther's books burned in, 187-
    8
  theologians of, 186-7
  University of, 5, 60, 96, 248
Low Countries, 5, 6, 9, 13, 118,
  141, 147, 168-9, 187, 192,
  257
Lucian, 134, 135, 140, 208, 209,
  261
  Erasmus's translations of, 103,
    105, 139, 147
  Icaromenippus, 139
Lucretius Caris, Titus, 78
  De rerum natura: 150
Lupset, Thomas, 137, 182, 187
Luther, Martin, x, 12, 27, 39,
    47, 57, 78, 106, 145,
    152, 196, 211, 218, 220,
    222, 231, 232, 233, 235,
    237, 250, 253, 261, 10a,
    10b
  Babylonian Captivity, 190
  Bondage of the Will, 206
  death of, 244
  compared with Erasmus, 91-5

and Erasmus, 172-80, 186-91,
    193-4, 198-209, 212, 216,
    223, 248, 252, 254
  their break and antagonism,
    202-9
  and excommunication, 129,
    187-91
  and Novum instrumentum, 162,
    165, 166
  visit to Rome of, 123-5
  Sermons, 174
  his 95 theses, 173, 176, 186
  and tolerance, 229-30
  taken to Wartburg, 191
  at University of Wittenberg,
    165, 173, 199, 244
  and Zwingli, 229
Lutheranism, 78, 93n, 118, 231
Lutherans, 228, 229, 230, 232,
  239, 247
  burning of, 187, 193, 220
  and the Pope, 198-9
  and sack of Rome, 222
  schools, 209

McConica, James Kelsey, x
  Humanism and Reformation Poli-
    tics in the Reigns of Henry
    VIII and Edward VI, 256-7
Machiavelli, Niccolò, 8, 33, 113,
  120, 153, 154
  Discorsi, 156
  Il Principe (The Prince), 156
Maertensz, Dirck, 166, 184
Mainz
  archbishop of, 164
  Erasmus in, 145
Manetti, Gianozzo, 99
Mantua, court of, 63, 95
Marburg, conference at, 229

Margaret, Erasmus's mother, 2, 3, 12, 24, 25

Margarethe, Erasmus's house-keeper, 253

Marot, Clément, 212, 257

Mary, queen of England, 73, 192, 213, 243, 258, 259

Mary, queen of Hungary, 95, 234, 236, 246, 250, 253

Massacre of St Bartholomew, 110, 129

Matrimony: In Praise of (Erasmus), 65

Matsys, Quentin, 166-7, *frontispiece*

Maximilian I, Holy Roman Emperor, 9, 157, 158

Medici, Cosimo de', 66, 68, 69

Medici, Giulio de', *see* Clement VII

Medici, Lorenzo de', 12, 20, 42, 44, 118, 126, 150-1, 172
death of, 114
and Platonic Academy, 66-9, 211

Melanchthon, Philipp, 232, *8b*
and Erasmus, 103, 165, 206, 239, 244, 254
and Luther, 175, 186, 231

Method of Study, A (Erasmus), 139, 140, 238, 241, 243

Michelangelo Buonarrotti, 106, 108, 113, 116, 125
David, 113

Michelet, Jules, 107, 109

Middle Ages, 16, 23, 41, 67, 82, 134-5, 149, 202, 217
medieval Church, 46, 58, 59, 69, 83, 170, 178, 219, 230, 250-1

medieval Latin, 17

medieval learning, 18-19, 22

medieval pedagogy, 20-1

medieval piety, 46

medieval theology, 18, 27, 58, 89

Mithras, cult of, 148

Montaigne, Michel Eyquem de, 121, 213, 257
Essays, 121, 213

Montesquieu, Charles Louis Secondat de, 156, 257

Montfaucon, Bernard de
Diarium italicum: 261

More, Sir Thomas, 66, 68, 137, 139, 149, 153, 187, 197, 206, 208, 250-2, *6*
beheading of, 250, 254
canonization of, 251, 252
as Chancellor of England, 228
resigns as, 245
Dialogue Concerning Heretics, 252
and Erasmus's visits to England, 73-5, 80, 101-3, 130, 131, 133, 137, 167
translation of Lucian, 105, 147
and Luther, 173
and *Novum instrumentum*, 164-165, 182
Utopia, 166, 211, 213, 252

Montaigu, Collège de, 48, 49, 51-3, 99, 137, 212
Erasmus at, 49-72

Mountjoy, William Blount, Lord, 80-2, 137, 208, 249
patron of Erasmus, 64-5, 84-5, 128-30, 136

Mountjoy—*continued*
Erasmus as guest of, 73, 74, 101, 142
Musurus, Marcus, 118, 123

Nagyvárad, peace-treaty of, 246
Nancy, battle of (1477), 9
Naples
Erasmus visits, 128
Neacademia of Venice, 117-18
New Testament, 77, 79, 96, 99-100, 157-66, 170
annotations of Erasmus, 34, 110
Annotations of Valla, 97-100
Greek texts of, 79, 83-4, 116, 140, 181
teachings of the Gospels, 13, 36, 77, 89, 94, 158, 183
Erasmus's translations of, 143, 147, 153, 157-66
Vulgate, 99-100, 157, 165, 181
see also Novum instrumentum
Nicaea, Council of, 177
Nicholas V, Pope (Tommaso Parantucelli), 38, 57, 99, 149
Nominalism, 14, 58-9
Oxonian, 110
Novum instrumentum, Erasmus's translation into Latin of Greek New Testament, 157-166, 168, 169, 183, 198, 257
annotations to, 163
Apocalypse, 159, 163
Apologia, third preface to, 157
and Colet, 164
critics of, 180-3
Greek manuscripts for, 159-60
condemned as heretical, 258
translations from, 162, 166
and Zwingli, 223

Occam (or Ockham), William of, 46, 55, 59, 73
Œcolampadius, Ioannes, 159, 198, 199, 224-6, 233
meeting with Erasmus in Basle, 226
Oláh, Cardinal Miklós, 236, 244, 246
On the Civility of Boys (Erasmus), 238
On the Education of a Christian Prince (Erasmus), *see Institutio principis christiani*
On the Education of Boys (Erasmus), 123, 238, 241, 243
On Fluency (Erasmus), *see De copia*
On Plenty (Erasmus), 243
On Preparing for Death (Erasmus), 248
On the Purity of the Church (Erasmus), 253
On the Sweet Concord of the Church (Erasmus), 247
On the Writing of Letters (Erasmus), 213, 238
On Ways of Confessing (Erasmus), *see Exomolegesis*
Opera Omnia (Erasmus), *8a, 11a, 11b*
Origen, 40, 69, 77, 86-9, 94, 96, 108, 253
Erasmus edits works of, 87, 253
Orleans
Erasmus in, 81-4
Outlines of Friendly Conversation (Erasmus), 209
Oxford, 88, 101, 137
Erasmus in, 75-80

pacificism and Erasmus, 12, 72, 107, 111, 148-53, 217-18, 221, 257, 262, 263
  Colet's support, 149
  Erasmus's pacifist booklets, 192
Padua, 20, 66, 118, 123
  Erasmus in, 122-3
Panegyric for Philip, Duke of Burgundy (Erasmus), 97
Parabolae (Erasmus), 147
Parantucelli, Tommaso, *see* Nicholas V
Paraphrases on the Acts of the Apostles (Erasmus), 202
Paraphrases of St John (Erasmus), 213
Paraphrases of St Matthew (Erasmus), 192
Parc, Premonstratensian monastery of, 97-8
Paris, 5, 52-3, 56, 61, 63
  Erasmus in, 49-72, 80-2, 84-5, 95-6, 98-101, 105
patristic literature, Erasmus's work on, 218, 246, 247, 252-3
  see also: Jerome
Paul, St
  Colet on the Epistles of, 75-9 *passim*
  Erasmus and, 89, 91, 102, 143, 163
  Luther on the Epistles of, 165
Paul III, Pope (Cardinal Alessandro Farnese), 126, 172, 179, 249, 253
  offers Erasmus cardinalate, 249
Paul IV, Pope, 178, 258, 259

Peasants' Revolt, 198-200, 206, 221
  Erasmus's attitude to, 199-200
  Luther's attitude to, 200
pedagogy, 16, 20-1, 22, 23, 27, 45, 107, 110, 194, 241, 243-244
  Erasmus and, 238-44
Peter, Erasmus's brother, 2, 4, 9, 25, 26
Petrarch (Francesco Petrarca), 19, 36, 108, 111, 114, 116, 262, 1
  Africa, 42
  admiration for Cicero's writing, 16, 214
  De contemptu mundi, 41
  as father of humanism, 16-17, 35, 204, 241
  Italian sonnets, 42
  and Padua, 20, 66
Pflug, Julius, 231, 244, 257-8
  Three Dialogues on Religion: 257-8
Philip (the Handsome) of Burgundy, archduke of Austria, 9, 97
Phillips, Margaret Mann, x
  Erasmus and the Northern Renaissance, x
philology, 16, 22, 23, 70, 107, 110, 157, 158, 181, 214
philosophia Christae of Erasmus, 144, 148, 157-8, 164, 169-70, 177-8, 183, 213, 232, 246, 256, 258
Piccolomini, Aeneas Sylvius, *see* Pius II
Pico della Mirandola, Gianfrancesco, 66, 110

Pico della Mirandola, Giovanni, 17, 18, 36, 49, 63, 65, 66, 91, 103, 111, 114, 116, 126, 149, 239
 and Ciceronian Latin, 214-15
 Influence on Erasmus, 218, 253
 accused of heresy, 87n
 On Human Dignity, 17-18, 71, 204
 and humanists, 109-10
 and neo-Platonism, 70-2, 108, 156
 dreams of religious and political unity, 145, 172, 177
Pirckheimer, Willibald, 168, 208, 240, 249
Pistorius, Simon, 220, 244, 257
Pius II, Pope (Aeneas Sylvius Piccolomini), 39-40, 50, 235, 236, 243
 Commentari, 40
 Euryalus and Lucretia, 39
 In Europam sui temporis, 40
Plato, 33, 46, 49, 66-71, 76, 116, 131, 153, 241
Platonism, 35, 37, 62, 86n, 89, 120, 178, 217
 neo-Platonism, 35, 36, 59, 62, 63, 86n, 90, 92, 108, 110, 156, 177
 Erasmus's relation to, 66, 79, 109
 Florentine, 65-72, 74, 94, 110-11
 neo-Platonist theology, 77, 78
 Platonist Renaissance, 260
Platonic Academy, Florence, 20, 37, 63, 66-9, 114

 foundation by Cosimo de' Medici, 66
Pletho, Gemisthos, 68, 69, 71, 91, 217
 Laws, the, 68, 217
Plotinus, 69, 76, 122
Plutarch, 140, 147, 153, 241
 Erasmus's translation of his treatises, 147
Poggio Braccolini, Gianfrancesco, 31, 36, 102, 103, 111, 236
 Contra hypocritas, 37
 and Erasmus, 37, 66, 91, 110, 114, 209
 Facetiae, 37
 and Latin classics, 17, 42
Poland, influence of Erasmus in, 171-2, 258, 259
Poliziano, Angelo, 42, 49, 65, 111, 114, 116, 118, 126, 3b
 objection to Ciceronian style, 214
 and Erasmus, 36, 66, 110, 121
 as leader of Florentine neo-Platonism, 70
 Miscellanae, 121
Pontano, Giovanni, 42, 110, 209
 Dialoghi, 110
Praise of Folly, The (Erasmus), 11, 103, 107, 111, 124, 126, 130-5, 140, 142, 145, 191, 197, 209-10, 211, 257, 260, 261, 8a
 writing of, 130
printing
 of books, 47, 53
 and Erasmus, 119, 147
 in England, 73

in Venice, 116-20
press, benefits of, 231
Protestantism, 93, 143, 179, 252
Protestants, 178, 191, 209, 222,
    224, 225-6, 229, 237, 244,
    248, 257, 259
Pulci, Luigi, 42, 57, 103
    Morgante, 57, 103

Querela pacis (Erasmus), 151-3,
    168
condemned by Sorbonne, 152
Quintilian, 33, 241

Rabelais, François, ix, 52, 114,
    135, 239, 246, 257, 261
    Gargantua, 21, 58, 103, 213
    Pantagruel, 213
    Theleme, 211
Raphael, 113, 125
Reade, Charles, 3
    The Cloister and the Hearth: 3
Reformation, 12, 20, 39, 91, 129,
    152, 170, 176, 178, 191, 195,
    201, 203, 207, 211, 217-18,
    229, 261
    Counter, 120, 152, 178
    in Germany, 230
    Swiss, 221
    and theology, 230-1
Reformed Church, 260-1
*Refutation of the Errors of the
    Inquisitor Beda* (Erasmus),
    219
Renaissance, 40, 41, 66, 68, 103,
    107, 109, 133, 139, 196, 211,
    231, 239
    division into two, 107-11
    end of, 222
    in Florence, 113

Renaudet, Augustin, ix, 108,
    129, 137
Reuchlin, Johannes, 54, 65, 103,
    108, 146, 159, 186, 211, 212,
    243
Rhenanus, Beatus, first bio-
    grapher of Erasmus, ix, 82,
    95, 117, 183, 185, 196-7,
    198, 209, 253, 254
Rhine, river, 183
    Erasmus's voyage up, 144-6
Riario, Cardinal Raffaello, 126,
    129
Rochester, bishop of, *see* Fisher,
    John
Rogers, Servatius, *see* Servatius
Rome
    Erasmus in, 123-9
    impressions of contemporary,
    123-6
    sack of, 222
Ronsard, Pierre de, 42, 257
Rotterdam, 2, 5
    statue to Erasmus in, 143, 257,
    11b
Rousseau, Jean-Jacques, 151, 208
Rovere, Cardinal Giulio della,
    see Julius II
Rucellai, Bernardo, 114, 115
Ruysbroeck, Jan van, 13, 14, 91

Sadoleto, Cardinal Jacopo, 110,
    208, 243
St Bertin, monastery of
    Erasmus at, 86-8
St Paul's School, 78, 101, 238
Sallust, 33, 62
Salutati, Colluccio, 19, 35-6, 102
Savonarola, Fra Girolamo, 39n,
    47, 49, 56, 75, 103, 239

Scaliger, Julius Caesar, 4-5, 121, 216-17, 254

Scarabaeus (Erasmus), 168

Schmalkalden, League of, 230

scholasticism, 18, 35, 45, 46, 52, 53, 54, 57, 69, 73, 169, 170, 244
  dialectics of, 41
  philosophy of, 57
  and scholastics, 18, 20, 33, 34, 35, 42, 45, 58, 73, 77, 96, 108
  theology of, 13, 46, 51, 57-9, 92, 163, 177, 202, 204

Scotism, 14, 58-9, 89, 137

Scotus, Ioannes Duns, 34, 46, 59, 71, 73, 86, 87, 179

Secundus, Ioannes, 42, 250

Seneca, Lucius Annaeus, 141, 147, 153, 241

Servatius, Rogers of Rotterdam, 32, 85, 86, 103-5, 115, 142-3

's Hertogenbosch, 10, 25, 26
  Erasmus at school in, 25-6

Sickingen, Franz von, 193, 200

Siena, 73
  Erasmus in, 123, 129

Sigismund II, king of Poland, 171, 246

Smith, Preserved, ix, 122

Socrates, 36, 40, 94, 132, 239, 253

Sorbonne, 13, 17, 32, 34, 48, 70, 77, 81, 86, 96
  Erasmus at, 49-72, 80-2, 84-5, 95-6, 98-101
  Erasmus's enemies in, 169
  Erasmus's *Colloquia* condemned by, 212
  Erasmus's *Querela* condemned by, 152
  theological faculty of, 52

Spain, 8, 15, 225, 248, 253
  influence of Erasmus in, 170-1

Spalatin, Georg, 188, 189, 199

Spinoza, Baruch, 122, 217, 260

Sponge to Wipe off Hutten's Aspersions (Erasmus), 201

Standonck van Mechlin, Jan, 51, 53, 84

Steyn, monastery at, 26, 27-30, 33, 34, 36-41 *passim*, 43, 45, 57, 61, 100, 103-4, 143, 235, 238
  Erasmus at, 26-43, 55, 85

Strasbourg, 11
  Erasmus in, 146, 173

Stuart, Alexander, 4, 122-3, 129, 142. 253

Suleiman the Magnificent, 221, 228-9, 235

Swiss Confederation, 6, 8, 153
  Catholic/Protestant war in, 229, 232-3

Swiss reformers,
  Erasmus's relations with, 223

Szydlowieczki (Schydlovietz), Christopher, 171, 197

theology, 93
  and Anabaptists, 234
  of Colet, 77, 78, 79
  Erasmus's study of, 49, 56-7, 79, 84, 102
  and Luther, 176, 177, 202-6, 230
  scholastic, 13, 46, 51, 57-9, 92, 163, 177, 202, 204
  and theologians, 58, 60, 180, 183, 190, 205, 232

Thirty Years War, 110, 129, 221, 259

Thomas Aquinas, St,15, 29, 34, 46
    47, 55, 71, 87, 179, 186, 204
    and Aristotle, 59
    attacked by Erasmus, 251
    and More, 75, 251
    Summa Theologiae, 148
    and war, 150
Thomism, 14, 58-9, 219
tolerance, Erasmus's views on,
    12, 72, 107, 110, 186, 217-
    218, 232, 257, 262, 263
Tournehem castle, Erasmus at,
    64, 65, 86, 88-95
Transylvania, dukedom of, 171,
    225, 258, 259
Trent, Council of, 1n, 93n, 162,
    231, 244, 258
Turks, 6, 60, 128, 150, 197, 221,
    228, 234-8
    threat of, 171, 229, 230, 234
    wars of, 149, 221-2, 234

Unitarians, 93n, 213, 234
United Provinces of the Nether-
    lands, 154n, 259
Utrecht, 5, 24, 49
    Erasmus in choir of cathedral
    at, 24-5
    Erasmus ordained by bishop
    of, 43
Utrecht, Hadrian of, *see* Hadrian
    VI

Valla, Lorenzo di, 31, 36, 38-9,
    54, 66, 83, 91, 97-100,
    110, 111, 114, 159, 204,
    214, 242
    *Annotations to the New Testa-
    ment*, 97-8, 159, 244
    De libero arbitrio: 38, 204

De voluptate, 38
Elegantiae, 38, 54
    Erasmus's annotations to,
    45, 50, 54, 238
Vasari, Giogio, 178
    Lives of the Painters, 178
Venice, Republic of, 6, 8, 11,
    117, 118, 194
    Erasmus in, 117-21
    and Julius II, 123, 128, 141
Vienna, Council of, 100
Villon, 42, 61
Virgil, 19, 29, 33, 46, 62
Vitrier, Jean, 86-8, 92, 149
Voltaire, François Marie Arouet
    de, 102, 103, 132, 135, 153,
    156, 178, 256, 261, 262
    *Dialogue Between Lucian: Eras-
    mus and Rabelais in the
    Elysian Fields*: 261

Warham, William, archbishop
    of Canterbury, 73, 102, 128,
    130, 136, 167, 249
    death of, 246
War is Sweet to the Inexperienced
    (Erasmus), *see Dulce bellum*
Werner, prior of Steyn,, 43 49,
    56, 57, 81, 85, 103
Wessel, Johan, 15, 43, 243
Wicelius, Georgius, 208, 220,
    231, 244, 257, 258-9, 268
will of Erasmus, bequests in, 253
Winchester, bishop of, *see* Fox
Winckel, Peter, 9, 10, 25, 26
Wycliffe, John, 91-2, 158, 204,
    209

Ximénes, Cardinal Francisco,
    129, 168, 170, 181

Zasius, professor, 98, 224

Zerbolt of Zutphen, Gerard, 14–15, 91

   The Reformation of the Faculties of the Soul: 14–15

   Spiritual Ascensions: 14–15

Zuñiga, Juan Lopez, 181–2

   Impieties and Blasphemies of Erasmus of Rotterdam: The, 182

   Suspect and Scandalous Assertions of Erasmus, 182

Zwingli, Ulrich, 57, 91, 93, 159, 162, 179, 201

   death of, 233

   and Luther, 57, 91, 199

   influence of *Novum instrumentum,* 153, 165, 223, 229

Zwinglians, 172, 208, 222–5 *passim,* 229, 230 247